WITHDRAWN

THE JAMES
From Iron Gate to the Sea

RIVERS OF AMERICA BOOKS

(already published are:)

THE
RIVERS OF AMERICA

As Planned and Started by
CONSTANCE LINDSAY SKINNER

Present Editors
CARL CARMER
JEAN CRAWFORD, *Associate*

Former Editors
HERVEY ALLEN
FAITH BALL, *Art*

The
JAMES
From Iron Gate to the Sea

by

Blair Niles

Illustrated by
EDWARD SHENTON

RINEHART & COMPANY
INCORPORATED

New York   *Toronto*

F
232
J2N696j

DEDICATED

TO MY NIECE

ARGYLL PRYOR RICE

AND

MY NEPHEWS

HENRY GORDON RICE

AND

ROGER PRYOR RICE

Preface

ACCORDING to the original editorial plan for the Rivers of America, the volume on the James was to treat only of the Tidewater section of the river. Under the new editorship of the series it has been decided to include within a single volume the entire river; as the river itself is contained within a single state.

To this end I have been asked to expand my original book on the subject.

And I have thought necessary, not only the addition of the new material, but also a recasting of the whole book, in order so to integrate the Piedmont and Valley regions of the river with the Tidewater section, that the story, like the river, should flow from its beginning to the present; flowing through time, a continuous stream of human living.

In preparation for this new portrayal of the James, I have done much additional research, and, not considering it sufficient to have been born and "raised" in Virginia, I have returned again and again to the James River country.

I have added more than forty thousand words, and have, at the same time, cut some twenty thousand from the original volume; bringing the subject matter strictly within the James River watershed.

New chapters are: *Immigrants and Labor; The People's Man; When England Was Still "Home"; The Valley; Looney's Ferry; "It was not lonesome on the River in those Days."* Other chapters have been revised and enlarged to take their places in my design for the whole river.

I have seen the book as the biography of the watershed of the James; presented from the angle of its significance in that stream of life which is an important tributary of the

ix

larger stream which, for lack of a more concretely descriptive name, we call civilization.

In telling the story, it has been my desire to convey the liberty-loving resilient spirit of James River, which has been alien always to the era of cynicism, now surely destined to perish in the light of that vision of freedom and of faith which has come to men in the foxholes, to men fighting on perilous seas, and in the air.

Contents

THE JAMES
From Iron Gate to the Sea

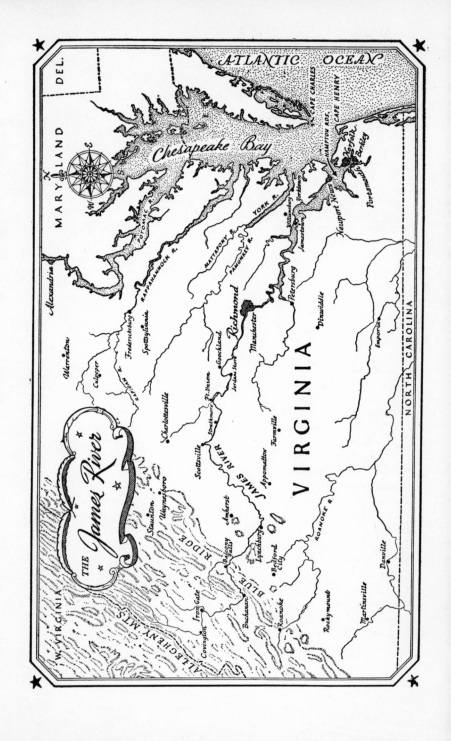

Iron Gate

The River

A LITTLE below Iron Gate, at the southern end of the great Valley of Virginia, in a mountain-rimmed world with the bold range of the Alleghenies on the west and the billowy curves of the Blue Ridge on the east, the Jackson and Cowpasture rivers unite, and the result of their union is James River.

The Cowpasture has wandered down from the north-west, winding through valleys, between ranges of hills and lesser mountains; following so devious a route that the Indians called it the Walatoola—the river that bends. On its way it has gathered to itself the waters of the Bullpasture River, of creeks and brooks, and of the clear cool springs for which its valley is noted. No towns pollute the clarity of the Cowpasture River, which mirrors unmarred the tranquil country through which it journeys.

I first saw the river on an autumn day. The wooded hills, which still retained much of their foliage, were reflected in copper and gold upon its placid surface; maples and hickories and oaks, dark patches of pines and cedars, the silvery skeletons of sycamore trees and the pallid trunks of the beach,

3

with subdued green willows overhanging the water. The sun
was a bright white globe in a foam-flecked, deeply blue sky,
where an occasional turkey buzzard soared high. All this was
repeated in the river depths; softly blurred by the quivering
life of the water. It was as though the river, gazing upward,
recorded in its own fashion whatever impressed it.

The countryside was so still that every least sound was
registered and remembered; the tiniest of bird voices, the
brittle rustle of fallen leaves, the low murmur of the river
where it ripples over rocks, the distant cawing of crows, the
far-off bark of a dog, and the companionable salute of
roosters. Stacks of corn and hay dotted the quiet fields. Here
and there crooked rail fences outlined pastures where horses,
cattle, or sheep grazed monotonously. Wood, ready for winter
fires, was piled outside the scattered farmhouses, and children
played with hair flying in the wind.

The mere memory of the Cowpasture River tranquillizes
the spirit.

The Jackson is a stream of altogether different temperament. Like the Cowpasture, it too flows through the Valley of
Virginia, but it has not that serene leisure which makes so
significant the name of the Cowpasture. The Jackson is called
after the energetic pioneer, William Jackson, who in 1746
took up so large a tract of land along the river that for three
miles it flowed through his property. It was wilderness country in those days and the settlers lived ever in the menace of
Indian vengeance, but William Jackson wore the wig and the
buckles of a formal personage.

As for his river, it hurries with the air of an important
engagement to be kept, while the Cowpasture dawdles. The
very springs of the Jackson River valley differ from those
of the Cowpasture valley; the Jackson's springs being warm,
in some cases hot, while the Cowpasture springs are cool. And
at Covington the Jackson becomes charged with the froth
and the sulphurous odor of the West Virginia Pulp and Paper
Mill which makes of that town an industrial center.

But both rivers share the memory of Indian tribes gath-
ering at their hunting grounds; of Indians on the warpath,

the Iroquois coming down from Central New York through
Pennsylvania, and passing through the Valley of Virginia on
their way to attack the Catawbas; memory, too, of pioneer
whites braving the red man, and the wilderness. The valley
can never forget battle and massacre and savage torture,
though today tranquillity rests upon it like the shimmering
haze of Indian summer.

It is two miles below Iron Gate, near the border of
Allegheny and Botetourt counties, that Jackson River, still
acrid and frothy from the paper mill at Covington, meets
the Cowpasture, which comes so quietly around rolling
wooded hills as almost to seem like a pool, rather than a river;
a pool painted in the muted tints of late autumn foliage.
The two streams sweep about a green islet, and unite; and
there, more than three hundred miles from the sea, James
River is born. It happens at a quiet spot, hidden by trees
from the road, and from the bridge which a short distance
below crosses the newly born river. Both Cowpasture and
Jackson appear suddenly around wooded points of land so
that their approach is not visible from the tiny strip of
pebbled beach where one may stand to look upon the birth
of the James.

The aboriginal Indians had no settlement in this part of
the Valley of Virginia. But their "Great Path" crossed the
Potomac and traversed the Valley from north to south,
crossing the James near the southern boundary of its watershed, where Looney's Creek coming up from the south joins
the James.

At that time the open grasslands of the Valley attracted
huge herds of buffalo; shaggy brown beasts standing on squat
legs, cocking their ridiculous twelve-inch tails, pawing the
ground, grunting and snorting with rage at the sight of man,
when what you expected of such powerful creatures was a
deep bellow. So they were described by William Byrd when
he explored the Virginia frontier more than two centuries

ago. Their flesh, he said, was "so good that a cardinal legate might have made a comfortable meal upon it in Carnival time."

In this Virginia wilderness there were also in abundance deer, elk and bear, wild turkeys, vast numbers of cranes, migrating flights of pigeons in such quantities that the branches of trees broke beneath their weight, and yelling packs of wolves followed Byrd's expedition. Wild turkey stewed with venison he found to be so delicious that "we no more tired of it than a man wearies of an engaging wife because of her being a constant dish."

When the pioneer white men settled in the Valley they called the grasslands of the buffalo "The Pastures"; and the streams which watered them came to be known by the names of the pastures: the Bullpasture River, the Cowpasture River, the Calfpasture River.

Save for occasional rapids, the James is as tranquil a stream as the Cowpasture, all the way to Balcony Falls. At long intervals a flat-bottomed open ferryboat provides crossing for passengers; generally moored waiting at the riverbank, but occasionally being poled in slow transit across the gleaming mirror of the water. From the north and the south, the east and the west—for the James is a serpentine stream, frequently changing its direction—other rivers and creeks add their waters, and the James widens as it proceeds on its way across the state.

At Buchanan it passes close to its southern watershed; there the remains of the once famous James River Canal appear; the old towpath, the dry bed of the canal, the disintegrating locks. At Balcony Falls the James boldly cuts a gorge more than a thousand feet deep through the Blue Ridge Mountains, and there the water level falls two hundred feet in four miles. Here the engineers of the canal met—and overcame—their greatest problem. The river later enters that rich region between the mountains and the Tidewater which we call the Piedmont, and, passing the Peaks of Otter, finally arrives at the city of Lynchburg, standing high above the water on the south bank of the James.

Beyond Lynchburg, passing close to historic tragic Appomattox, the James flows through wide quiet lowlands, the river willow-fringed for mile after mile, on its way to Richmond, with one bank paralleled by the towpath and the dry bed of the abandoned canal. On the hilltops is often a plantation house with tall white columns and surrounded by a flock of small outbuildings, like a hen in the center of a brood of chicks. And about the railroad stations cluster houses, usually white, the church spires appearing abnormally high, in a region where houses rarely exceed two stories.

When the James reaches Richmond it has crossed Virginia from west to east, and has arrived at the Falls. There, for a distance of seven miles, it rushes around great obstructing boulders, foaming about wooded islets scattered among the rocks. The land rises steeply above the Falls, and the city of Richmond stands upon this elevation, looking down upon the dashing torrent of the Falls.

The Falls mark the head of tidewater, and the geographical limit of that civilization established by the early planters—those Venturers who, at Jamestown on James River in the year 1607, founded the first permanent English settlement in the Western Hemisphere, thirteen years before the Pilgrims landed on Plymouth Rock.

At the Falls a great change takes place in the nature of James River, which has been gradually descending from the mountain region of the great Valley, from the hills about Lynchburg, through rolling country to the heights above the Falls, where all elevation comes to an abrupt end. The river now traverses the level coastal lands. Below Richmond it becomes suddenly a wide, tawny, tidal estuary, taking its color from the soil through which it and its lower tributaries pass.

On both banks are the ancestral Tidewater homes, sites of homes that are no more, and of immortal historic events. On the north bank is Shirley, the beautiful colonial house where Light-Horse Harry Lee came riding down the avenue of trees to court Anne Carter, who was later to become the mother of Robert E. Lee. And there Lee spent the happiest days of his youth. Near Shirley is Turkey Island, where William Randolph, king's councilman, established the original home of the Randolphs in Virginia, and built what has been described as "a goodly house, with a portico on three sides, surmounted by a dome visible a great way off to the navigators of the James River, the whole surmounted by an aerial structure called the 'bird cage because many birds do hover and sing about it.'" All destroyed by shellfire in the needless tragedy of the "War Between the States."

In the far-off time of William Randolph, when in England King Charles had, as they say, "come back to his own," Henry Isham, Gent., and his wife Dame Katherine lived at Bermuda Hundred, on the opposite bank of James River. And William Randolph, rowing across to smoke a pipe of tobacco with Henry Isham, fell in love with Mary Isham, the pretty daughter of the house, who played for him upon the "cittern."

In their marriage old traditions were united, for William Randolph traced his descent from "the great Earls Murray," and Mary Isham from "Magna Charta barons." Through the seven sons and two daughters of their marriage they became the ancestors of all the Virginia Randolphs and their descendants—among whom were Thomas Jefferson, Richard Bland, and Robert E. Lee.

And not far from Turkey Island, on the north bank of the James, is Westover—the imposing colonial home of the Byrds; and across the river on the south bank, Jordan's Point, where lived the statesman and historian Richard Bland, whom Thomas Jefferson called "the wisest man south of the James." It was at Jordan's Point that Nathaniel Bacon gathered his forces before leading them in that attack designed to put an end to Indian outrages against the colonists. Also on the south bank are Upper and Lower Brandon, and Claremont, said to be a replica of Claremont in England.

And then, at last, there is Jamestown, on the north bank—and lovely, gracious Carter's Grove.

When you fly a thousand feet above James River, you see not only that river, but a wide sweep of Tidewater Virginia. Parallel rivers flow eastward toward Chesapeake Bay. Up from the south and down from the north lesser rivers pour their waters into the main streams: into the Rappahannock, the York, and the James; and creeks contribute to the rivers, and brooks feed the creeks.

Airplane view establishes things in perspective, each in its place, relating land and water. You realize why it was that three hundred years ago when the Virginia Venture established the first permanent British colony in the New World, horses played no part in the conquest; for this network of streams formed the only highways; penetrating in every direction primeval forests. Horses, which on the trails of Mexico and Peru terrified the natives as supernatural creatures, had no value in the conquest of this roadless region of forest and flowing stream, where for a hundred miles inland the tides of the sea ebb and rise in the rivers.

The great forests of the past were long ago replaced by plantations, but groves of trees stand about the old mansions, trees march down village streets, and if it happens to be a blithe autumn day when you fly over this Tidewater country at intervals in the landscape wooded areas will be painted scarlet and gold, harvest fields will lie serene in the sun, dotted with stacks of hay and corn, and strewn with yellow pumpkins, no bigger than oranges as you see them from the plane.

Dropping down to fly low over the James you draw near to the great story of the river; passing over the broad mouth, through which sailed the little fleet that brought the first Venturers from England.

Jamestown Island, where they first settled, looks from the air like a great open fan lying upon wide amber waters. A bridge connecting the island with the peninsula forms the handle of the fan; and the fan's decorations are a grove of trees at one end, at the other a square ivy-covered tower, a monument, and two statues set upon velvet grass at the foot of the terraced embankment of an abandoned fort.

General Lee had the fort built during the Civil War, the tower was part of the ancient church of old Jamestown, the monument commemorates the founding of the colony, the statues are of Captain John Smith and Pocahontas. Sculptured in bronze, the winsome Indian princess, her hands outstretched, is moving toward John Smith, who stands looking out over the river. Once he said of the first American colonists: "They have been my Wife, my Hawks, my Hounds, my Cards, my Dice and in total my best content." It is of them that his statue seems forever to dream, gazing out upon the James River.

When your plane again climbs you look beyond the James, across the narrow peninsula, to York River; your eyes pause to dwell upon Williamsburg standing midway between the two streams, and then upon Yorktown where Cornwallis surrendered to George Washington, and the independence of the United States was won; the founding of America and its independence lying within a dozen miles of each other, both visible from the air at the same moment.

It is this Tidewater James that I think of always as the "dear ole muddy Jeems."

Describing the region of the James River watershed, Thomas Jefferson, in his famous *Notes on Virginia* prepared for the French statesman, said: "Our country being much intersected with waters and trade brought generally to our doors, instead of being obliged to go in quest of it, has probably been one of the causes why we have no towns of any consequence." And Jefferson lists as included within the James watershed: "Norfolk, Portsmouth, Hampton, Suffolk, Smithfield, Williamsburg, Petersburg, Richmond, the seat of our Government, Manchester, Charlottesville and New London."

But to complete the picture you must continue westward to the origin of the James, below Iron Gate in the great Valley of Virginia; you must visit Buchanan, Clifton Forge, Covington, Lexington, Warm and Hot Springs. For the James and its tributary waters flow through the southern part of the Valley, cutting a passage through the Blue Ridge Mountains, before the James crosses the Piedmont section of Middle Virginia, and finally rushes over the "Falls" at Richmond, down to Tidewater.

Though the James is wholly contained within the state of Virginia, it is not a local river, for it belongs to the nation; not to the native-born only, but also to those who have come from many lands to become citizens of the United States. So much of significance to our country has happened in the James River watershed that this river cannot belong to one state alone, but must belong to all.

When I had written the final word of this book, I again went back to Virginia; this time revisiting the Tidewater James. And everywhere I saw proof of the truth of that sentence: *So much of significance has happened in the James River watershed that this river cannot belong to one state alone, but must belong to all:*

It was October of 1944, and we were crossing the ferry between Willoughby Point and Old Point Comfort. The sun was setting over the wide serenity of Hampton Roads, when suddenly the ships of a great convoy were "standing in." On all sides we were now surrounded by ships; battleships, destroyers, tankers, freighters; coming to anchor in Hampton Roads, at the mouth of James River. I knew that the men who manned them had come from all over the country; united in a great common purpose. German prisoners crowding the decks of some of these incoming ships were symbolic of that purpose; as the sunset was symbolic of the dying day of totalitarian tyranny.

In that same October men from nearby Army and Navy camps walked the streets of Williamsburg, visiting the restored Capitol, the Governor's Palace, the Wren building of William and Mary College, and old Bruton Parish Church. Streets which once knew George Washington, Thomas Jefferson, Richard Bland, the "Antiquary," and passionate

Patrick Henry, now knew the youth from all the states of the Union; while for them—for youth dedicated to pay the bitter price of war—restored Williamsburg was fulfilling the dream of its founder, Dr. W. A. R. Goodwin, whose hope it was that through the restoration "the future may learn from the past."

Youth, which is to shape the future, thus looked upon the Williamsburg of America's great past; their presence a living, daily testimony to the fact that *James River belongs, not to the native-born only, but also to those who have come from many lands to become citizens of the United States.*

The Graveyard — Jamestown

CHAPTER ONE

"To Overcome Is To Live"

NO ONE WAS ever indifferent where Captain John Smith was concerned. And though he has been nearly three hundred years dead, his robust personality has come striding down the centuries, still winning devotion, still making enemies—still living. The echo of his voice seems never to die away, nor his brave eyes to dim; and he remains confident, arrogant, daring. He proclaims a philosophy of strength, he is impatient with the slothful and the futile. "To overcome is to live"—that is the motto on his coat of arms. From time to time in the world there appear such men; and inevitably they are hated as well as loved; the truth about them lying somewhere between those two extremes.

13

John Smith was born in England of respectable yeoman parents, but at an early age he became a soldier of fortune, traveling up and down the continent of Europe. His adventures seem as incredible today as our winged journeys would have appeared three hundred years ago. But Smith lived in that fabulous age when life itself was melodrama, so that such exploits did not then appear too extraordinary. In the James River story they have a place only because they show the *Arabian Nights* quality of one phase of his mind, and in that quality lay much of his gift for dealing with the aboriginal Indians, in whose land the British sought to establish a colony.

According to Smith, he was for a time soldier in the service of Prince Sigismund of Transylvania. The armies of the prince and of the Turks were encamped outside the town of Regall when a challenge announced that, "in order to delight the ladies who did long to see some court-like pastime," one of the Turkish captains defied any captain to combat with him for his head. And Smith took up the challenge. Both armies then assembled in battle regalia to look on, and veiled ladies crowded the city walls. At the very first thrust of the lance the Turkish captain was unhorsed, and Smith cut off his head. On the next day the Turks dared Smith to a second combat; again the armies assembled and veiled ladies watched from the city walls. They saw both lances shattered, saw the combatants turn to pistols to decide the issue, and saw Smith behead his foe. Now—ever in the tradition of gallantry—Smith offered the Turks yet another chance, giving them the choice of weapons. They selected battle-axes, and in the struggle Smith's ax fell to the ground, but at once he drew his sword and a third Turk lost his head.

Some time later Smith was taken prisoner in battle, and in the market place of Axopolis he was sold into slavery. His purchaser was, as is fitting in such a story, a prince, who sent the new slave to his wife, the Lady Charatza Tragabigzanda in Constantinople. This princess became so much interested in the new slave that, fearing he might be resold, she sent him away to her brother, the Pasha of Nalbritz, begging the pasha to treat him kindly. The pasha did not spoil the story by obeying her, and Smith received from him no more consideration than the most wretched slave; even to the degradation of having an iron collar put about his neck. Finally Smith murdered his tormentor, dressed himself in the garments of the dead man, and mounting his master's horse, rode away; far out into the Scythian desert, for he must put himself beyond the reach of any who might identify the mark on his collar. So he rode for many days, until at last he arrived at a Russian stronghold, where he was able to free himself from the damning evidence of the slave's collar. He traveled then safely and with much enjoyment through Russia and Poland to Leipzig, where providentially he found Prince Sigismund. It was then that the prince granted him a coat of arms, bearing three Turks' heads and the motto "Vincere est vivere:" "To conquer—to overcome—is to live."

How much of all this is true?

Well . . . there is in London, officially registered in the College of Arms, a document in Latin wherein Sigismund gives Smith safe-conduct to his own country, and grants him a "shield of arms, the figure and description of three Turks' heads, which, with his sword before the town of Regall, in single combat he did overcome, kill, and cut off, in the Province of Transylvania." It is all written out by hand, and in the upper left-hand corner of the page there is a copy of the crest granted to Smith by Prince Sigismund. At the bottom of the page there is a certificate, dated August 19, 1625, and signed by Sir William Segar, Garter King at Arms, stating that the above is a true copy of the original document.

Being the sort of man he was, Captain John Smith, when he arrived in England, joined the group of Venturers who sailed with Christopher Newport to found a colony in Virginia. The English were now determined to carry out Sir

Philip Sidney's advice "to check the dangerous and increasing power of Spain . . . in the New World by planting English Protestant settlements there which would increase until they extended from ocean to ocean."

The enterprise had limitless possibilities. It might easily carry a man eventually to the court of the great Kubla Khan; for Newport's instructions read that when it should please God to bring the voyagers to the coast of Virginia they were to settle upon a river, and the river they selected must bend toward the northwest; for thus they would soonest find the other sea.

The Other Sea . . . it was in those times always the passage to the rich, fabulous Orient that adventurers sought.

Newport was to choose a stream bending to the northwest. And the new settlement must be located well inland from the river's mouth; since if they should sit down near the sea they would be more open to attack. For a colony formerly planted in that part of the world under the patronage of Sir Walter Raleigh had disappeared so completely that it was never known whether its members lived or had all perished. They had been established upon an island called Roanoke, and some years later a ship had been sent seeking news of them. Arriving near to the island in the darkness of night, and waiting there until the morning should break, those on board the ship had played upon trumpets and sung familiar songs of the homeland, hoping for response to their serenade from those on the island. But there had come no answer, and with the dawn they had discovered the island to be deserted.

Because of this tragedy, Captain Newport was cautioned to select for the new colony a place easily defensible. His instructions concluded with the admonition that the settlers were not to offend the natives, and that in none of their letters home were they to write of anything that might discourage future colonists. A strange circumstance of the undertaking was that Newport carried a sealed box containing the names of those on board who were to act as a governing council in the new land. The box was not to be opened until their arrival, and of course throughout the voyage there was much speculation as to which men were to rule.

The voyage was long. For six weeks adverse winds kept the three little ships actually within sight of England, and it was five months before they finally arrived on the Virginia coast. Even before they reached the Canaries, where they took on water, John Smith had contrived to make for himself enemies who charged him with plotting to be king of the colony which they were to establish. And for the remainder of the way he journeyed as a prisoner. But he had won devotion as well as hatred among the voyagers. "It is because they envy his reputation," his friends said, "that this scandalous accusation had been made against him."

As for Smith, it did not matter that he voyaged as a prisoner in irons; for there flowed strong in him the vigor of a young body, disciplined to hardships and accustomed to danger. He was as sturdy of body as of mind, a muscular bronzed man with a light beard, and horizontal mustaches, like a line drawn to underscore the bold strength that looked out of his eyes. And did he not believe that to overcome is to live?

A great storm blew Newport's little fleet toward the shore of Virginia. Sailing between the capes which stand watch at the entrance of Chesapeake Bay, they explored a river flowing through so pleasant a land that with great admiration they praised God. It was spring, and the forests rising in lofty majesty on the banks were freshly green. Flowers bloomed and birds sang; new songs and unfamiliar flowers. Even the fact that on the night of their first landing they were attacked by savages did not dishearten them; after all, the fellows had run howling before British guns.

One of the Venturers—George Percy, eighth son of Henry Percy, eighth Earl of Northumberland, wrote: "This River which wee have discovered is one of the famousest Rivers that ever was found by any Christian, it ebbs and flowes a hundred and threescore miles where ships of great burthen may harbour in safetie. Wheresoever wee landed upon this River wee saw the goodliest woods, as Beech, Oke, Cedar, and Vines in good abundance which hang in great clusters on many Trees, and other Trees unknowne, and all the grounds bespred with many sweet and delicate flowres of divers colours and kindes. There are also Strawberries, Mulberries, Rasberries and Fruits unknowne, there are many branches of this River, which runne flowing through the woods with great plentie of Fish of all kindes, as for Sturgeon all the World cannot be compared to it. In this countrey I have seene many great and large Medowes having excellent good pasture for any cattle. There is also great store of Deere both Red and Fallow, there are Beares, Foxes, Otters, Bevers, Muskrats and wild beasts unknowne . . . Wee set up a Crosse at the head of this River naming it *Kings River,* where wee proclaimed *James* King of England to have the most right unto it."

With similar bright optimism did the James River country appear to Captain John Smith, to Wingfield and Martin, Ratcliffe, and Bartholomew Gosnold; a river, they said, "for breadth, sweetness of water, length navigable into the country, deep and bold channell, so stored with sturgeon and other sweet fish as no man's fortune hath ever possessed the like. And as we think if more may be wished in a River it will be found."

And this beautiful river, which before the coming of the British Venturers had been known as Powhatan's River, had now become the James, in honor of their rickety, popeyed, tyrannical, bigoted king, James the First; and the capes they called Henry and Charles in compliment to his two sons.

On the north bank of the river, about sixty miles inland, they selected a peninsula as the spot where they would settle, naming it Jamestown. Between two trees they stretched a canvas sail, and there good Master Robert Hunt, who had come to look after their souls and to convert the heathen, conducted their first religious service.

Newport had already opened the sealed box containing the names of the Council, and when the prisoner, John Smith, discovered that he himself was among those appointed he demanded a trial of his case, and his enemies being unable to prove the charges against him, he was triumphantly acquitted.

Before going back to England to secure supplies and additional colonists, Captain Newport explored their river as far as the falls, taking with him a selected number of men.

Along the way a chief came to greet the explorers, carrying in one hand his bow and in the other a pipe of peace, that they might choose whether they would have war or peace. At another point a chief met them marching at the head of his people, playing as he came upon a reed flute, and wearing a crown of deerskin dyed red, with two long feathers in his hair placed like horns on either side of his crown. "His body was painted all with crimson, and his face blue, his ears all behung with bracelets of pearl, and in either ear a bird's claw." This man, they said, received them in a "modest, proud fashion."

There was much banqueting with music and dancing, because it was thought that the strangers were come merely as guests, and it was not yet suspected that they intended to make permanent settlement in the land.

Everywhere along the river they heard of the great Chief Powhatan, whose name people spoke with awe; and when they returned to Jamestown they found that in their absence a large company of Indians had attacked their settlement, wounding many and killing two. In spite of this, when Newport sailed away to England he carried to the London Company an enthusiastic letter bearing the signatures of all the members of the Virginia Council.

The lovely Virginia spring passed, and there fell upon Jamestown a withering heat, as strange to Englishmen as the brilliant unfamiliar fireflies which pricked the hot darkness of the night. August came and with it a strange new disease, a fever which they called the "country sickness."

The river shimmered in the summer heat, the tides rose and ebbed. Sometimes there was no sound but the soft lap of the water, the buzz of the mosquito, and the groans of the dying.

England must have seemed to them as far away as the stars. Their minds must have gone back to her; remembering only what was happy; remembering tunes played on the viol and the virginals, remembering the boisterous life of the taverns, the strength of old liquor strong enough "to make a cat speak," the baying of hounds, the huntsmen's horns, the flight of falcons, and the bagpipes and drums of Christmas festivities; forgetting how rich were the rich and how poor were the poor, forgetting the sharpers and the money-lenders, the "roaring boys and roysterers" who made the streets a peril, forgetting the beggars, forgetting the cruel power of a monarch who could keep even the great Sir Walter Raleigh a prisoner in the Tower.

But Captain John Smith, looking out over the broad deserted James, thought: Who would live at home idly, or think himself any worth, to live only to eat, drink and sleep, and so die?

By the autumn only thirty-eight of the hundred and four that had come out of England remained alive; though weakened by sickness and by their scanty diet of barley, sodden in the river water.

Smith was now cape merchant of the colony, and actively engaged in trading with the Indians. No one else had his gift for dealing with them. From the beginning he had set himself to learn their language, but there was more in it than that. It seemed as though this man possessed some secret understanding of the inner mind of the savage. Those who lay at Jamestown alternately shaken with chill and scorched with fever begged him to explore farther. Only a little distance away, they hoped, everything might be better. Smith might even come upon the passage to that other sea, and so they would all arrive at the riches of the East.

Thus he took the barge and eight men and went to discover in the region drained by the Chickahominy: to discover and to trade for corn. Forty miles up the Chicka-hominy, he left the barge to await his return, and proceeded by canoe with two of his countrymen, and a couple of Indian guides. By the time they had gone twenty miles they were wearied with dragging the canoe over fallen trees and sub-merged logs, so that Smith with one of the Indians set out to see what might be observed on foot.

He soon heard a whoop and at the same time felt that he had been struck by an arrow. Indians poured out of the forest and Smith fired, killing two of them. But all at once he realized that he and his guide were standing on a quaking bog into which they were fast sinking. He threw away his weapons and surrendered himself to Indian mercies, hoping that by the time they had helped him to dry ground, he would have thought of some trick by which he might gain his life. Suddenly he remembered his pocket compass; if he could make this appear to them as a magical thing he might divert their attention from the amusement of murdering one John Smith.

As soon as they were safe out of the bog he produced his compass, and the warriors crowded close to see the mys-terious little needle which, however you turned the compass, pointed always in the same direction. And while they stared, Smith's Oriental imagination spun for them a discourse upon the movement of the stars, on how "the sun did chase the night round about the world continually, how great was the Land and the Sea, how diverse the Nations," and other important matters.

Not that he expected them to comprehend, but because he understood the effect of sonorous phrases, of the influence of many words, and of a bold confidence shown by those in peril. Still, in the end they bound him to a tree as though they intended to begin the torture.

Yet they hesitated. For this man had the manner of an important—perhaps a magical—person. It might, after all, be unwise to kill him, at least just yet. . . . And the chief among them, who was Opekankano, brother to Powhatan, gave the order to unbind him. Also, Opekankano would further examine the marvelous instrument and learn more about it.

It was winter, the season of hunting, when great circles of fire were lighted in the forest and Indians killed the beasts trapped within the rings of flame. From hunting camp to hunting camp, from village to village, Smith was marched through the country, and everywhere crowds gathered to gaze at the bearded captive who seemed not at all to understand that he was a prisoner to be delivered into the hands of mighty Powhatan.

Finally Smith was conducted into the presence of Powhatan, lord of the land. The chief received him, lying proudly on a bed a foot high, upon which were spread ten or twelve mats. A young woman sat at his head and another at his feet; surrounding him were many warriors, and standing back of them other young women, all with chains of beads about their necks, their heads and shoulders painted red. And among them was little Pocahontas, Powhatan's favorite daughter, the child of his old age.

Smith sent home to England a "Relation" of this interview with the Indian king, though all that happened did not appear in his account as it was first published in London; for it had been forbidden to write anything that might discourage future colonists. At any rate, Smith somehow arrived at an understanding with Powhatan, since he was permitted to return in safety to Jamestown.

And in the Indian vocabulary, which he compiled, there was this sentence: "Bid Pocahontas bring hither a little basket, and I will give her beads to make her a chain."

Captain John Smith

CHAPTER TWO

"If the Little Ant and the Sillie Bee..."

FROM that interview with Powhatan, Smith returned to Jamestown to find himself accused of murder. The same enemies who had charged him with intriguing to make himself king of the colony now declared that he had led his companions into a trap and was responsible for the fact that two of them had been slain by the Indians. So, on the very day of his safe return to Jamestown he was tried, convicted, and sentenced to be hanged. Although men like the knightly Percy and the saintly Robert Hunt protested, Smith's enemies were determined. In the morning he was to hang.

But on the tide, flowing full and strong up the James, Captain Christopher Newport was arriving from England. His return had been so long delayed that in Jamestown men had begun to think he had perished on the wintry Atlantic, like Sir Humphrey Gilbert who had gone down with his ship in a tempestuous sea, while in the darkness his confident voice had shouted to the sailors: "Be of good cheer, my friends!

We are as near to Heaven by sea as by land!" In the same fashion perhaps, Newport had perished. Or, it might be that he had been captured by some roving pirate, or by the Spaniards. Yet here he was again, borne up on the swelling tide of James River; bringing rescue to Captain John Smith.

A few days later the frail, reed-thatched village that was Jamestown burned to the ground. But a greater misfortune still was that somebody discovered yellow earth, which was eagerly pronounced gold. Hadn't Cortez found gold in Mexico, and Pizzaro in Peru? Why, the very cooking utensils of those countries were of solid gold! Therefore there must be gold also in this bright yellow Virginia sand.

After that there was no more rebuilding of the burned houses and no one could be made to take an interest in planting corn. Jamestown was gold-crazy. Newport, who was due to return to England in a fortnight, remained fourteen weeks, loading the yellow dirt into his ships, his crew consuming most of the food sent out for the colonists. "There was no talk," Smith said, "no work, but dig gold, refine gold . . ."

Before sailing for England with his yellow dirt, Newport went with Smith to pay a ceremonious visit to old Powhatan, who set them forth a banquet of wild fowl and venison, corn bread, nuts and persimmons. When they had feasted, and had been entertained with dance and song, Smith would trade English gewgaws—bells and mirrors and beads—for the corn which he knew Jamestown was soon to need desperately.

Powhatan was haughty. He would not condescend to peddle, he said, trifle by trifle. If the English would lay out their goods, he would offer what he thought suitable. Newport fell unsuspiciously into the trap and for the whole collection Powhatan gave only four bushels of corn. But there remained, by accident, a few blue beads not included in the transaction. With Oriental subtlety Smith suavely explained that they had not been offered because blue beads might be worn only by royalty. Then away skyrocketing went the value of blue beads. Royalty must have blue beads. A chief's wife felt herself disgraced without a few of the royal blue beads. In the end the blue beads brought more than two hundred bushels of corn. But Powhatan scored at the last by giving Newport only twenty turkeys in exchange for twenty swords.

Of course, after Newport had departed for England, Powhatan wanted to continue trading turkeys for swords on the same terms. But Smith would not trade swords at any price; from the beginning he understood that the English could not trust the friendship of men whose land they were appropriating for themselves. No, he would not sell swords at any price. Then the Indians, visiting the fort at Jamestown, tried to sneak off with some of the coveted weapons. Smith captured and imprisoned two of them. And Powhatan sent his craftiest ambassador, accompanied by the little Pocahontas, to intercede for their release. They brought gifts, venison, and pones of corn bread baked in the ashes.

So it happened that Pocahontas came to the settlement at Jamestown; a gay child, turning cart wheels in the square before the fort. She was still too young to have put on the apron of the Indian woman, or the mantle prettily fashioned of feathers which she would wear when she was grown-up. She was just a child, delicately made, graceful and merry, whirling naked in the square.

Smith called her the "Nonpareil." For among the Indians, he said, there was never anyone who could compare with Pocahontas, Powhatan's "dear and darling daughter, who exceeded all; not only in her feature and countenance and proportion, but in her wit and spirit." Truly the Nonpareil.

Pocahontas easily won the release of the captive Indians, and for herself whatever might please a little girl. After that, throughout the hard hungry winter, she would cross over her father's river and walk twelve miles through the woods to Jamestown, bringing corn and game; over and over saving the colony from starvation.

Whenever Smith felt that he could safely leave Jamestown he explored one by one the Tidewater rivers; seeking

always that passage to the other sea, and that mine of gold
for which the early London backers of the Virginia Venture
clamored. He found no gold and no sea, but he mapped the
country and made a record of its plants and animals and of
the customs of its people.

In the September following their second summer on
James River, Captain John Smith was elected president of
the Governing Council. And a month later the river tide
again brought a ship.

One Thomas Forrest, Gent., was aboard and with him
his wife, Madam Forrest, and her little fourteen-year-old
serving maid, Ann Burras; the first Englishwomen to arrive
at Jamestown. And while Ann was smiling upon the woman-
less men, knowing in her feminine heart that almost any one
of them was ready to make her Jamestown's first wife, Smith
was reading the ultimatum sent by the London Company.
The company found itself displeased with the colonists; their
quarrels and intrigues were not to be tolerated. Also, the
company demanded practical results. The settlers had produced none. The shipload of yellow sand had proved to be
merely yellow sand: "A drunken ship," Smith had called
it, "freighted with so much gilded dirt." The passage to the
other sea had not been found, and there was no news of the
lost colony. One at least of these three things, the company
insisted, must be accomplished; otherwise Jamestown would
be abandoned, no more supplies would be sent out, and no
more colonists.

As if that were not ironic enough, Captain Newport
brought with him a copper crown: it was the fancy of King
James that Powhatan should be crowned as a great foreign
potentate with whom he, James, was allied. It was fantastic
. . . unbelievable. Smith, as president, with a delegation of
colonists, went to Powhatan to invite him to Jamestown for
the ceremony of coronation.

The monarch was away, and while Smith and his companions waited the Indians made a celebration in his honor.
They built a great fire in the forest clearing and spread mats

for their guests to sit upon. It was night and the autumn foliage flamed red and gold in the flashing firelight, when out of the shadows a troupe of thirty young girls came dancing into the light. The Englishmen who were present said that their bodies were painted, some red, some black, some parti-colored. The Indian women were described by another as "remarkable for having small round breasts . . . so firm that they are hardly ever observed to hang down, even in old women. . . . They keep their skin clean and shining with oil . . ." and "commonly go naked as far as the naval downward, and upward to the middle of the thigh, by which means they have the advantage of discovering their fine limbs and complete shape."

The leader of that troupe of dancing girls who danced in the firelight wore a pair of "fair stag's" horns on her head, and an otterskin at her girdle. As they danced singing about the fire, the flames illumined their figures.

They danced in a narrowing circle close about Smith, singing over and over: "Love you not me? Love you not me?" And it was Pocahontas who led those singing dancers.

The firelight shone on her sleek young body, on her long braids of black hair, on the stag's horns she wore, and on the otterskin at her girdle. She was all of the forest, with the bright eyes of its creatures and their silent, agile movements; she was a little wild thing, incredibly supple and swift, with an Indian girl's dainty hands and feet, and the beautifully sculptured body of her race. And this little princess of the wilderness sang: "Love you not me? . . . Love you not me? . . ."

On the following day Powhatan arrived.

No, he would not visit Captain Newport at Jamestown. "I am a king," he said, "and this is my land. If your Father Newport would see me, he can come to me here in my own house."

And because he must carry out the royal orders from London, Captain Newport came, Indian prestige triumphing over British. But he had difficulty in placing the crown on Powhatan's brow, since the Indian would not lower his head to receive it. For here was a man so full of majesty that as long as he lived every Englishman admitted into his presence felt his regal dignity. "He is but a naked savage," they would say, bewildered, "yet how proudly majestical."

The gifts presented and the crowning over, John Smith sat down and wrote to the London Company: a "rude answer," he called this letter in which he put before the company just what were the conditions in a colony fighting the cruel wilderness battle. "As for the coronation of Powhatan," he wrote, "by whose advice you sent him such presents, I know not, but give me leave to tell you I fear they will be to the confusion of us all." Smith sent the letter by the hand of Captain Newport when he sailed for England.

Among the new immigrants come out to colonize Virginia many had been booked as "gentlemen," and in addition the passenger list had included a perfumer, two goldsmiths, a jeweler, and six tailors; very few were sturdy laborers. With such men Smith, now president of the Governing Council, cleared the land of primeval forest so that corn might be planted and houses built; with such men he must maintain a colony on the banks of a wilderness river, menaced continually by savages who at one moment seemed friendly, at the next were treacherously hostile. And he could not appeal to the motive of private gain, for the colonists were at that time allowed no individual stake in the enterprise. But at least he would not tolerate idlers living upon the toil of the industrious. "No empty porringers," he decreed, "will be filled from the common kettle unless the owner has by toil earned his meal, or has been prevented by illness. . . . He who will not work shall not eat."

Out of Jamestown's bitter struggle for survival in Virginia, John Smith thus grew in stature, from the mere soldier of fortune to the pioneer planting a colony in the wilderness. He had begun to think and evolve a philosophy. "If the Little Ant," he thought, "and the Sillie Bee seek by their diligence the good of their commonwealth: much more ought man."

In December, not three months after her arrival at Jamestown, little Ann Burras, the servant girl, married John Laydon, one of the early settlers. And so was founded the first of Virginia's families. But already fear of that famine which Smith had foreseen was in every man's eyes: What were they to do in the months before another ship could arrive with supplies?

And Smith thought: Perhaps there will be no other ship. For he had not forgotten the London Company's threat of abandonment and he remembered his own letter to the company, that letter which he had called a "rude answer." Altogether, it might well be that Newport would never return. And Jamestown must have food. Somehow he, Smith, must get corn for Jamestown. It was his responsibility. If the Indians would not trade of their own will, they must be made to trade. For, "no persuasions," as his friends expressed it, "would persuade him to starve."

He took the barge and sailed up and down the river from one village to another. But Powhatan had commanded his people to barter no more with the English. Even that tribe which had contracted to deliver to Smith four hundred bushels of corn would now part with only a hundred. . . . And Jamestown must have corn or perish.

It was at this time that Powhatan sent a messenger to say that he would like to see Smith; also he wanted men sent to build him an English house: he wanted a rooster too, and a hen, strange new creatures in his country; and he desired swords and guns and a grindstone. In exchange for these things he would give corn.

Smith dispatched men to build the house, and then, taking along a group of dependable colonists, he sailed the barge and the pinnace down James River and into the bay. It was Christmas, and in the Chesapeake they were delayed by a blizzard. While it lasted they were the guests of a small tribe of Indians unfriendly to Powhatan. They sat together around a cheerful fire in the smoky wigwam and ate oysters. "Powhatan has sent for you," the Indians said, "to murder

The Statue of Captain John Smith
gazes upon the James at Jamestown

you. He will seem to show you kindness, but do not trust him."

With these warning words in their minds the English sailed out of the bay, and into that river on whose bank the great chief had his headquarters. When they arrived at his landing they found the river frozen far out from shore, but they broke their way through ice to the bank and established themselves in a vacant house, Smith then sending to Powhatan to say that they were come.

On the following day the king received them, and what happened at that interview has been told by certain of the men whom Smith took with him. And I give the conversation that took place between them precisely as it was recorded by those present:

"Corn?" Powhatan had no corn for anyone. What made them think he had corn to trade?

"Powhatan"—Smith was stern—"I am surprised you have forgotten that we are here at your own invitation . . . you must have a short memory."

The Indian laughed. There might perhaps be a little corn, but only in exchange for swords and guns. There would be no corn to barter for other things.

("Do not trust him," the Indians on the Chesapeake had said, "for he plots to murder you.")

"Powhatan," Smith continued, "to testify my love I sent you men for the building of your house, neglecting mine own. You have returned my friendship by forbidding your people to trade with us. As for swords and guns, I told you long ago I had none to spare. You must realize that those I have can keep us from want . . . yet steal from you, or wrong you, I will not. Nor will I break that friendship which we have mutually promised. Not unless you force me to it by bad usage."

Powhatan listened. He would spare Smith what corn he could.

"And yet . . . yet, Captain Smith, yet some doubt have I of your coming to my country . . . that doubt makes me not so kindly to receive you as I would. For many do inform

me that your coming is not for trade, but to possess my
country. For this reason my people dare not bring you corn.
They see you and your men armed. And so they dare not
bring you corn. If . . . if you would free us of this fear,
leave your weapons on board the boats in which you have
come. Here they are needless, for we are all friends, and forever Powhatans."

("Do not trust him. Have no faith in him, for he plots
to destroy you." Was this, perhaps, why he was so eager
to have the weapons left aboard the boats?)

"Seeing you thus armed, Captain Smith, my people dare
not bring you corn—"

So the old Indian chieftain and the young florid-bearded
British captain talked throughout that day, and again on
the following day.

"To free us from fear, leave your weapons aboard the
boats in which you have come—"

This great ruler over thirty tribes, feared up and down
the Tidewater rivers, actually pleaded with John Smith. Both
were making a desperate fight: the old chief seeking a way
to save his land from those who would possess it; the young
captain, with equal desperation, fighting for corn to save
Jamestown from starvation.

"To free us from fear, leave your weapons. . . . Why
are you jealous of our loves? . . . Come in friendly manner
to see us, and not thus with your guns and swords."

"Powhatan, the vow I made you of my love, both myself and my men have kept. As for your promise, I find it
every day violated by some of your subjects. Yet we have
no desire for revenge. Else had your people known the cruelty
we use to our enemies, as well as our true love and courtesy
to our friends . . .

"Your people, when they come to Jamestown, are received with their bows and arrows. And, as is the case with
you, so it is our custom also to wear our arms . . . as for
provisions, do not imagine that we shall starve without
your aid."

(Yet in only a few days Jamestown would be without

food. Corn . . . corn . . . he *must* have corn for Jamestown!)

"Do not think, Powhatan, that we shall starve without your help."

Powhatan laughed.

"Captain Smith, I have never dealt so kindly with any chief as with yourself. Yet from you do I receive the least kindness of any. Captain Newport gave me swords, a bed . . . what I desired, ever taking what I offered."

("By whose advice you sent him such presents"—Smith had written to the London Company—"I know not, but give me leave to tell you I fear they will be to the confusion of us all.")

"Captain Newport gave me what I wished. Only you refuse to do what I ask. Only you. Yet you would have from me whatever you desire. You call me father, as Captain Newport is your father . . . but if you intend so friendly as you say, send away your arms that I may believe you."

(Was he trying to prolong the talk until his warriors had assembled? And would the men on the barge and the pinnace arrive before that happened?)

"You must know, Powhatan, that as I have but one God, I honor but one king, and I live here not as your subject, but as your friend . . ."

Leaving some of his women in talk with Smith, Powhatan went out of the room and fled secretly away, and while they talked Indian warriors surrounded the house.

Then, so Smith's friends tell the story, "with sword and pistol, he made such a passage among the naked Devils that those next him tumbled one over another, and the rest made haste to escape."

He gathered his followers together in that house on the riverbank where they had lodged. In the afternoon a messenger came to Smith, with Powhatan's excuses and the gift of a chain of pearls. Also corn was provided with men to carry it down to the boats, but as it was low water the boats could not then get away.

Waiting in the house on the river for the tide to turn, the English heard the Indians making merry, with music and dancing and games. But still the ebb tide kept them waiting. Darkness fell. And Pocahontas came softly through the night. Smith was in danger and Pocahontas, Powhatan's favorite daughter, came to warn him. Those who were present have told the story:

"Pocahontas," they say, "Powhatan's dearest jewel and daughter, in that dark night came through the irksome woods and told our captain that great cheer would soon be sent us . . . but that Powhatan and all the power he could make would then come and kill us all . . . if we would live, she wished us presently to be gone.

"Such things as she delighted in, we would have given her, but with the tears running down her cheeks, she said she durst not be seen to have any, for if Powhatan should know of it, she were but dead. . . . And she went away by herself as she came.

"Then within less than an hour, eight or ten lusty fellows came with platters of venison and other victual . . . but the captain made them taste every dish, which done, he sent some of them back to Powhatan to bid him make haste, for he was prepared for his coming."

Having been warned, the English could not be taken by surprise; and at high water they sailed away.

Meanwhile in London the colonists who had returned to England with Newport had joined with those of the London Company who were petitioning King James to grant to Virginia a new charter under which the method of governing the colony was to be reorganized. The company was disturbed about the Venture. Much money had been spent and there was nothing to show for it. Yet that fellow John Smith was writing arrogantly, actually calling the company to task. And certain of the colonists who had returned to England were spreading talk of Smith's cruelty to the Indians, which was embarrassing, because from the beginning it had been understood that converting the "Naturells" to Christianity was a prime object of the enterprise. Clearly something must be done about all this or the whole investment would be lost.

Also it was argued that the length of the voyage must be cut and Virginia brought nearer to England. A straight route would save a thousand miles over the roundabout West Indies voyage. And that would make easier the supervision of the colony. The company thought that young Captain Samuel Argall was the man to undertake this finding of a more direct route between England and Virginia, for he had a reputation for getting what he went after.

Let Captain Argall take his ship out and see if it might not be possible to make a direct and clear passage in the eye of the wind.

Duly arriving in the eye of the wind, Argall brought Jamestown news of the new charter. The original charter had set up a superior council in London, appointed by the king. This superior council, in turn, appointed the local council in Virginia, and that local council elected its own president. The new charter drafted by the great Liberal leader, Sir Edwin Sandys, transferred from the king to the London Company the direction of Virginia's government, and in place of a president elected by the local council, there would be a governor appointed by the London Company in England.

But Captain Smith—people asked—his term as president had not expired . . . what of Captain Smith?

Oh, that was changed . . . everything was changed. The company itself was reorganized, and many great men added to its directors. Virginia, the new charter declared, extended for two hundred miles to the north and to the south of Point Comfort, while to the west it reached to the other sea, though how far that was nobody knew. The company was raising new funds. Broadsides had been written and sermons preached about Virginia. London had gone quite wild, and everybody was buying shares in the Venture. Lord Delaware was to be the governor and already a great expedition of nine vessels, with supplies and five hundred settlers, was ready to sail: with Sir Thomas Gates coming out on the

Sea Venture to represent Lord Delaware. Smith was no longer president.

That might be, Smith said, but until he had official orders he would continue to govern. In the meantime he was anxious to move Jamestown to a more healthful location: to that end he made excursions up and down the river.

In August part of the expected fleet of nine ships arrived. They had passed through a hurricane which had lasted two days and two nights, and the *Sea Venture,* bringing Sir Thomas Gates, had disappeared, lost perhaps in the tempest. And Smith, though he had found so lovely a site that he called it "Nonesuch," was unable to move the colony, for he had been seriously burned in a gunpowder explosion and was forced to go for treatment to London in one of the returning ships.

He left ten weeks' provisions in the storehouse, and there were hogs and goats and sheep, and ever so many chickens, a horse too, and six mares. The colony now numbered nearly five hundred, among them women and children. More than fifty houses had been built, and a good palisade to protect the settlement from attack. So things were when Smith said farewell to Jamestown.

Seeing him go, his friends mourned: "thus we lost him that would never send us where he would not lead himself, that would never let us want what he could by any means get us. . . . 'Since,' as he once said, 'we are not born for ourselves, but each to help the other.' . . ."

What his enemies felt was expressed by George Percy, who called him "a vainglorious fellow . . . sounding his trumpet as the hypocrites do" . . . a fellow who appropriated "to himself many deserts which he never performed, and stuffed his relations with many falsities and malicious detractions of others."

Pocahontas~Ruins of the
Ambler house at Jamestown

CHAPTER THREE

Pocahontas: From Eyewitness Records

IT MUST have seemed to Pocahontas very long ago that the white man had come. In actual time the dogwood had bloomed but twice, and but three times, high in the golden autumn haze, had the geese flown south. But so many things had happened that surely it was long ago, for the whole world was altered since the day Captain John Smith had been brought a prisoner to her father.

Before that she had been just a merry little girl. She had known, of course, that one day she would be a woman: then she would paint her body a lovely red, she would hang pearls about her neck, and put white aigrettes in her hair. She would have a husband too; he would be a chief, perhaps as great as her father. And she would have children.

One day, of course, her father would die, and according to custom, his brother, Opekankano, would rule. But always there would be Indian villages along the riverbanks, with houses made of saplings woven together, and mats hanging

at the doors. Inside there would be the fire that must never
be allowed to go out. Always people would light the darkness
with burning torches of pine, and when it was cold they
would dress in skins. These things had always been, just as
the rivers had always flowed, the sun always rose and set,
and the summer followed the winter: the happy summer
when wild roses and sunflowers bloomed in the village, and
women were busy in the cornfield and the garden: cultivat-
ing the corn in rows, with beans and peas, pumpkins and
cymblins between the rows; and in the gardens growing
muskmelons, passion vines, gourds, and tobacco.

It had been in the season when the trees were green and
strawberries ripe in the forest that news had reached her
father that white men were landed in the next river. But
no one had been alarmed; the older people remembered that
white men had come before, but they had not stayed long.
These men also would not stay . . .

The spring passed. The rains of early summer fell upon
the crops. As usual, in the morning the breeze was sweet
but with the day it died away. Then the hot summer came
when the heat was heavy and the air still. Often in the late
afternoon thunder rolled and boomed and fire flashed in the
sky. Sometimes there was heard the great crash of a tree falling in the forest. And people said that in the next river the
white men were dying. Soon there would be none left. Perhaps by the time the northwest winds spread frost upon the
ground and the geese flew south all the white men would
be dead. It might easily be that that would happen.

But it was not so.

Frost powdered the earth. Chinquapins and persimmons
ripened. Cranes in vast numbers passed over, headed south,
and darting like arrows high across the sky flocks of geese
called Cohunk! Cohunk! They, too, were going south. But
the white men remained, though scarcely fifty of them were
left alive.

Cold winter came. The snowbirds arrived, fluttering
black and white in the low bushes. In the far depths of the

forest, bears went into their holes, so fat with the small sweet
wild grapes of autumn, and the honey of wild bees, that they
waddled when they walked. The trees were naked, and it
was not easy for the woods creatures to hide. It was winter
and still the white men had not gone. The season of hunting
had come. Wild turkeys with wings outstretched ran in terror from the hunters' fires, and with stricken eyes the deer
fled. But it was of no use; they might as well have stood still,
for in the end the hunters killed them.

From such a hunting party Captain John Smith had
been brought to Powhatan. It had been a beautiful thing to
see how he scorned danger, almost as though he did not know
that Powhatan was famed for his cruelty, that men had not
only death to fear from him, but a death of hideous agony.
Surely this white man with the big light beard must have
heard of Powhatan's cruelty. Yet he had seemed so careless
of his danger that he could entertain them all with marvelous
tales; such tales as Pocahontas had never heard. He could
laugh and tell tales. Then what pains he had taken to learn
the words: "Bid Pocahontas bring hither a little basket, and
I will give her beads to make her a chain . . ."

It did not seem possible that he was dead. But that was
what people were saying. Captain Smith, they said, was dead.
Pocahontas could not believe it. For a long time even Powhatan did not think it could be true. Yet Captain Smith did
not come to trade, insisting that he must have corn. Corn
for Jamestown seemed always more to him than his own
life, for he so often risked his life for corn.

Now nothing was any longer as it used to be. Her happy
visits at the place they called Jamestown . . . her visits, too,
were past. There was no one like Pocahontas, Captain Smith
used to say: he had given her the pretty name "Nonpareil,"
and he had taught her to call him "father." But all that was
over, like her childhood.

Perhaps it was on the night when she had bound the
antlers to her forehead, put on the otterskin apron, and
painted her body; perhaps it was then that her childhood was

finished; that night when in the torchlight she had danced, singing "Love you not me?"

Now people were saying, "He is dead. He was burned with their gunpowder; he is dead." And everything was changed; even the songs people made up were different. They used to sing about love and about hunting, making the words as they sang. Now they made up songs about the white men, songs of scorn and hatred.

"Ho," they sang: "see how in spite of their guns we kill these men."

And a chorus jeered: "Whe! Whe! Yah, ha, ha!"

"As for their Captain Newport, he never deceived us by his gifts or by the crown for Powhatan."

"Whe! Whe! Yeh, ha, ha!"

But Powhatan had fallen into deep melancholy. Above every other village in his kingdom, he had loved Werowocomoco, that village to which Smith had been brought prisoner. Now Powhatan took no more pleasure in his village: so long as there were white men in the next river, he could not know peace.

Lately the white men's ships had brought women as well as men; it was plain, therefore, that they had come to stay.

Pocahontas saw her father sit brooding in fear. Everywhere in all the villages of his kingdom there was fear. The whisper of fear was on all the rivers.

And now again the geese flew south, calling Cohunk! just as though the world were as it used to be. So winter was come. The Indians talked of dreadful things happening at Jamestown. The colonists were starving and in their despair thirty of them dared to come to Powhatan. And Pocahontas had never known her father to condemn men to a slower horror of torture.

After that no more white men came to the village. Before the winter was over it was known to the watchful Indians that those in Jamestown were too weak from hunger even to seek acorns in the forest, and that they were burning

the timber from their houses because they lacked strength
to cut firewood in the forest.

"Whe! Whe! Yah, ha! ha!"

The Indians sang in exultation. It was only a matter of
time now—a very little time—and the white men would be
gone.

Then news came that once more the tide bore ships up
the river . . . But to the mournful beat of drums the ships
took on board the starving colonists. Guns were fired in last
salute, and the ships dropped down the river. For three days
Jamestown stood, deserted.

"Whe! Whe!" . . . at last the white men were gone.

But again there were ships in the river. The two so
lately sailed had returned, and with them were three more.
The three had brought food in abundance, and many colonists. A new chief, too, had come; a great man gorgeously
arrayed, quite different from Captain Smith, who had no
such glory of dress. Indians went to Jamestown to stare, and
to trade. But Pocahontas was not among them. For Captain
Smith was no longer there.

The news brought to Powhatan had been quite true: the
terrible "Starving Time" in Jamestown, the two ships which
had rescued the survivors, and the abandonment of the settlement with melancholy salute of guns. It was true also that
within three days the ships had returned together with three
more.

The first two ships were the *Patience* and the *Deliverance*, built in Bermuda by the shipwrecked men of the *Sea
Venture*, which had foundered on the rocks of that island.
With the three new ships came Lord Delaware himself,
arrived in the mouth of the river at the melancholy moment
of Jamestown's abandonment. His fleet brought salvation;
abundant provisions and colonists, among them, in addition
to "knights and gentlemen of quality," many artisans and
laborers.

Crops were immediately planted, new buildings begun, and old ones repaired. Lord Delaware loved flowers and he had the church "kept passing sweet" with blossoms: When he went on Sunday to service he was escorted by all the councilors, captains, and other officials and gentlemen . . . with a guard of fifty halberdiers in livery of bright red cloaks. The lord governor himself sat in a velvet chair, with a velvet cushion before him upon which to kneel; very different from plain John Smith in his heavy breeches and leather jerkin, with his own hands felling forest trees and building houses.

But for all its new prosperity, the men of Jamestown suffered, and often died, from the baffling country sickness. Lord Delaware himself became so ill that he went home to England, and Sir Thomas Dale governed in his name.

John Smith had had no authority to alter the system under which he ruled. All supplies and all products of work had been held in common; but Governor Dale, with his greater power, allotted each man a plot of ground for his own personal use. The chroniclers of the day recorded the effect: "Formerly," they say, "when our people labored jointly together, the most honest would hardly take so much true pains in a week as now for themselves they will do in a day."

(Similarly of the New England Pilgrims, William Bradford later recorded that not until the plan of holding property in common was abolished did the colonists become thrifty and industrious.)

Jamestown began to thrive, but Indian raids increased: they stole cattle, hogs, tools, guns and ammunition; whenever possible they took prisoners whose fate was often a death of lingering horror.

Then Argall, trading in the Potomac for corn, chanced to hear that the princess Pocahontas was there visiting friends. This gave Captain Argall (described by those who knew him as an "ingenious, active and forward-looking young fellow") a shrewd idea; he would abduct the princess and take her to Jamestown. With Pocahontas in their possession, he reasoned, the English could force Powhatan to restore their stolen property and to free those white men who were his prisoners.

Argall's first move was to win the chief, Japazaws, in whose family Pocahontas was a guest. He invited Japazaws to visit the ship; and among the things he showed him there was a beautiful copper kettle. The more Japazaws thought about that kettle, the more he coveted it.

Ralph Hamor, who was at the time secretary for the Jamestown colony, tells the story: Japazaws desired the copper kettle. Very well, Argall would let him have it, on the condition that he persuade Pocahontas to visit the ship. Japazaws hesitated. Argall promised that no harm should come to the princess. The kettle was beautiful and shining. Japazaws would see what he could do, provided that Pocahontas was not to be harmed. Argall repeated that assurance.

Japazaws confided the scheme to his wife. It was a lovely kettle.

Mistress Japazaws told Pocahontas how greatly she longed to visit the white man's ship. Actually she had never been aboard a ship. If only Japazaws would permit her to visit this one! The lady played her part well; she pleaded and cajoled. Japazaws was obstinate. Mistress Japazaws wept. Japazaws conceded that if it pleased the princess Pocahontas to accompany his wife he would consent. And Pocahontas agreed.

Supper was served them on board. Captain Argall was entertaining, and Pocahontas suspected nothing, so that it was a simple matter for Japazaws and his wife, after supper, to slip away with the bewitching kettle.

"As for Pocahontas," Hamor writes, "much ado there was to persuade her to be patient . . . and with extraordinary courteous usage to Jamestown she was brought."

The English at once sent a messenger informing Powhatan that his daughter was in their possession and that they would hold her until he was willing to ransom her in exchange for the English prisoners, the stolen swords and guns and tools. Three months passed without a reply from

Powhatan, and then seven of the prisoners, a few muskets, and some corn were returned.

Another messenger was dispatched to say that Pocahontas was well and kindly treated, but she would not be freed until the remainder of the prisoners and the goods were received. And again months elapsed with no word from Powhatan.

Governor Dale himself then went into Powhatan's river with such vessels as happenel to be anchored at Jamestown. The governor equipped these ships with armed men, and he took with him also the princess Pocahontas. If the Indians were as bold as they pretended, let them fight for her; or let them return the men and the stolen articles they were holding. Otherwise, he declared, the English would burn their houses, take away their canoes, break their fish traps, and do whatever damage they could.

At Powhatan's headquarters Dale found that the chief had gone inland, and men had to be sent to present to him the governor's ultimatum. Powhatan's reply was that the prisoners had all run away; but on the following day he would return the guns and the tools. Meanwhile, instead of keeping his word, he sent four hundred armed warriors, daring the English to come ashore.

Then, since it was April and the season for planting corn, Governor Dale went back to Jamestown, announcing that he would give the Indians until harvest time to meet his demands. If they failed, he vowed to return and destroy them utterly.

And little Pocahontas grieved. If her father had loved her, she cried, he would not value her less than swords and guns and axes.

Meanwhile, in London, the Spanish ambassador was writing to his king, Philip the Third of Spain, urging that the English in Virginia should be "destroyed with the utmost possible promptness," begging his king to "command that such a bad project should be uprooted now while it can be done so easily . . . an end should be now made of the few who are there, as that would be digging up the Root, so it could put out no more." Philip replied that in this the Spanish Council of State agreed, and that the Windward Fleet would be made ready and forthwith proceed to drive out all who were in Virginia.

But Spain was slow and the ambassador in London wrote again and again: "It will be serving God and your Majesty to drive those villains out from there, hanging them in time which is short enough for the purpose." Orders should be given, he said, to have the insolent people quickly annihilated.

Philip had recommended that a detailed account of everything concerning the Virginia colony be obtained from well-informed men, and a certain Don Diego de Molina, with two companions, arrived at the mouth of the James, permitting themselves to be captured, in order that they might report to the king of Spain precisely the condition of the British colony in Virginia; Spain's representative in England being at the same time cautioned to employ "all necessary skill and dexterity" to keep from the English king the purpose for which the three men had been sent to Virginia, and to use "all diligence" to the end that they be set free when their mission had been completed.

And, concealed in the soles of shoes and in coils of rope, Molina smuggled out of Jamestown those reports which he sent back to his sovereign. He wrote that with from eight hundred to one thousand soldiers Jamestown could be reduced with great ease—or even with five hundred soldiers; for, he said, there was no expectation there of aid from England, and that it was "most important to stop the progress of the hydra in its infancy, because it is clear that its intention is to grow and encompass the destruction of all the West, as well by sea as by land, and great results will follow I do not doubt . . . This Nation by itself will be very powerful . . . the rich are so greedy and selfish that they even cherish a desire for the Indies and the gold and silver there."

But Spain was dilatory.

In England more and more people were smoking, though the clergy opposed the habit and King James called tobacco a "filthy weed." But Jamestown was not prospering, for smokers everywhere preferred the tobacco grown in the Spanish colonies: something must be done to improve the Virginia product.

John Rolfe, who was himself addicted to smoking, was raising his own tobacco and experimenting in its cultivation. He could give his undivided attention to the problem, for he lived alone in Jamestown. During the months in Bermuda, while the *Patience* and the *Deliverance* were being built, his first child had been born and died, and in a short time his wife, too, was dead. Rolfe was therefore alone; smoking and experimenting in the growing and curing of tobacco.

Then Captain Argall brought Pocahontas a captive to Jamestown. She was a young woman now, and still the Nonpareil that John Smith had christened her when she was a child; still gentle and tender, still small of stature. Governor Dale put her under the charge of the Reverend Mr. Whitaker to be educated and converted.

Don Diego de Molina must have looked with some amusement upon the deliberate fashion in which the Reverend Mr. Whitaker went about his task. Spanish conquistadores would have baptized and christened her at once; the British method must have appeared needlessly tedious to Molina. But that was not, of course, his concern; his business was to act as spy for his Spanish Majesty to smuggle out of the country those reports which he sent back to his sovereign, concealed in the soles of shoes and in coils of rope.

Meanwhile something other than conversion or spying, or experimenting with tobacco was happening in that settlement on the north bank of the James where the tides rose and fell and men toiled to found a colony in the wilderness. For not all the attention of John Rolfe, "honest young gentleman of good behaviour," was now devoted to tobacco. There came a day when he put into the hands of Governor Dale a long letter. The letter opens with an involved preamble, as though its writer hesitates to arrive at the real purpose.

"Did not my case," he says, "proceed from an unspotted conscience I should not dare to offer to your view and approved judgment these passions of my troubled soul . . ."

(You cannot help wondering, as you read, whether Governor Dale already knew what Rolfe was so reluctant to put into words, or whether it would come to him as a surprise.)

"Let this," Rolfe continues, "this, my well advised protestation which I have made between God and my own conscience be sufficient witness at the dreadful day of judgment . . . to condemn me if my chiefest interest and purpose be not to strive with all my power of body and mind . . . for the honour of our country, for my own salvation and for the converting to a true knowledge of God and Jesus Christ, an unbelieving creature, namely Pocahontas! . . ."

(Poor little Pocahontas! So it is you who are the cause of this fearful day-of-judgment matter!)

"Pocahontas," the letter continues, "to whom my heart and my best thoughts are and have a long time been entangled and inthralled in so intricate a labyrinth, that I was even awearied to unwind myself there-out."

(Suddenly the words ring with a sincere passion. "I was even awearied to unwind myself there-out.")

"To you, therefore, most noble Sir, the patron and Father of this country, do I utter . . . this my long continued affection which hath made a mighty war in my meditations. And here do . . . truly relate . . . that I forgot not to set before mine eyes the frailty of mankind and his proneness to evil . . . nor was I ignorant of the heavy displeasure which Almighty God conceived against the sons of Levi and Israel for marrying strange wives . . ."

(You can picture Rolfe busy about his tobacco, and all the time torn by this battle between his heart and his tradition.)

He tells the governor how he has prayed to be preserved from sin, fearing that his love was but the wicked instigation of the devil. "But," he laments, "when I thought I had obtained my peace, behold but more temptation . . . besides the many passions and sufferings which I have daily and hourly; yea, and in my sleep, endured, awaking me to astonishment . . . pulling me by the ear and crying: 'Why dost not thou more endeavour to make her a Christian?' "

Then his heart again cries out above all other considerations, and he speaks of the great appearance of love which Pocahontas shows toward him, and of the "capableness of her understanding, her aptness to receive any good impression . . . besides her own incitements stirring me up. . . . " What should he do! he exclaims. Should base fear of displeasing the world influence him, when perhaps this is a task God has set him to do? The letter concludes, complacently remarking that Rolfe does not so undervalue himself as not to believe a more worthy match possible for him.

But, in spite of that, and in spite of the suggestion that his alliance with Pocahontas would be of value to the colony, love shines through the lengthy pompous letter, breaking forth now and then into a genuine cry from the man's heart.

So it came about that Pocahontas was baptized— christened Rebecca, the Lady Rebecca—and married to John Rolfe. It is said that Don Diego de Molina, the Spanish prisoner, was among those of quality present at the wedding. Whether or not that was actually the case, he was at the time in Jamestown. And again he must have wondered at the difference between Spanish and British conquerors; for without scruple the conquistador took the aboriginal woman, by marriage or otherwise, as the case might be. But the marriage itself was of real concern to Molina, and to his sovereign, Philip of Spain. For the marriage made peace between the colony and the Indians.

Actually two of the bride's brothers and an uncle came to the wedding. Jamestown rejoiced, and Governor Dale wrote home to London that Pocahontas lived lovingly with her husband. Others who knew her said that "by the diligent care of Master Rolfe and his friends, she was taught to speak such English as might well be understood . . . that she was instructed in Christianity, that she was become very formal and civil after the English manner . . . And that she had by Rolfe a child whom she loved most dearly."

Aboard the ship *Treasurer,* Rolfe and his lady sailed for England. Other passengers were Governor Dale and Don Diego de Molina, whose sovereign had at last negotiated his release from captivity in Jamestown. And when the *Treasurer* had safely arrived, there was Captain John Smith returned from a voyage to New England. So Pocahontas, who had thought him dead, met once more the hero of her childhood.

In a letter to Queen Anne, John Smith described the scene. He wrote, because he would have the queen understand how much the Virginia colony owed to the princess, Pocahontas.

His letter went back to the day when he was brought before Powhatan for judgment. There had been present Powhatan's beloved daughter, Pocahontas, then but a child—a child of "compassionate and pitiful heart," who "hazarded the beating out of her own brains" to save him from the death to which her father condemned him. And in that hard winter of famine Jamestown would have starved but for Pocahontas, who "with her wild train, came to Jamestown as freely as to her father's house," bringing corn and venison. Again a year later she risked her life, he says, coming unaffrighted through the dark woods to warn him of danger.

And, "humbly kissing her Majesty's feet," Smith begged that she will do some honor to so great a spirit as Pocahontas, cannily adding that such attention on the part of the queen will be to the advantage of England's colony on James River. He himself, he explained, could not do for Pocahontas all that she so well deserved, since he was about to sail again for New England. But, having heard that she was at Branford with some of his friends, he had gone there to see her, and he described how, when he saluted her as "Lady Rebecca," she had turned from him without a word, hiding her face and remaining thus for some hours.

When at last she spoke, it was to reproach him: "You did promise Powhatan that what was yours should be his, and he the like to you. You called him father, being in the land a stranger. By the same reason, so must I do to you."

Smith then explained that his formality came from respect for her position. But she cried out: "Were you not afraid to come into my father's country, and cause fear in him and all his people but me? And fear you here that I should call you father? I tell you that I will. And you shall call me child. And so I will be forever and ever your Countryman . . ."

Pocahontas had forgotten nothing. All was remembered: the stones upon which Smith's brains were to be beaten out; that release from death which she had won for him; the pretty new name that he had given her—the Nonpareil. And remembering, she had turned away in silence, covering her face.

Unless he had forgotten all, how could he greet her as the Lady Rebecca!

Surely he, too, remembered; he could not forget the wide shining river and the slender body of a little savage princess glistening in the sun.

You seem actually to see her as she lifted her head again to exclaim: "They did tell us that you were dead and I knew no other 'till I came to Plymouth!"

Lady Delaware herself presented Pocahontas to their Majesties, and all agreed that by the "Decency and Grace of her Deportment she charmed the whole Court . . . Persons of Quality took her up, and she was guest at Masks, Balls, Plays and other Public Entertainments, all of which wonderfully pleased and delighted her."

An artist painted a portrait which represents her with brilliant crimson lips and skin of a faint copper hue. He shows her with huge thoughtful dark eyes, set beneath straight black brows and above high cheekbones. She is wearing a dark hat so banded in gold as to give the effect of a coronet. A mantle of brocaded red velvet embroidered in gold gives only a glimpse of her gown with its rows of gilt buttons up the front. Above the scarlet mantle flares a stiff ruff of white lace, and white lace cuffs finish the sleeves. In one hand—a small, beautifully formed hand—she is carrying a little fan of ostrich plumes.

The great historian, Purchas, met her and she made a deep impression upon him. "The Indian princess," he says, "did not only accustom herself to civilization, but still carried herself as the daughter of a King . . . I was present when my honourable and reverend patron, the Lord Bishop of London, entertained her with festival and state and pomp beyond what I have seen in his great hospitality afforded to other ladies."

What Pocahontas herself thought of London can never be known. But surely she compared James I with her father. King James must have been a shock to one whose people held a high standard of physical perfection and of prowess; for the legs of this king appeared too weak to carry his body; his tongue was too thick for his mouth; his puffed lips never quite closed over his teeth; his protuding eyes rolled in a vacuous stare; and his gaudy clothing was seldom clean. She must have thought it strange that such a man as James should be king of the English, and that they should have given his name to so noble a river as the Powhatan.

The English visit came finally to an end. The last splendid entertainment was over. A London gentleman, writing to Britain's ambassador at The Hague, related what there was of court gossip. The "Virginia Woman—Pocahontas," he said, had been most "graciously used" by the king. There had been recently a gorgeous masque at which she had been present, and "greatly pleased." But now the "Virginia Woman . . . was upon her return, though sore against her will. . ."

Pocahontas had had her glittering hour, and Rolfe was taking her back to his plantation on the James.

It was March and at home in Virginia there would be spring in the air. Fish would be running in the river, and bears coming out of their holes, and turkeys gobbling. In sheltered spots flowers dared to bloom, people would soon be planting corn and sowing tobacco seed. The white magic of dogwood would soon gleam in the forest and all the trees would unfurl their leaves. Then before you knew it the hot summer would come, with buzzards soaring high in the lazy heat, while on the plantation everybody was busy ridding the tobacco of the big green caterpillars.

The years would pass, with her baby soon growing into a small boy and then into a man. And always there would be the river flowing wide and strong, and the tides rising and falling in the river.

The ship which was to take Rolfe and Pocahontas to Virginia dropped down the Thames to Gravesend. Suddenly then Pocahontas fell desperately ill . . . "And it pleased God at Gravesend to take this young lady to His Mercy, where she made not more sorrow for her unexpected death than joy to the beholders to hear and see her make so religious and Godly an end." In these words Rolfe and Captain Argall recorded her death.

And when news came to John Smith that Pocahontas was dead and buried at Gravesend on the Thames, he must have remembered how she had cried out: "I tell you I will call you father, and you shall call me child, and so I will be forever and ever your Countryman."

The tender tale of little Pocahontas and her hero shines like a personal memory out of the old records; so vivid that it seems strange its truth should have been doubted. You wonder that anyone could ever have questioned that she saved Captain Smith from death.

Such a rescue was in keeping with an established Indian custom. And without admitting the child-worship which Pocahontas felt for Smith, how is it possible to account for her coming a year later through the "dark irksome woods"

to warn him of her father's plan to massacre him and his
companions? Smith himself alludes only casually to this, but
it is related in detail by several of the Englishmen present
when it happened. And it is Smith's companions, not Smith
himself, who describe that dance in the autumn forest when
Pocahontas said: "Love you not me?"

For more than two hundred years the famous episode
of the first rescue was accepted; never questioned even in
attacks upon Smith by bitter personal enemies, eager to make
a case against him because they considered him vainglorious
and unjust in his criticism of them.

Then an American historian observed that this rescue
was not mentioned in that brief *True Relation* which Smith
sent back from Virginia to a friend in England in the summer
of 1608. Since that discovery, historians have argued, dis-
agreeing about the truth of the rescue. But it must be remembered that Smith was writing under the ban which
commanded the colonists to record nothing which might
alarm possible settlers, and that even after his manuscript
reached England it was censored before publication; for in a
foreword the editor explains: "Something more was by him
written, which being (As I thought) fit to be private, I
would not venture to make public." Also, the Pocahontas
incident is not the only event thus omitted from the *True
Relation*.

All this seems to answer those who have thought the
rescue invented by Smith at a later date in order to exploit
himself when Pocahontas was the popular sensation of
London. But if that were the case, why didn't his letter
enlarge upon it? The rescue had immense romantic value; yet
his letter to Queen Anne tells it in the fewest possible words;
in one short sentence. And in his subsequent works, though
then free from censorship, Smith mentions it but briefly.

When you add together every line written of Pocahontas
by those who actually knew her, though their words are few,
she comes convincingly to life in their pages. No one writer
tells the complete story, so that in order to get the whole
picture you must assemble what each has contributed: Anas

Todkill, the soldier; William Phettiplace, captain of the pin-nace; Wyffin and Pots, who wrote "gentleman" after their names; Hamor, who was secretary of the James River colony; Rolfe, her husband; Governor Dale, the Reverend Mr. Whitaker; Purchas, the historian, who knew her in London, and—Captain John Smith. In what these men have written there is no conflict in opinion; or in any fact, except a slight variation in their estimate of her age. Out of this eyewitness testimony the girl Pocahontas emerges lovely and tender and human, while the story itself is a tale of timeless beauty.

The Church
at Jamestown

CHAPTER FOUR

Immigrants and Labor

ROLFE left his little son to be brought up in England, and sailed alone back to his home on James River. He was become a great man. Pocahontas had been the sensation of London, and together they had been entertained by "persons of quality"—actually received by their Majesties. Also Rolfe was now secretary of the James River colony, and his experiments in the cultivation of tobacco had developed a variety that was competing successfully with the Spanish product. Even the London gallants who refused to smoke any but the "right stuff" at last accepted Virginia tobacco. There must have been comfort for Rolfe in the knowledge that he—John Rolfe—had achieved this for the desperate little colony on the James.

Now the urgent need was labor for the tobacco plantations.

At that time in England the poor were so poor that, if an entire family toiled from morning until night throughout all the days of their lives, the most for which they could hope was to live on brown bread and cheese. And there were many who must starve for lack of work. Hordes of vagabonds had become so great that people were forbidden to move from one parish to another without official permission, and destitution had driven throngs of children upon the streets. No one might follow a trade without having previously served an apprenticeship, and since relatively few could be placed as apprentices, agriculture was the only means of existence for the majority. But agriculture did not provide work for the great numbers who sought it. Accordingly, wages were whatever was decided upon by the local landowners; the laborer must accept their terms, or join the legion of hungry unemployed.

The dream of man's "inalienable right to life, liberty, and the pursuit of happiness" was, in the seventeenth century, as yet unborn.

Sir Edwin Sandys of the Virginia Company in London wrote to the king's secretary to say that the city of London had selected, from the "superfluous multitude, one hundred children to be transported to Virginia, there to be bound apprentices upon very beneficial conditions." But "some of the ill-disposed children," Sir Edwin added, "declare unwillingness to go. The city wanting authority to deliver and the Virginia Company to transport these children against their will desire higher authority to get over the difficulty." And obviously the difficulty was surmounted; for the transportation of homeless children began, shipped out to serve for a period of years as indentured servants; free, when their terms were completed, to make for themselves a new life in a new land.

The first shipment reached Jamestown in 1619; in the same year that John Rolfe, as the colony's secretary, recorded the arrival there of a Dutch ship bringing "twenty negars" which were sold to the colonists; in exchange, some said, for food for the famished sailors aboard the Dutch vessel. And when the demand for labor in the American settlements was realized in England, kidnaping became a flourishing business, even though its penalty was death for the kidnaper. In the seaport towns youths and children were lured aboard ships, smuggled out of England, and shipped to the colonies to be sold as servants. People spoke of the kidnapers as "spirits," and when anyone mysteriously vanished it was whispered that he had been "spirited away."

In the England of the seventeenth century those guilty of what were considered serious crimes went to the gallows, but there were some three hundred lesser offenses for which men and women received jail sentences. Many such prisoners, under pressure of the need for laborers, were now transported to New World colonies to serve terms of from seven to fourteen years as indentured servants. Political and religious prisoners were often similarly transported.

Early in the century, therefore, involuntary servitude, both black and white, was established in England's New World colonies.

At the same time, tales of the opportunity waiting in the New World were carried back across the seas, and in England men and women who had no hope to feed upon began to dream. Those with a little property sold their all and bought passage, impoverished and ambitious gentry too, and the younger sons of the nobility, left the past and sailed away into the future.

But for the really poor there was but one way to get to America. They could voluntarily bind themselves as indentured servants, as redemptioners trading some years of liberty for the chance to become at the termination of their indenture free men in that world of new opportunity.

This brought about voluntary, as well as involuntary, servitude in the plantations on the banks of James River, and, later, in all England's American colonies.

Copies of indenture papers are preserved in the archives of the time. Here is one of them:

"This Indenture made the 6th day of June in the year of our Lord Christ 1659, witnesseth that Bartholomew Clarke of the City of Canterbury, sadler, of his own liking and with ye consent of Francis Plumer of ye City of Canterbury, Brewer, hath put himself apprentice unto Edward Rowzie of Virginia, planter, as an apprentice with him to dwell from ye day of the date above mentioned unto ye full term of four years from thence next ensuing to be complete and ended, all which said term the said Bartholomew Clarke well and faithfully the said Edward Rowzie as his master shall serve, his secrets keep, his commands most just and lawful he shall observe, and fornication he shall not commit nor matrimony with any woman during the said term, he shall not do any hurt unto his master, nor consent to ye doing of any, but to his power shall hinder and prevent ye doing of any at cards, dice, or any unlawful games he shall not play; he shall not waste the goods of his said master nor lend them to anybody without his masters consent, he shall not absent himself from his said masters service day or night, but as a true and faithful servant shall demean himself to the said Edward Rowzie . . ."

In return for these four years of life in which Bartholomew Clarke was to deny himself all connection with women, all the ordinary amusements of the average man, four years in which night and day he was to be at the disposal of his master, that said master was to pay his passage money out to America, was to provide him with "competent meat, drink, apparel, washing and lodging," was to see that he was instructed in the "mystery, art and occupation of a planter," and at the end of the four years the said master was to make over to Bartholomew Clarke, "fifty acres of land and all other things which according to the custom of the country is or ought to be done."

These things which, according to the custom of the country, were done upon the expiration of an indentured man's term seem to have varied with the length of his service, including, in addition to a piece of land, agricultural tools, a cow, twelve months' supply of corn, some personal clothing, and occasionally a house.

Early in the seventeenth century there arrived in Jamestown, sent out by the Virginia Company in London, a shipment of young women destined as wives for the colonists. The company wrote that these girls had been selected with extraordinary care; testimonials to the character of each being enclosed.

"We are all desirous," said the letter from the London Company, "that marriage be free according to the laws of nature"; no girl to be married against her will, and no husbands to be considered except such as were free men, or tenants with means to maintain wives; and upon marriage each husband was to pay to the London Company a hundred and twenty pounds of tobacco to meet his wife's passage money.

William Bullock remarked quaintly that, if a freed servant has been diligent, and "if he looke up to God he may see himself fit to woo a good man's Daughter." Mr. Bullock also had encouragement for women immigrants to the Jamestown colony. "If they come of honest stock," he said, "and have a good repute, they may pick and chuse their husbands out of the better sort of people." In fact many a young fellow would bind himself as a servant for a year in order to pay the transportation costs of a wife. And Bullock advised fathers in England to send their daughters to Virginia; since there they would not have to give, but would receive, portions for their girls.

John Rolfe had lived to see the forest cleared and tobacco plantations established up and down the James. At Jamestown, wooden houses stood in two neat rows; there were three stores framed together, and a certain Mrs. Jane Pierce was boasting of the fine figs in her garden. Old Powhatan had died and Opekankano had succeeded him, but Powhatan's death seemed not to affect that peace with the Indians, which had not been seriously disturbed since the day Rolfe married Pocahontas, although it was still necessary to maintain a strong palisade around Jamestown, while in case of need guns might be fired from the church tower.

It was in this period of hopeful prosperity that Rolfe let his eyes dwell upon Jane, daughter of the prosperous Mrs. Pierce. She would be a worthy match, for no man was more respected in the colony than her father, her mother was a notable housewife, and of all the houses on the river none compared with the Pierce house in Jamestown.

Rolfe had now something new to dream of while he smoked; Jane would make some man a good wife. Rolfe believed in a man's marrying advantageously, and for Rolfe to dream was to act. Inevitably, therefore, Miss Jane Pierce became the third Mrs. John Rolfe, and Jane was doing very well for herself too, for in July of the year 1619 the first legislative body ever assembled in North America met in the Jamestown church. It consisted of a Council appointed in London, and a House of Burgesses made up of elected representatives from boroughs which extended now for seventy miles along both banks of the James River. John Rolfe, secretary of the colony, had been elected member of that first House of Burgesses. Miss Jane was marrying an important personage. In his starched ruff and bright-hued coat, he must have been an impressive bridegroom, as well as a worthy match.

Three years later, upon a spring day in 1622, John Rolfe, like other men, was busy on his plantation. All were preparing ground for tobacco, and no one had any reason to feel anxiety. Only the week before, the Indian chief, Opekankano, had sent a message saying that he held peace between the English and the Indians to be so firm that the sky should sooner fall than their accord be broken.

George Thorpe was confident that Opekankano was on the point of being converted to Christianity. And what a great thing that would be! For, of course, all the heathen chief's people would then accept the Christian religion. George Thorpe had been a member of Parliament representing Portsmouth, and he was also a man of property. He had sold out his estate, given up his position in the world, and come to the James River colony resolved to devote all that he was and all that he had to the conversion of the Indians. In 1622 he had been working among them for two years, full of hope and without suspicion. The Indians had shown fear of Thorpe's big English mastiffs, and without hesitation he had ordered them shot. Opekankano was about to be converted to Christianity. Thorpe felt his sacrifice was to be rewarded even beyond his hopes.

In James River the tides gently rose and ebbed. The balmy March air quivered with the promise of spring.

Then . . . suddenly, without warning, the dreadful thing happened.

The tale was related by one of the survivors. On the fatal morning, he said, Indians came into the plantations in the manner of friendly visitors, coming unarmed. And some among them sat down to breakfast with the white men; suddenly, all fell upon the colonists, murdering them with their own weapons or with whatever tools happened to be at hand. They butchered the old and the young, the men and the women; butchered them in the houses and in the fields. Three hundred and seventy-four were slaughtered.

But there is no record that a single Negro lost his life. It was as though the Indian recognized a brotherhood, a kinship between all whose blood flowed dark.

And Jamestown escaped. An Indian boy called Chanco lived at the time in the home of a colonist whose plantation was across the river from Jamestown. The night before the massacre, Chanco's brother came and lay with him. In the quiet dark he told his news: command had gone forth from Opekankano that in the morning every Indian was to rise up and slay the white man; not one white man was to be left alive.

Chanco waited until his brother slept, then crept stealthily out of his bed. He had decided to warn that white man with whom he lived, for, he said, the man had used him always as a son. And in the first light of dawn this man rowed across the wide river to give the news to Jamestown.

But there had been no one to warn John Rolfe away on his plantation . . . and after that day nothing was ever again heard of him. And George Thorpe, who to please the Indians had had his mastiffs shot, Thorpe was among the slaughtered.

Yet undismayed, immigrants continued to flow westward across the sea; to New England now as well as to Virginia.

The Indian massacre postponed the building of a university on James River; otherwise colonization went ahead as if there had been no massacre. A quarter of Virginia's English population had perished but more hurried to take their places.

It was the seventeenth century, and those who came to settle, involuntarily or of their own free will, in America, left an England where human beings could be convicted of witchcraft, and condemned to die on the gallows, where Puritans were called "vipers," and those who refused to conform to the established church were beaten and imprisoned, where a king was so cowardly that he dressed in padded clothes as a protection against possible assassination, so rickety that he had the "sidling gait of a crab," so goggled-eyed that he must have looked like a frog in the green garments which he affected. Yet this travesty of a man declared that "God makes the king, the king makes the law"; his power coming by "Divine right direct from God." If it was blasphemy to question what God could do, this king said, so it was presumption to question any act of the king.

In this seventeenth century England there was little liberty, no justice, no mercy. A servant who assaulted his master was sentenced to be "imprisoned for a year, to be flogged on two market days . . . to be put one day in the stocks, and on his knees in the open church to beg pardon of his master and afterward to be reimprisoned." Unruly and disorderly servants and apprentices were sent to houses of correction. And there is on record in the archives of Middlesex County, in England, the admission by a master that he "hath most uncivilly and inhumanly beaten a female servant with a great knotted whipcord, so that the poor servant is a lamentable spectacle to behold."

Under such conditions men and women and children lived and worked in that England from which voluntary and involuntary labor emigrated to Britain's American colonies; emigrated to live at first often under hard conditions, but always with the hope of eventual freedom, with the hope of a new life, a life of opportunity.

As was the case with the free Virginia colonists, many indentured servants died, succumbing to what was called the "country sickness"; and there must have been in addition many who had not the fortitude to survive the conditions of their servitude, who, as a happier century would say, just lacked the guts to take it.

For that there is the evidence of young Richard Frethorne, obviously sent by his father as an indentured servant to Virginia; probably with the hope that in the great New World lay opportunity for his son beyond anything 'that he might have in England.

Young Richard, in the terrible year of the massacre, wrote his father from Martin's Hundred on the James, giving a homesick, mournful picture of his life.

For a "mess of water gruel and a mouthful of bread and beef," he said, he had to work "early and late." He had "no spice or sugar or strong waters." As for clothing, he complained that he had "nothing at all, not a shirt to his back, but two rags, but one poor suit, but one pair of shoes and one pair of stockings, one cap, and his cloak stolen from him by one of his fellows."

He spoke of having met a man who had shown him much kindness, and this man, he said, was amazed that his father had sent him out as a servant to the company.

Young Richard begged his father to redeem him, or at least to send him money and provisions. For his misery was such that he thought "no head had been able to hold so much water as hath and doth daily flow from mine eyes." And Richard did not live many months after the date of his despairing letter.

Among those indentured servants who could not accept the conditions of their servitude, many ran away; some seeking freedom and some with the hope of placing themselves with better masters.

Other colonies had now been established in North America. The Pilgrims had come to New England, the Dutch to New York, the English to New Jersey, Delaware, Pennsylvania, Maryland, and the Carolinas. And, as in the James River colony, there were indentured servants; crossing the ocean under conditions of "terrible misery . . . stench . . . fever . . . dysentery;" to become servile chattels for varying periods of time, but upheld by the thought that in the end they were to be free, that opportunity never to be dreamed of in the Old World was to be theirs in America.

Founded upon that hope, the system of voluntary indenture continued for many years. And these redemptioners were advertised for sale in the various colonies; not only as agricultural workers, but as weavers, tailors, shoemakers, blacksmiths, carpenters, millers, butchers, masons, and schoolteachers.

"Prisoners of Hope," the novelist Mary Johnston called them.

Redemptioners . . . some years of toil, and then freedom.

The system continued, because so many in seventeenth century England longed to escape from the ills they knew, to gamble on the chance of a better fate across the water. There was hope in the very name "redemptioner."

Memory of the sort of England from which the New World colonists emigrated inevitably shaped life on the plantations on the banks of James River, as in all other British settlements; for the bright dawn of man's inalienable rights was not to light the world until another century should be born.

Side by side with the system of indentured labor, African slavery came into being, though its growth was slow. For forty years after the arrival of the first Negroes at Jamestown, in 1619, there were but three hundred Africans in all Virginia; even as late as 1671 there were three times as many white indentured servants as Negroes; in 1683 there were nearly twelve thousand white redemptioners and only three thousand blacks. In the early days a Negro on an isolated Virginia plantation might actually have grown to old age, and died, without ever seeing another of his kind. It is not strange that there was born in the heart of the race the lament:

> Sometimes I feel like a motherless child,
> A long way from home.

Later in the century, after the formation of the Royal African Company, it was the policy of England to stimulate the importation of Negroes from Africa and to discourage the indenture of white servants. Virginia retaliated by putting a tax on every African imported, but a mere colony was no match for the cupidity of the Royal African Company in which the powerful Duke of York was a stockholder.

In the beginning slavery as an institution was not legally recognized in Virginia; the records show that in those days Negroes, like white redemptioners, were "sold" for a term of

years; at the end of which they, also, received their freedom.
The County Court records in Virginia cite many Negro
indentures, for varying terms of servitude: in one case for as
short a period as three years. There are records of free
Negroes who in their turn had indentured servants. In the
County Court of Northampton County there is on record a
case brought by the Negro, John Caso, against Anthony
Johnson, his master, a Negro imported from Africa before
1622, who in 1653 was the owner of a large tract of land on
the eastern shore of Virginia. John Caso's suit declared that
his indenture to Anthony Johnson had been for a period of no
more than seven or eight years, but that Johnson had kept
him in servitude for seven additional years after freedom had
been due him. Johnson replied that there had been no indenture and maintained that he had John Caso for his life. The
court ruled in favor of the Negro master.

While another case on record shows that a white man who
had kept a Negro beyond his time of service was ordered by
the court to free the Negro, and to pay him four hundred
pounds of tobacco in compensation for the excess time that
he had served.

As the colonists of the seventeenth century had brought
to America memories of the England from which they had
emigrated, so the African also brought memory of the Africa
he had known.

From the narratives of early travelers and traders we
can piece together what these Africans remembered:

Francis Moore, in the employ of the Royal African
Company, described his landing at the mouth of the Gambia
River: "As we sailed up that river near the shore, the country
appeared very beautiful, being for the most part woody, and
between the woods were pleasant green rice grounds, which
after the rice is cut, are stocked with cattle . . . we landed at
James Island . . . about ten leagues from the river's mouth
. . . in the middle of the river that is here at least seven
miles broad." Of this island, he said: "Upon it is a square
stone fort regularly built with four bastions; and upon each

are seven guns well mounted that command the river all
round; besides, under the walls of the fort, facing the sea, are
three round batteries on each of which are four large cannon
well mounted, that carry balls of twenty-four pounds
weight . . ."

On the Gambia River the Royal African Company had
several factories, or depots, of trade and a fleet of sloops and
longboats, which, Francis Moore said, were employed in
"carrying goods up to the factories and bringing from them
slaves, elephants teeth and wax."

The country was well-cultivated; there were plantains,
oranges and limes; and the natives "jocose and merry,"
dancing to the music of drums, "sometimes for four and
twenty hours together."

When one of their kings wanted goods or brandy, he
would dispatch a messenger to the governor at the Royal
African Company's fort, asking him to send up a sloop with
a cargo of goods. And "against the time the vessel arrives,
the king plunders some of his Enemies towns selling the
People for such Goods as he wants, which commonly is
Brandy or Rum, gun powder . . . firearms and cutlasses for
his soldiers . . . coral and silver for his Wives and Mistresses
. . . If he is at war with no other King, he falls upon one
of his own Towns, and makes bold to sell his own Most
miserable Subjects."

According to Francis Moore, there were years when the
traders brought down to the Royal African Company at this
one fort as many as two thousand slaves, who they said were
prisoners of war. And "their way of bringing them is tying
them by the neck with Leathern thongs, at least about a
Yard distance from each other, having generally a Bundle of
Corn, or Elephants Teeth, on each of their Heads. Thirty or
Forty in a String."

The captives were brought often from seven hundred
miles back in the country, and when they were assembled in
the slave markets, Moore said, "surgeons examine them,
naked, both men and women. Those approved as good are set
on one side . . . meanwhile a burning Iron with the Arms

or Name of the Companies, lies in the Fire, with which ours are marked on the Breast . . . Then stripped and stark they are sent on board . . . six hundred or seven hundred sometimes on a single Vessell, crowded as close as possible."

An Official of one of the Dutch companies said that it was the custom of his company to hire, for a large sum of money, one Negro nation to take up arms against another and to take as many captives as possible, to be sold to the slave traders. The director of a French factory at Senegal declared, "the greater the Wars, the more Slaves are procured."

And William Snelgrave, captain of a slaver, described still other means of providing slaves for the trade. Most crimes among the Africans, he said, were punished by fines: those who failed to pay were sold as slaves, which was the fate also of debtors who did not pay their debts, while in cases of famine parents would sell their children.

In the seventeenth century the Negroes in England's American colonies were so close to Africa that to many these memories were personal; actual experiences, not yet secondary memories related by parents or grandparents. The beat of wild drums still throbbed in their ears. The worship of African gods crossed the seas to America; greegree charms were still held potent, protecting those who wore them from sickness, from the casters of spells and from ill luck, protecting against panther-men and hyena-men; ensuring good crops, good hunting and fishing, giving men success with women, and giving to the women children.

Africans newly come to America could remember, too, the hypnotic ecstasy of dancing; dancing into insensibility under the strong light of a tropic moon. Those who had been taken captive in war had looked upon the human sacrifice of prisoners to propitiate the victors' gods. Many among the captives of war had journeyed from the interior of Africa to the slave factories on the coast. On the long trek they had seen those too weak to continue the march cut out of the line, and left to die beside the trail. The march had taken them through the great forest, the vast, ominous forest where it was so dark that when they had at last come out upon the river their eyes could scarcely bear the sunlight.

Later, throughout the long horror of the voyage to America, all had shared the fear that upon arrival in the strange land for which they were bound they were to be eaten. And some could remember the wild despair of mutiny; the howling mad despair and the cruelty of punishment which had quelled mutiny.

Children born of Negroes brought from Africa listened to those reminiscences of the great dark home of the race. And the memories were handed down.

Looking from the year 1944 across time to the seventeenth century, the conditions under which the white indentured servant and the African labored in America appall us.

Bartholomew Clarke's indenture papers show the degree of servitude to which he bound himself, his complete renunciation of all personal liberty; the entire loyalty which he pledged to his master; even to the keeping of his master's secrets. And, turning the yellowing pages of bound volumes of the statute books, you may read the punishments which might be inflicted for any breach of that covenant.

It was, for example, ordered by the General Court that a servant "for scandalous false or abusive language against his master, have thirty-nine lashes publicly and well laid on." Resistance to overseer or master added two years to a redemptioner's term of servitude. The violation of each stipulation of the indenture contract carried its own special penalty.

Back in England, in the city of Canterbury, Bartholomew Clarke had "of his own liking" pledged himself to fulfill every obligation set down in the indenture pact, and to refrain from each of its prohibitions:

"Fornication he shall not commit nor matrimony with any woman" during the period of his indenture.

And the indentured servant found guilty of fornication was fined five hundred pounds of tobacco. It was, of course, practically impossible for such a servant to pay the fine, but it might be advanced by his master, and the servant's term of indenture extended by half a year in recompense. But should the master be unwilling, and the servant unable, to pay, then the servant was to receive "upon his or her bare back twenty-five lashes well laid on."

If a bastard child resulted from the intercourse of two redemptioners, the law declared that the sheriff, as soon as he learned of the fact, was required to arrest the woman and "whip her on the bare back until the blood came." Also she must pay a fine of two thousand pounds of tobacco, or remain in servitude to her master for two years after the termination of her indenture. In addition to punishment for the offense itself, the father was put in security for the support of the bastard child, who otherwise was indentured to the parish to serve until his twenty-fourth year.

There were laws, too, to enforce the prohibition against marriage. A clergyman who performed the ceremony was fined ten thousand pounds of tobacco, unless the redemptioners had certificates giving the consent of both their masters. And should a secret marriage have taken place between redemptioners, both were required to serve their respective masters for an entire year after the expiration of their indenture; while if a free person were proved to have clandestinely married a redemptioner, he was to pay to the master fifteen hundred pounds of tobacco, or to serve him for a year; at the same time that a year was added to the redemptioner's original term.

In the papers signed before leaving England, Bartholomew Clarke had further agreed *"not to absent himself from his master's service day or night."*

He found that runaways were pursued with hue and cry, a reward offered for their capture, at one time as much as a thousand pounds of tobacco, while any constable failing to make "diligent search" for such fugitives was fined two hundred and fifty pounds of tobacco.

For running away twice, the law decreed that "every Constable into whose hands the said fugitive . . . shall by any commissioners be committed shall be and hereby is enjoined by vertue of this act to whip him severely and convey him to the next constable (Toward his master's home) who is to give him the like correction and soe every constable through whose precincts he passeth to doe the like."

It was still the seventeenth century and none of all this was as yet shocking to emigrants come out from England to colonize the wilderness of America; for in the various colonies along the Atlantic coast there were similar laws, restraining the liberty of indentured labor, and punishments equally harsh.

With the passing of years, laws were enacted to give some protection to the indentured servant.

"Whereas [said the Law] the barbarous usage of some servants by cruell Masters bring soe much scandall & infamy to the country in general, that people who would willingly adventure themselves hither are through feare thereof diverted, and by that meanes the supplies of particular men & the well seating of his majesties country very much obstructed. Be it therefore enacted that every master shall provide for his servants competent dyett, clothing and lodging, & that he shall not exceed the bounds of moderation in correcting them beyond the merit of their offences, and that it shalbe lawful for any servant giving notice to their masters (haveing just cause of complaint against them) for harsh and bad usage, or else for want of diet, or convenient necessaries to repaire to the next commissioner to make his or her complaint, & if the said commissioner shall find by just proofs that the said servants cause & complaint is just, the said commissioner is hereby required to give order for the warning of such master to the next County Court where the matter in difference shalbe determined, & the servant have remedy for his grievances."

It is obvious that the protection given the indentured servant by this law could be pretty flimsy. It was his word against his master's, with the prejudice naturally in the master's favor. But there are in the records many cases where the servant did find protection. And the actual conditions of servitude must have been generally more lenient than appears in the harsh letter of the law; for William Byrd casually remarks in his *Diary* that Governor Spotswood "had made a bargain with his servants that if they would forbear to drink upon the Queen's birthday, they might be drunk this day. They observed their contract and did their business very well and got very drunk this day. . . ."

"*And in the end thereof—*" so Bartholomew Clarke's indenture read— "*And in the end thereof fifty acres of land to be laid out for him, and all other things for which according to the custom of the country is or ought to be done.*"

For this had he bound himself to four years' service on a James River plantation.

A redemptioner could look about and see the success he might himself one day achieve. From the "fat rich soile" a planter might so succeed that "he hath a fine house and all things answerable to it." There was, for example, a certain Captain Mathews on James River who "sowes yeerly store of Hempe and Flax and causes it to be spun; he keeps Weavers . . . causes cattle to be dressed, hath eight shoemakers employed in their trade, hath forty negroe servants, and brings them up to trades in his house . . . He hath abundance of kine, a brave Dairy, swine, a great store, and Poultry . . . lives bravely . . . a true lover of Virginia . . . worthy of much honour."

Such was the redemptioner's ambition. And there were among them men elected members of the House of Burgesses, and it often happened that an indentured servant won the affection of the planter to whom he was bound. The court records are full of instances in which these planters acted as attorney for their indentured laborers, and in every way assisted them in establishing themselves at the end of their terms, often making it possible for them to earn the means of shortening the period of their servitude. Also men who had come over as indentured servants married into the family of their masters; so often that such a marriage was not a matter for special comment.

A certain Charles Lynch, for example, was, as a boy in Ireland, kidnaped, shipped to the James River colony, and sold for a term of years to Christopher Clark, a wealthy Quaker planter. Ten years later he had married the Quaker's daughter, Sarah, and settled at "Chestnut Hill," a large estate on the James. About a mile above Chestnut Hill, their son, John, later established a ferry across the river, and there, on the south bank, was founded the city of Lynchburg.

Descendants of Charles Lynch, the kidnaped indentured immigrant, mingled their blood with that of pioneers in the Valley of the upper James, and that of the Huguenot refugees —Fontaine and Maury.

Even in the dark seventeenth century, where we of today move aghast, already the glory of America lay like the faint light of coming dawn upon James River; because in spite of all that now appalls us, there was opportunity, for at least some of the unfortunate.

Historians agree that it is impossible to say when Negro slavery began in the James River colony. Certainly for twenty years after the first Africans were brought to Jamestown, Negroes were sold as servants for limited periods, under the same conditions as white indentured servants, with the difference only that many of the whites had voluntarily indentured themselves.

Evolving from that difference, slavery as an institution came about gradually. Since African indenture was never voluntary, it inevitably followed that Negroes were sold for increasingly long terms of servitude; until it grew to be the custom for traders to sell for life; slavery being established by custom long before it was legally recognized. It was forty years after that Dutch ship had brought the twenty "Negars" to Jamestown before Virginia's first legal act recognizing slavery as an hereditary institution; then at Jamestown, in December, 1662, it was declared by law that *"all children born in this country shalbe held bond or free only according to the condition of the mother."*

Previously the laws regulating the punishment of indentured servants had applied equally to whites and blacks, regardless of color. Now that slavery was legally sanctioned, there came to be a difference in the laws. It was ruled that white servants running away in company with Negro slaves must not only serve additional time themselves, but must serve the time lost by the absconding Negroes whose servitude, being for life, possessed no time. And as the slave was without time, his punishment must always be by the lash. With increase in the numbers of slaves there were of course greater numbers of absconding Negroes at large, and fear on the part of the whites led to greater severity in their punishment. The statute books cannot now be read without a sense of dark sick horror, excelled only by the horror of the fetid slave ships which made fortunes for those who transported human cargo from Africa to America.

In this the seventeenth century, whatever of human kindness, of affection, or of mercy existed in the world was to be found in the individual: these things had no place in governments, or in the conduct of nations; and public opinion was not yet sufficiently aroused to restrain the cruel from horrifying excesses. Man—whether he had come from Africa, from England, or from the continent of Europe— was not then shocked by cruelty.

Meanwhile, back in England, King James had beheaded Sir Walter Raleigh under charge of treason. James was ambitious to marry his son, Prince Charles, to the daughter of the king of Spain. The Spanish king detested Raleigh, who not only had been one of the captains responsible for the defeat of the Spanish Armada, but had later attacked treasure galleons bound for Spain from the New World. It was evident that James hoped Raleigh's execution would appease Spain and induce her king to give his daughter as wife to Prince Charles.

It is an ugly story, for it was freely said that at the same time that James released Raleigh from the Tower, and sent him to seek El Dorado, Spain had been secretly informed of the expedition's destination, so that Spanish forces had been lying in wait for Raleigh; not only forcing him to return to England, but also charging him with having violated England's peace pact with Spain; for which crime the treacherous James had beheaded him—the great Walter Raleigh.

To his record of bigotry and treachery James added revocation of the charter he had granted to the London Company; the Virginia colony becoming a royal province, with the crown appointing its governor, though the House of Burgesses still remained an elected body.

Then, having performed no good act, but that authorizing the immortal King James version of the Bible, he died, a drunken glutton.

Charles I succeeded him. Captain John Smith died, unmarried to the end, and was buried on the south side of the choir in the Church of St. Sepulchre in London. Upon his tomb was engraved his coat of arms, with the three Turks' heads and the motto "Vincere est vivere"—to overcome is to live. Charles I ruled under his father's doctrine of divine right of kings. When Parliament refused large appropriations, he dissolved Parliament. In order to get money he revived monopolies and levied illegal taxes. But in the end he was forced to reconvene Parliament in order to secure funds. It was this Parliament which organized an army under Cromwell, making war upon Charles, and defeating him. Charles was brought to trial, condemned as a "tyrant, traitor, murderer and public enemy"—and beheaded.

Many of the Cavaliers who had supported him fled to Virginia, and among these fugitive royalists were the ancestors of patriots in the American Revolution—George Washington, George Mason, Edmund Pendleton, Richard Lee, Peyton and Edmund Randolph, James Madison, and James Monroe.

Cromwell died, the crown was restored, and Charles II came to the throne. Now it was the turn of Roundheads and Dissenters to be persecuted, and if possible to escape to America. Charles II died and his brother, James II, became king. Rebels were hanged, or sold into service on the plantations of the West Indies and the American colonies. James II was forced to leave the throne, and England invited his daughter Mary and her Protestant husband, William of Orange, to reign.

In France, in 1685, the Edict of Nantes was revoked: Protestants were no longer permitted to worship God in their own fashion; their rich properties confiscated; they themselves condemned to imprisonment in dungeons; sentenced to the hideous toil of the galleys, chained, naked, to their oars, and when fainting from exhaustion, restored to consciousness by the lash; while still others were hanged, drawn and quartered. For in France, too, it was the seventeenth century.

Half a million Huguenots fled from this persecution, some of whom, finding a haven on James River, settled in Norfolk and Surry counties, and at Manakin Town on the south bank of the James, a short distance above the present city of Richmond. They came singly, in families, and in such groups as those led by the Marquis de la Muce, by de Joux, by Louis Latane, and by Pastor Richebourg. They were given grants of land, "tax-free for several years to come," as well as "donations of money and provisions."

In a Memoir, one of these refugees, of nearly two centuries and a half ago, described his experiences.

He was impressed by the fact that "the planters live along the waters. None of the plantations, even the most remote is more than one hundred, or one hundred and fifty feet from a creek, and the people are thus enabled not only to pay their visits in their own canoes, but to do all their freight-carrying by the same means; by the little sloops employed by the ships which come to load tobacco."

Horses, he says, were used for travel "only when the water was rough, or when one had a fancy to journey by land. There is neither town nor village, save the one called Gernston. For the rest, there are only single houses, each standing in a plantation. There one finds such a grand quantity of tobacco that one hundred and fifty ships are yearly required to transport it. . . .

"The gentlemen called cavaliers are greatly honored and respected," and are "moreover most civil and honest." The soil was fertile and the climate good. It was a hospitable land, where, he said, one might travel cheap: there were no hotels but everywhere he had been made welcome, given food and drink, and good cheer; where there were horses they had been put at his disposal.

This Memoir, he explained, was written that he might inform the Huguenot refugees of this pleasant and healthful retreat. Amusingly, he himself returned to Europe. For he had read a certain prophecy predicting the re-establishment of Protestantism in France, the restoration of property and the end of persecution. He wanted to be on hand when all this took place. Moreover, he explained, he had not left his native land to spend the rest of his life to practice his religion in an alien tongue. And in America so few spoke French. Still it was a delightful country in which other Huguenots might settle: he recommended it to them.

It was out of these varied elements that the settlement on James River became a flourishing colony in whose making each played his part: merchants and seamen, yeomen, gentry and nobility, indentured servants, the condemned, political and religious fugitives, Englishmen, Scotchmen, Welshmen and Frenchmen, and the Negro out of Africa; the jungle savage, the unlettered peasant, university men of Edinburgh, Cambridge, and Oxford.

The new land they made cost them toil and pain, death, massacre and starvation, great loneliness and the ache of homesick hearts. But all these obstacles went down before gallant courage.

In addition to immigrants, ships now brought out furniture and finery, seeds and pigeons, beehives and mastiffs and occasionally horses, even though the highways of Virginia long remained its rivers and its creeks. Quinine was introduced from Peru; at last the colonists had a cure for that country sickness which had cost so many lives. And of such buoyant spirit were the James River colonists that even in that first hard perilous century they were so given to elegant dress that, in order to discourage too great finery, a law was passed providing that each Sunday at church every man should be assessed according "to his own and his wife's apparel."

But for tobacco it is possible that none of all this would have been. John Rolfe's experiments in the cultivation and curing of tobacco had saved the colony on James River. Now life revolved about tobacco; "the bewitching weed," William Byrd called it. It was an exigent weed. As an old Virginian long ago said: "If you have not a large stock of patience and perseverance, with a will to learn and a resolution to keep trying until you succeed, you have missed your calling, and had better try something else. For there is no royal road to success in tobacco raising. But if you possess the true essentials—hope, time and lasting pluck—you will succeed soon or late, and what is better, reap a full reward for honest faithful toil."

For tobacco requires much of soil, and much of man.

In March, before the dogwood is white in the forests, the cultivator of tobacco is making ready plant patches where the seed must be sown. The best spot was thought to be in the woods, with a southern exposure and if possible near a stream. The plant bed must be cleared of all growth, and then burned over in order to kill the roots of grass and weeds, the ground then plowed over, and finally broken up with hoes and rakes until the soil is of a fine soft texture. The seed, mixed with dry ashes, is sown and pressed into the earth; with piles of brush laid over the bed as a protection against possible late frosts.

The fields to which the young plants are later to be transplanted have to be prepared with equal care; broken up, manured, shaped into mounds three or four feet apart, and about a foot and a half high; the height of a man's knee, as the old-timers put it.

All this must be finished at the end of the month, for the plants will then be ready for transplanting: "when the fourth leaf has sprouted," the old-timers used to say, "when the fourth leaf has sprouted and the fifth is just showing itself." But you must wait for a shower of rain, since the ground must be soft, so that the little plants may be pulled up without danger of breaking their tender roots. You must wait for rain.

In the tobacco fields then, a man would walk ahead carrying the young plants in a basket, dropping one upon each of the hillocks. Another would follow, making a hole in the center of the mound with his finger, placing in it the plant, and carefully pressing the earth about the roots. A shower was equally important in the planting, for the soil must be moist about the delicate young roots.

Men may stand erect and stretch their tired muscles when the planting is done. But they may not really rest, because the growing plants demand increasing attention.

The earth about their roots must be constantly shifted, in order to supply the needed nourishment. The hillocks must be kept free of weeds. Leaves near the ground must be removed, and when later the flower stalks appear men must go up and down the long green rows, topping the plants, nipping off with the thumbnail the stems which would otherwise flower and consume some of the nutriment, all of which must go to producing big luxuriant leaves. To this end, the number of the leaves must be limited, and any new suckers which the roots put forth must be pruned away. Nine leaves to a plant, the Virginia growers said: nine leaves produce the best result. With the coming of summer, big hawk moths appear, flying low; come to lay their eggs upon the sturdy tobacco leaves which march in rows of lush tropical green up and down the plantations. Tiny worms hatch in thousands upon thousands from these eggs; voracious worms devouring the tobacco leaves. From the moment the first moth is seen fluttering over the fields there can be no rest for growers of tobacco. A hopeless war must be waged on the moths. Countless eggs will be laid in spite of all that man can do. The eggs will hatch, and the season of "worming" tobacco will come, inevitably.

The worms gorge themselves until they are sufficiently tired to lie motionless on the leaves; resting their pale-green bodies prone upon the surface, their heads lifted above the leaf, held in this posture immobile as though carved out of jade.

Men and women and children must pass between the rows, looking for the worms and killing them. Sometimes flocks of turkeys would be driven into the fields, for, it was said, turkeys could be taught to eat the worms,

"Worming" tobacco is wearisome work. The sun lies hot upon the blazing shadeless fields. It would be good to run away and plunge into the rippling water of the river flowing drowsily through the steaming plantation low-grounds. The heat shimmers in dizzy waves. And there are thousands of worms to be picked from the tobacco leaves and crushed underfoot. Thousands and thousands of worms . . . And every worm that escapes death will, when it reaches its full growth of some four inches, burrow into the ground where it passes through a pupa state, then to be reincarnated as a moth; again to lay eggs on tobacco leaves, again to hatch as a worm, with an insatiable appetite which only tobacco leaves seems to satisfy. Thousands upon thousands of worms, reaching their maturity in three to four weeks' time . . . Only three to four weeks before they are reincarnated as egg-laying moths.

The days are long and hot, and the voice of the river

under the willows is tantalizingly cool, temptingly idle. A river, accomplishing important work, yet knowing neither time nor toil. Nothing to do; not even to flow, for gravity attends to that; a river, the idlest thing alive in the world . . .

While the workers "worming" tobacco must not miss a single worm. One surviving worm may mean nobody knows how many more to eat up the tobacco crop. The day is long, and it is wearying to stoop all the long day over the rows of tobacco, under the hot sun, with the cool river so near. The fat squashy bodies of the worms become loathsome in the long day. It would be easier, perhaps, if the river were not so near.

And then the summer has gone; time to think about cutting tobacco. That is a task for men of experience: if it is cut too soon the tobacco will rot; on the other hand, it must all be in the barns before frost.

After the cutting comes the curing, the sorting, the stripping, the packing and "prizing"—and then at last the hogsheads are ready for shipping.

In the late autumn, when in great V's pointing south the wild geese have passed overhead, ships would arrive in the river, bringing to the colonist those luxuries which tobacco had purchased for him in London, at the inflated prices made possible by England's Navigation Acts.

The ships would lie in the channel of the James sometimes all winter, while their cargo of tobacco was assembled. Because of the Falls at the head of tidewater, and because of the involved windings of the James just below the Falls, the larger ships would anchor ten or fifteen miles downriver. Scows and sloops and canoes would bring the hogsheads out to the waiting ships.

After the number of plantations had increased along James River, tobacco warehouses were established at intervals on the banks, where the tobacco might be received and examined before loading it aboard the ships.

So the cycle was finished, only to be repeated over and

over, year after year. In those days men lived in terms of
tobacco. The rich counted their income in pounds of tobacco.
The free men toiled in the tobacco fields in order to become
rich. A redemptioner might tick off the period of his servitude
by the number of its sowings and plantings; so many seasons
of hoeing and "worming," so many cuttings and curings and
shippings of tobacco, and then he would be free, to begin
sowing and planting and harvesting for himself. Only those
who were slaves for life had no incentive to count off the
cycle.

Tobacco paid the passage of colonists and of wives to
populate the land. Tobacco bought indentured servants, and
later African slaves. Tobacco built and furnished houses,
purchased finery, paid the salaries of parsons and the fees of
physicians, paid the fines of those convicted of crime, and
the rewards for the capture of absconding servants and slaves.
Tobacco paid taxes and was involved in disputes between the
colonies and England.

Tobacco was part of the Virginia landscape: the rising
smoke in late spring meant the burning of the plant patches;
the patient figures in the summer fields moved between rows
of exotic green tobacco leaves; tobacco barns stood forth
gaunt and ill-proportioned. The very air was scented by the
life cycle of tobacco: by wood smoke, and the fragrance of
that sweet-scented tobacco for which the James River region
was famed.

Planters and laborers and slaves alike lived in the rhythm
of tobacco.

Bacon's Castle

CHAPTER FIVE

The People's Man

YOUNG NATHANIEL BACON'S plantation was at Curle's Neck, on James River, twenty miles above Jamestown. There, in the year 1675, he was living with his wife, Elizabeth, daughter of Sir Edward Duke. It was the year of portents, when Virginians marveled at "three prodigies" which they looked upon as "ominous presages," because of the disasters which followed soon after.

There was first the great comet, observed every evening for a week or more. It appeared in the southwest, "streaming like a horse's tail westward," until it set in the northwest.

The second prodigy consisted of flights of pigeons, "in breadth nigh to a quarter of the mid-hemisphere, and of their length there was no visible end." When these pigeons came to rest upon the trees their weight was so great as to break down the branches. Men shot them in great numbers.

But the old planters were fearful, because, they said, "the like was seen in the year 1640 when the Indians committed the last massacre." And until now it had not been seen again.

The third portentous prodigy was a vast swarm of flies, about an inch long and the size of the tip of a man's little finger. The flies rose out of the earth. They devoured the young leaves at the tops of the trees, and then they vanished as suddenly and mysteriously as they had appeared.

These were the three prodigies in which the old planters read prophecy of disaster. But surely no prodigies of ill omen were needed, for disaster was already upon Virginia. Taxes were high, the price of tobacco was low, King Philip's Indian War had broken out in New England, and like a forest fire the flame of Indian rebellion against the white man was spreading southward from settlement to settlement. Already it had reached the Potomac, where the flame was fed by reprisals on the part of some of the surviving whites, who killed four of the Indian "great men." Hideous atrocities had brought these reprisals, and the reprisals brought more atrocities.

There was terror on the plantations along the Rappahannock, the York, and the James: terror of the tomahawk, the scalping knife, of being beaten to death, and of ghastly, nameless tortures. In January of 1676, within a radius of ten miles, thirty-six whites were murdered in a single day. Whole families now abandoned their homes to take refuge in more protected places.

Virginia's governor at that time was Sir William Berkeley; a courtier affecting velvet and gold lace, and so extreme a reactionary that he declared he would limit all learning to the very few. If he could have his way there would be under his rule no printing presses and as little preaching as possible; for, he said, learning has brought disobedience and heresy into the world. He was fanatically a king's man; a royalist, who believed in the monarch's divine right. All his favors went to those of like mind, all his official appointments went to them, and he continued to keep in power for sixteen years a House of Burgesses with royalist

sympathies; adjourning it from year to year and never issuing
a writ for a new election. The laws passed by this Assembly
were naturally such as would concentrate power and wealth
in the hands of very few. At the same time, Charles II was
granting vast tracts of Virginia land to his favorites. The rich
were becoming richer, and the poor, poorer.

Then came the three prodigies, and the terror of the
Indian uprising sweeping southward from New England. The
specter of that fiendish torture, in which the North American
Indian apparently delighted, haunted every isolated plantation
along the James, and Governor Berkeley was petitioned to
organize an expedition against the Indians. Now the uprising
had reached the Falls in James River, and every day brought
tales of new victims, new horrors inflicted upon the white
colonists.

In a manuscript which later came into the possession of
Thomas Jefferson, and is now preserved in the Library of
Congress, one Thomas Mathew, member of the House of
Burgesses in the year of the three prodigies, describes at
first hand what happened along the James in the time of the
comet, the pigeons, and the swarming flies:

"Frequent complaints of bloodshed," he wrote, "were
sent to Sir William Berkeley . . . which were as often
answered with promises of assistance . . . Those at the heads
of James and York rivers . . . grew impatient at the many
slaughters of their neighbors and rose for their own defense
. . . chusing Mr. Bacon for their leader . . . humbly
beseeching a commission to go against those Indians."

But their petitions were in vain and, wondering at the
cause, people began to say that, on account of his monopoly
of the beaver and otter fur trade, the governor was protecting
the Indians rather than the colonists. And much was said of
Berkeley's well-known greed and of the demands made upon
the aged governor by his bewitching young wife.

Among the colonists slain was Nathaniel Bacon's overseer, "whom he much loved, and one of his servants whose
blood he vowed to revenge if possible."

It was to Bacon's interest, obviously, to placate the

governor rather than to protect and avenge the defenseless. Had he done so, his future in the colony would have been brilliant, for he had all the worldly qualifications that Sir William Berkeley admired and delighted to honor. He was of the family of the great Lord Bacon; he was married to Sir Edward Duke's daughter; and Nathaniel Bacon, Senior, president of the King's Council in Virginia, was his cousin. This elder Nathaniel was, moreover, rich and childless, and young Nathaniel might have been his heir. All this had won for him the governor's welcome to the colony, and a seat on the King's Council.

But young Nathaniel seems never to have hesitated: he was from the beginning the people's man. Allied to Britain's aristocracy, educated at Cambridge, graduated in the law at Gray's Inn, with the background of Friston Hall in Suffolk where he was born, and the further prestige of European travel, Bacon had known nothing of hardship, nothing of the struggle so familiar to pioneer planters along the James. He was said, too, to have been so extravagant that his marriage to Elizabeth Duke had been opposed by her father.

But in Virginia the troubled people knew him at once as their man. When they assembled to put down the Indian menace—even without Berkeley's permission, should that be necessary—it was young Nathaniel Bacon to whom they turned. When he appeared at the meeting at Jordan's Point called to organize a punitive expedition, he was greeted with shouts of "A Bacon! A Bacon! A Bacon!"

It was Bacon whom they would have lead them into danger; Bacon, the rich young aristocrat who would defy the powerful Sir William Berkeley if there was no other way to protect the people. They knew instinctively that Bacon would hazard all, that he would not count the cost to his own personal fortune, any more than he would consider the physical peril of the expedition. He stood before them, young and slender, his long black hair framing his swarthy face. And they knew him for their man: impetuous, audacious, reckless of self-interest.

The anonymous author of *Strange Newes from Virginia*

spoke of him as a "remarkable Gentleman who has of late beconed the attention of all men of understanding who are anyways desirous of Novelty, or care what becomes of any part of the World besides that themselves live in . . . a Person indued with great natural parts . . . notwithstanding his juvenile extravagances . . ."

His enemies—the king's men—described him as "of an ominous pensive, melancholy aspect, of a pestilent and prevalent logical discourse tending to atheism . . . of a most imperious hidden pride of heart, despising the wisest of his neighbors . . . and very ambitious and arrogant."

Bacon, they said, "seduced the Vulgar and most ignorant People (two-thirds of each County being of that sort) Soe that theire whole hearts and hopes were now set upon him." And another said that his followers were "a rabble of the basest sort of people."

Yet among these followers, denounced as "rabble," were many prosperous and of good family with much to lose by reason of being of liberal mind; such men as Richard Lawrence of Jamestown, an Oxford man locally known as "the thoughtful Mr. Lawrence," and a certain William Drummond, a Scotchman, who had been governor of North Carolina. In the case of the People vs. Sir William Berkeley, men like these supported Nathaniel Bacon.

And on the banks of James River drums beat for volunteers to go against the Indians under the leadership of young Mr. Bacon. It was the end of April and the dogwood white in the woods, as when Christopher Newport first sailed between the capes and into the river which the Venturers named the James, declaring it to be "one of the famousest rivers that ever was found by any Christian . . . for breadth and sweetness of water . . . as no man's fortune hath ever possessed the like." While far away, in a valley as yet unseen by white men, lying between ranges of mountains one day to be called the Alleghenies and the Blue Ridge, two streams were coming together to form this river of breadth and sweetness. The abundance of buffalo and elk and deer made

the valley a hunting ground, and the great Indian warpath
there crossed the hills and the streams, and spring was green
upon the waters when Nathaniel Bacon led his men against
the tribes of menacing Indians.

In June, Bacon's young wife, Elizabeth, wrote to her
sister in England—or more probably to her sister-in-law, for
the letter refers to Nathaniel Bacon as "your brother."
"Deare Sister:
"I pray God keep the worst enemy I have from ever
being in such a sad condition as I have been . . . The
troublesome Indians have killed one of our overseers at an
outward plantation . . . If you had been here it would have
grieved your heart to hear the pitiful complaints of the
people—the Indians killing the people daily and the Governor
not taking any notice for to hinder them, but to let them
daily do all the mischief they can . . . and the poor people
come to your brother to desire him to help them against the
Indians, and he being so very much concerned for the loss
of the overseer and for the loss of so many poor men and
women and children's lives every day, he was willing to do
them all the good he could; so he begged of the Governor for
a commission in several letters to him that he might go
out against them [the Indians], but he would not grant
one. . . . So your brother not able to endure any longer, he
went without a commission. The Governor being very angry
with him, put out high things against him and told me that
he would certainly hang him as soon as he returned. . . ."
And "what for fear of the Governor hanging him, and what
for fear of the Indians killing him brought me into this sad
condition, but blessed be God he came in very well with
the loss of a very few men; never was known such a fight
in Virginia with so few men's loss . . . They did destroy a
great many of the Indians thanks bee to God, and might
have killed a great many more, but the Governor were so
much the Indian's friend and our enemy that he sent the
Indians word that Mr. Bacon was against them that they
might save themselves. After Mr. Bacon was come in he was

forced to keep a guard of soldiers about his house, for the Governor would certainly have had his life taken if he could have had opportunity; but all the country does so truly love him that they would not leave him alone any where. There was not any body against him but the Governor and a few of his great men which have got their estates by the Governor. Surely if your brother's crime had been so great, all the country would not have been for him. You never knew any better beloved than he is. I doe verily believe that rather than he should come to any hurt by the Governor or anybody else they would most of them willingly lose their lives . . ."

Inspired by Bacon's defiance of the tyrannical Berkeley, in May the lower counties of Virginia had arisen, forcing the governor to authorize an election for the House of Burgesses: the first in sixteen years. Bacon was elected to represent Henrico County, and those opposing Bacon declared that certain among the newly elected were men "that had but lately crept out of the condition of servants."

Bacon wondered whether the governor would allow him to take his seat in the new Assembly, or whether he would be hanged, as had been threatened.

"But all the country," as Elizabeth Bacon had said, "does so truly love him that they would not leave him alone anywhere." So when Bacon went down the James by sloop to apply for the right to take his seat in the Assembly, forty armed men went with him.

Berkeley had them all arrested, but the public indignation so alarmed him that he promised Bacon's rich cousin, the elder Nathaniel, that he would pardon and set free young Bacon, on condition that he confess himself wrong to have headed a military expedition without the governor's consent. If Nathaniel would do this, his cousin declared, it would be for the peace of the colony. As Bacon himself put it, his cousin represented to him that it would be a generous act to acknowledge that it was unwarrantable to beat up drums without the governor's leave; and that if he would make such confession, Berkeley would not only pardon him and the men with him, but would permit him to resume his seat in the Council, and would also grant him a commission as general.

Thomas Mathew—in the manuscript signed "T.M."—describes how Bacon's "rich and politick" relative, Nathaniel the elder, "prevailed with his uneasy cusin" to consent to read before the governor a "written recantation" composed for him by his diplomatic relation.

Young Nathaniel agreed, reluctantly. But if a moment of personal humiliation would make it possible to secure for the colonists safety from Indian attack, he would sacrifice his own pride.

Thomas Mathew describes the scene, when upon a day in June, "The Governor stood up and said, If there be joy in the presence of the angels over one sinner that repenteth there is joy now, for we have a penitent sinner come before us, call Mr. Bacon, then did Mr. Bacon upon one knee at the bar deliver a sheet of paper confessing his crimes, and begging pardon of God, the king and the governor, whereto (after a short pause) he answered, God forgive you. I forgive you, thrice repeating the same words . . ."

Bacon himself said that he had followed his cousin's advice, "not suspecting the perfidious hatred of the governor who yett restored mee upon this to the Councell, granted mee his pardon as fully as any ever was granted, and by one of the Burgesses proclaimed mee Generall to satisfy and disperse the people who were so satisfied that they all retired peaceably. . . ."

Things "stood in this posture" (as Bacon would have expressed it) when the newly elected Assembly took their seats. That Assembly owed its existence to the uprising of the people inspired by Bacon's daring defiance of the governor. Their revolt had compelled Berkeley to dissolve the old royalist Assembly which he had kept in office for so long, and had forced him to issue a writ for the new election.

It was of this Assembly that the royal commissioners, later sent out from England to investigate Bacon's Rebellion, had contemptuously remarked that some of the counties had elected "free men that had but lately crept out of the condition of servants."

Certainly no more democratic group of legislators has ever met anywhere than that Assembly known as "Bacon's Assembly." The laws which it passed were called "Bacon's laws," and they shine like a bright light out of the somber shadows of the seventeenth century. They were prophetic of that new civilization which a new people was one day to establish in a new land.

The laws set a limit upon successive terms of political office. They ordered that the vestries be elected every three years; thus abolishing the indefinite continuance in office of those bodies of men whose power in matters of taxation and local government was at that time so great. The new law made it possible for every free man of the parishes to have a voice in the conditions under which he lived. The assembly decreed also that councilors and ministers were no longer to be exempt from taxation, and it repealed Berkeley's law limiting the right of suffrage to freeholders and householders; thus restoring to all free men the right to vote for members of the House of Burgesses.

These were the great democratic acts of "Bacon's laws."

Other acts were concerned with Indian affairs, and with the war to be carried on to protect the colonists from their raids and outrages.

Berkeley had promised that Bacon was to be commissioned a general of the forces to be sent against the Indians. But the governor, going back upon his word, now refused to sign the commission, and Bacon was privately warned that he was again in personal danger.

"I took the next horse," he said, "and went away alone. I was noe sooner gone but pursued and searched for. They feeling the very beds for me."

Three or four days after his flight news came that he was thirty miles up the river, at the head of four hundred men, and Berkeley sent out a call for the militia from both sides of James River, to come to the defense of Jamestown.

Thomas Mathew, from a window in the State House, saw Bacon enter the town with a file of fusiliers on either hand. The governor and the Council went out to him, and Mathew watched Bacon, "strutting between his two files of ,men with his left arm on Kenbow flinging his right arm every way both like men distracted . . . Mr. Bacon with outrageous postures of his head arms body, and leggs, often tossing his hand from his sword to his hat and after him came a detachment of fusileers . . . who with their cocks bent presented their fusiles at a window of the Assembly Chamber filled with faces repeating with menacing voices 'we will have it, we will have it.' "

They were come to demand from Berkeley the promised commission to go against the Indians, with Bacon as their leader.

Mathew says that one of the burgesses shook his handkerchief out the window as a signal of peace, shouting three or four times over, "You shall have it! You shall have it!" And a servant of Mathew's had managed to get sufficiently near to hear the governor's words and also those of Mr. Bacon. The governor, this servant said, "opened his breast, crying; 'Here! Shoot me! 'For God, a fair mark, shoot!' To which Bacon replied; 'No may it please your honor, we will not hurt a hair of your head, nor of any other man's. We are come for a commission to save our lives from the Indians which you have so often promised and now we will have it, before we go.' "

Rumor of another Indian raid arrived, and the following day at sunset Bacon came to Mathew, his hands full of commission papers signed by the governor, but left blank to be filled in as Bacon saw fit. And Mathew sat up all night writing in the names of those appointed officers as dictated by Bacon.

Then at the head of an expedition of a thousand men, Bacon marched in the direction of the Falls in James River.

Mathew says that the governor ordered the militia to "follow and suppress that rebell Bacon, whereupon arose a murmuring before his face, 'Bacon Bacon Bacon;' and all walked out of the field muttering as they went, 'Bacon Bacon Bacon,' leaving the Governor and those who came with him to themselves, who being thus abandoned wafted over Chesepiack bay thirty miles to Accomack."

And news was carried to Bacon that Berkeley had denounced him and his followers as rebels, and was now gone to Gloucester County to raise troops with which to pursue and capture them. Those who were with Bacon said that it "vexed him to the heart to think that while he was hunting wolves tigers and foxes which daily destroyed our harmless sheep and lambs, that he, and those with him should be pursued with full cry, as more savage than wild beasts."

He next led his men to a place called Middle Plantation, where he called a conference. There, in August, an oath was drawn up, pledging Baconians to stand loyally by their leader, to resist the governor, and even to resist any troops sent out from England until his Majesty should have been informed of the true state of affairs in the colony. The oath further pledged all to swear that Bacon's commission had been lawfully granted, and that what he had done had been in accord with the laws of England. Some hesitated to pledge the entire oath, since it was so dangerous a thing to promise resistance to troops that might be sent from England to support Governor Berkeley; defiance of royal troops being dangerous, perhaps to the point of madness. But Bacon held that it was essential; they must resist until his Majesty was informed, and a reply had been received from him. And the oath was pledged.

At this same convention at Middle Plantation, Bacon issued his Declaration of the People, in which their charges against Berkeley's tyranny were boldly set forth.

In Virginia it was now civil war, and Bacon the one "hope and darling" of the people, as was admitted by the royal commissioners.

As soon as the conference of Middle Plantation was concluded, Bacon resumed his exploration of swamps and forests in search of Indians. Meanwhile Berkeley was journeying by water from Accomac, sailing up James River with six hundred fresh soldiers, and taking possession of Jamestown. Upon hearing this, Bacon at the head of three hundred footsore, ragged men, depleted by hunger, fatigue and disease, marched resolutely forward in the direction of the town, taking with them some of the Indians they had captured. Thomas Mathew reports that people came out upon the highways to see Bacon pass, praying for his happiness, and giving thanks to him for his protection.

Near Jamestown, Bacon halted his men and made that appeal which comes ringing down through the years. He reminded them that they were marching against an enemy who had every advantage, while they were so few, so weak, so tired. And then he cried: "Come on, my hearts of gold! He that dies in the field, lies in the bed of honour!"

All that night, though the day's march had covered thirty to forty miles, Bacon and his men worked by the light of the September moon, felling trees, cutting bushes and throwing up earth, so that by daybreak they had constructed across the neck of the Jamestown peninsula a fortification upon which to install their guns. But now that daylight had come, they needed protection during the placing of the guns.

A certain Mrs. An Cotton of "Q. Creeke" now takes up the tale. Living in Virginia in those days which Thomas Mathew has called "frightfull times," she wrote her "Account of Our Late Troubles."

She describes how Governor Berkeley, returning from Accomac, had arrived in James River in five ships and ten sloops, how in the night the Baconians had left the town, how Bacon in swift marches had reached the neck of the peninsula and constructed there his fortification. And Mrs. Cotton relates that upon the following morning the wives of all the "prime men whose husbands were with the Governor . . . were presented to the view of their husbands . . .

upon the top of the small worke" which Bacon had "cast up in the night."

Since this was not mentioned in the official report of the royal commissioners, its truth has been questioned, but Mrs. An Cotton undoubtedly believed that the ladies were used as a protection, while Bacon had his guns set in place. When that work was completed, she says that he returned the gentlewomen to safety, and that the governor immediately attacked the little fort with six or seven hundred men.

"But," she comments, "it seems that those works which were protected by such charms (when a raiseing) . . . could not now be stormed by a vesture less powerful when finished than the sight of a few white aprons. . . ." For within two or three days Berkeley's men had taken to their heels and he had evacuated Jamestown, retreating down the river.

Bacon at once entered the town, and, "that the rogues should no more harbor there," the Baconians lighted the fire that burned Jamestown to the ground, preserving only the state papers and documents. Drummond and Lawrence, whose houses were among the best in the place, set the example by putting the torch to their own dwellings.

Bacon then returned to York River to make preparation for another expedition against the Indians, "which," Mrs. Cotton says, "while he was contriveing, Death summond him." And in October he died.

The royal commissioners state that he was attacked by a "Bloody Flux," and lay ill at the house of a Mr. Pate, near West Point on York River, where he died, "much dissatisfied in mind inquiring ever and anon after the arrival of forces from England, and asking if guards were strong about the house." Thomas Mathew considered his illness caused by continual exposure and fatigue.

Nathaniel Bacon died, and was buried in secret by devoted men who so feared that Berkeley might desecrate the remains of their dead hope that no one was told the place of his burial. It is possible that his body was committed to York River, as some believed. But no one was ever to know the facts. Perhaps those who might later have told had been among those executed. For, when Bacon was gone, Sir William Berkeley, velvet-and-gold-lace courtier, let loose upon Virginia all his jealous hatred of brilliant young Nathaniel Bacon, the People's Man.

Mrs. An Cotton's account, which is, by the way, in the form of a letter, lists many of Berkeley's victims: brave Colonel Hansford, "the first Virginian born that ever was hanged"; Captains Carter, Wright and Farloe, Esquire Bland, Colonel Cruse—all ending their days as Hansford had done; Major Cheeseman (whose wife had sought his pardon vowing that it was her fault that he had supported Bacon) was saved from a like fate only by dying in prison. Among the many others hanged by Berkeley's order, Mrs. Cotton writes of a "James Wilson (once your servant)" and of "Leift-Collonel Page (one that my husband bought of Mr. Lee when he kep store at your howse) all . . . executed . . . and several others on the other side of James River." She makes it clear that those who had recently been "servants" had an important part in Bacon's democratic rebellion.

Thomas Mathew describes the fate of Mr. Drummond, "sober Scotch gentleman of good repute." Drummond was captured a few days after Bacon's death and brought before the governor, who, Mathew declares, "complimented him with the ironicall sarcasm of a low bend, saying Mr. Drummond, you are very welcome, I am more glad to see you than any man in Virginia. Mr. Drummond, you shall be hanged in half an hour, who answered what your honor pleases . . . A gibbet erected (which took up near two hours) he was executed."

And Mr. Lawrence fled and was never again heard of.

Mathew concludes the story in these words: "The Governor went in the fleet to London . . . and by next shipping came back a person who waited on his honor in the voyage . . . from whom a report was whispered about that the king did say, that old fool has hanged more men in that naked country than he had done for the murder of his father, wherof the Governor hearing died soon after, without having seen his Majesty, which shuts up this tragedy."

Bacon was gone, his chief followers hanged; cursed as traitors. The reforms of "Bacon's laws" were repealed, and his memory branded with the words "Bacon, the Rebel." And none, over their own name, dared to contradict that verdict. But, anonymously, one who loved him put into verse, "Bacon's Epitaph made by his Man."

> Death why so cruel! What, no other way
> To manifest thy spleene, but thus to slay
> Our hopes of safety, liberty, our all. . . .
>
> Since thou, in him, has more than thousands slain
> Whose lives and safeties did so much depend
> On him, their life, with him their lives must end. . . .
>
> While none shall dare his obsequies to sing
> In deserved measures, until time shall bring
> Truth crown'd with freedom, and from danger free,
> To sound his praises to posterity. . . .

The years wore away, and at the end of the century Jamestown was abandoned and the capital of Virginia moved to the site of that Middle Plantation where Bacon had proclaimed his Declaration of the People, which included among the charges against Sir William Berkeley, that under his rule "what arts, sciences, schools of learning, or manufactures hath been promoted?"

Though Bacon's Rebellion ended in tragedy, its spirit triumphed. A hundred years after his death the immortal Declaration of Independence followed his Declaration of the People. A hundred years and the American Revolution was fought and won. But a hundred and twenty-eight years were to pass before Rufus King, minister from the United States to Great Britain, came across the manuscript of Thomas Mathew's account of *The Beginning, Progress and Conclusion of Bacon's Rebellion in Virginia*, purchased it and sent it to Thomas Jefferson, then president of the United States.

From an exact copy, made from the original by Jefferson himself, the account was first published in the Richmond *Enquirer*, September, 1804; with an editorial note explaining that Mathew had written in compliance with the wish and curiosity of a British minister, Lord Oxford; and not for the public eye.

The publication of this, and of the other manuscripts and state papers, provided the testimony which establishes Nathaniel Bacon the Rebel as Nathaniel Bacon the Patriot. For now, as the nameless author of the Epitaph dreamed, now at last is "Truth crown'd with freedom, and from danger free."

The James at Westover

CHAPTER SIX

When England Was Still "Home"

IT WAS in the year preceding those portents of comet,
pigeons, and swarming flies, and on what was then the wild
Virginia frontier, that William Byrd II was born; born within
sound of James River rushing over the boulders at the Falls.
His first home was the stone house which his great-uncle,
Thomas Stegge, had built on the south bank of the river. A
crude map in an old book of land titles shows the house, a
rectangular two-story building with its entrance at one end
and a chimney in the middle. It stands at the water's edge in
a bend below the Falls, and stretching away to the south and
west, the Indian Trading Path led more than four hundred
miles into the wilderness interior.

Soon after inheriting the Stegge estate, the first William

Byrd had married Mary, widowed daughter of Warham Horsemanden, an officer in the royal army who had fled to Virginia when the Puritans came to power in England. With the restoration, Horsemanden had gone "home," while his daughter remained in Virginia, with the sound of the Falls always in her ears, and her husband's caravans setting forth and returning along the Indian Trading Path; for William Byrd traded with the Indians, as well as being a merchant in James River. His caravans into the Indian country carried kettles and hatchets, guns and ammunition, rum and beads, and a certain blue cloth much coveted by the savages. These things were exchanged for beaver and raccoon and deer skins. The ships out of London which came to anchor in James River brought English goods and indentured servants; those out of Africa had cargoes of Negroes. And for all this the prosperous young man, William Byrd I, was an increasingly good customer, while those ships returning to England carried his hogsheads of tobacco consigned to London agents.

Then, in the first year of his son's life, there came those three prodigies which people considered so ominous, and when the child was two years old Indians were on the warpath against the white colonists. William Byrd I, as captain in the militia, was with Nathaniel Bacon that day at Jordan's Point when the people had cried out for Bacon to lead them against the Indians. The plantation known as "Bacon's Quarters," where his overseer had been murdered, was close by the Byrd home at the Falls. And Byrd sent his wife and the little William II to England to the Horsemanden kin, to remain until the peril was passed.

A statement called "Mrs. Bird's Relation," preserved among British state papers, gives still another eyewitness account of Bacon's Rebellion. In it she declares that "before ever Mr. Bacon went out against the Indians there were said to be above two hundred of the English murdered by the barbarous Indians, and posts came in daily to the Governor giving notice of it, and yett no course was taken to secure them, till Mr. Bacon went out against them," and that her husband "had 3 men killed by the Indians before Mr. Bacon stirred, which was made known to the Governor, who notwithstanding was so posses't to the contrary that he would not believe it to be any more than a meer pretence . . . to make war against the Indians, and that he said the 3 men were alive and well, and onely shutt up in a chamber to make the world believe they were murdered." She further affirmed that the country was well-pleased with what Mr. Bacon had done, and she believed "most of the councell also —so far as they durst show it . . ."

But when the rebellion declared as its object not only expeditions against Indians, but also resistance against Berkeley's tyrannies of taxation and suppression of the suffrage of free men, then the elder Byrd astutely made friends with the old governor, and when Mrs. Byrd returned with her small William to the house on James River she found her husband so prospering that soon he built a more commodious dwelling for his family, moving them from the south to the north bank of James River, but still within sound of the Falls.

Other children were born to the Byrds: Susan, Ursula, Mary, and Warham. England became no more than a hazy memory to William, a vague dream, while the Virginia frontier was reality: the rushing river, the tobacco fields, the caravans departing and arriving, the Trading Path, red men, tales of tomahawks and of being carried off into the wilderness, black savages newly arrived from African jungles, and ships coming and going between James River and what his parents called "home."

And he heard much talk of how he was soon to be sent "home," because how could he be raised among Indians and Negroes?

Then, it happened. Before he was ten years old he was put aboard a ship lying in the river and sent home to Grandfather Horsemanden. The ship sailed down the James, and out between the capes, to the sea where people said pirates were as thick as hornets. At intervals the younger children followed William to England, while their mother remained, often alone, at the Falls; for William Byrd I had been elected member of the House of Burgesses and was therefore frequently in Jamestown, now rebuilt since the burning.

From time to time there were other murders by the Indians, or someone was carried off by them into the wilderness; once smallpox was brought to the plantation by some new Negroes; several of the servants, and a guest staying in the house, died from it. Mrs. Byrd had certainly much to occupy her; still she must have been lonely, with the children so far away in the England she was never again to see. But she could comfort herself with the thought that they were being brought up at "home"; that William was at the famous school where, under Christopher Glassock, he was being trained as a seventeenth century English gentleman.

Then Byrd bought part of the Theodorick Bland Estate at Westover, farther down the river, and built a comfortable house there, where his wife would be safer and less lonely, and he more convenient to Jamestown than on his frontier plantation. Westover must have seemed strangely quiet to Mrs. Byrd who had lived for so long with the sound of the Falls in her ears.

Six years later William, her first-born, returned, now twenty-two, educated and traveled, not only in England, but in Europe; also he had been "called to the bar," and made a fellow of the Royal Society, of which his friend Sir Robert Southwell was president; for her William knew the best people at "home," as a Horsemanden should. And the very year of his return he was elected to the House of Burgesses, as it was proper that a Byrd should be. But Mrs. Byrd was to have no settled life with her children, for within twelve months William went back to London, Susan had married a London merchant, and Ursula who at sixteen had married Robert Beverly, the historian, died leaving an infant son.

In another year, the year that the capital was moved from Jamestown to Williamsburg at Middle Plantation, Mrs. Byrd died; in November when, on the lawn which sloped down to the James, fallen leaves rustled underfoot. She died and was buried in the graveyard of the little church which the former owner of the estate, Theodorick Bland, had built just a few hundred yards from the Westover mansion.

The England that was "home" to Mary Horsemanden Byrd's son William was an altogether different place from the England that was "home" to those so hopeless that they eagerly sold themselves into temporary servitude that they might put behind them its despair and sail into the bright new future which was possible to pioneers in the American colonies. That England from which went the indentured servant and the fugitive from political or religious oppression, never existed for William Byrd II. Even the plight of those younger sons who sought a future across the seas was outside his experience. He was part of a society which gave no thought to the social conditions under which the majority lived; his England was the England of ladies and gentlemen of leisure, in the latter part of the seventeenth century and the first quarter of the eighteenth.

These ladies and gentlemen were equally gorgeous in their dress. Both wore diamond buckles on their shoes, and silks and satins and velvets of gay hues. A man might wear a crimson suit with bright blue trimmings and gold lace, or henna color with silver buttons and silk fringe. Women wore flowered silk over gold- and silver-net petticoats. Vast wigs curled down over male and female shoulders. Canes and fans came into vogue, and the technique of their use was a profoundly serious matter. Pleasure was a profession. Dancing, flirtation, balls, dinners, the theater, cockfights, gambling, such fashionable resorts as Bath and Tunbridge Wells, were occupations of the first importance. London had at that time some two thousand coffeehouses, frequented by their patrons as centers of news and gossip, where men of congenial tastes met intimately. There were coffeehouses which were political centers, others where men in trade gathered, and still others where the literati congregated. Byrd was familiar with many coffeehouses, but he was particularly fond of Will's—known as the "humorists' coffeehouse."

Jonathan Swift said that the worst conversation he ever heard in his life was at this particular coffeehouse, where, he said, five or six writers entertained each other with their trifling compositions with as important an air as if the fate of kingdoms depended on them. Students from the Inns of Court and from the universities gathered and "listened to these oracles . . . their heads filled with trash under the name of politeness, criticism and belles lettres."

And there Byrd was to be seen almost daily; but still more engrossing was his life in Society. He drove from party to party in his own coach-and-six with a liveried coachman; went often to court, paid visits to his friends, the Earl of Orrery, the Duke of Argyle, Sir Robert Southwell, and others; called often upon the noble ladies of his acquaintance, but had time also for several mistresses. He was fond of going to the theater, and of playing faro, piquet, and billiards. He wrote verses, lengthy and flowery letters, often character sketches in the form of letters, addressed to the ladies and gentlemen whom he considered his friends: this correspondence usually conducted under imaginary names as was then the fashion. Byrd gave to his ladies such names as Zenobia, Bellamira, Facetia, Preciosa, Charmante, Vaporina, Minionet, Brilliante, Lucretia, Babbina, etc., etc.

Preciosa was told that he would warm her frigidity with his flames. "Were you only indifferent," he said, "indeed I should have some reason to fear my address might miscarry but now I see you nettl'd and angry, I am as sure of you, as if the curtains were drawn about us." Babbina he called "the brightest of all the fairys." Some of these effusions Byrd signed "your slave," others "Veramour," or "Inamorato L'Oiseaux."

The Duke of Argyle he addressed as "Duke Dulchetti Argyle," and Sir Robert Southwell as "Cavaliero Sapiente Southwell."

In addition to all this, Byrd acted as agent representing the Virginia colony at London.

The London in which this extravaganza was carried on by the elegant was a filthy city where at night gangs of amateur and professional rowdies roamed the badly lighted streets amusing themselves by knocking down watchmen, removing knobs from doors, clubbing harmless pedestrians, overturning sedan chairs, slitting noses and carving faces, thoughtfully providing themselves with knives for the purpose. Also, they considered it diverting to "set women on their Heads and wrong them in the most barbarous manner."

The prisons of Byrd's London were places of stench and horror. Contemporary writers described them as graves of the living, where criminals and debtors were equally at the mercy of their jailers, where women were flogged in presence of the court, their bodies bared for the purpose. But the public was indifferent to the revelations of these writers.

A modern author—E. S. Roscoe in *The English Scene in the Eighteenth Century*—writes of the public executions:

"If a stranger had hired a phæton and started from Tyburn turnpike and had happened to choose a Monday morning before 1783 . . . opposite the spot on which the Marble Arch now stands he would have noticed one or more gallows, and carts containing the condemned persons with arms pinioned and a rope round their necks and coffins by them, men and women murderers or simple thieves, received by jeers . . . and shouts from the excited and expectant populace. As each vehicle placed beneath the gallows moved away, a dangling body would have been seen against the sky. This would be seized by those who had been the friends of the executed man, who holding it, by their weight, sought to end his sufferings."

Such was the background of crime and punishment, of debt and misfortune, of fashion and frivolity—the social scene familiar to those who in the seventeenth and early eighteenth centuries emigrated from England to the colonies of America. Such was the "home" to which colonists sent their children to be educated.

William Byrd II was thirty, when in 1704 his father

died, bequeathing to him, the eldest son, his estate of thousands of acres of James River land. Returning at once to Virginia to take possession of his inheritance, Byrd was obviously a great catch for any colonial girl. His wealth was enhanced by the prestige of having been educated at "home," of having lived intimately among the "ton" of English society. And he was handsome, so dark and dashing that he came to be known as the "black swan."

Calling himself once more Veramour, he courted Lucy Parke, whose father's reputation has handed him down through the years as that "sparkish gentleman," Daniel Parke. Byrd wooed Lucy as "Fidelia," and "No courteour," he wrote her, "can gape for preferment with more impatience than I do to hear from you my charming Fidelia."

They were married and settled down at Westover on the James "two miles above where the great ships ride," and more than twenty miles below the Falls.

Westover was strangely quiet after London, where from morning to night the streets echoed with the cries of vendors, with the warning shouts of chair-carriers, of drivers of carts and coaches crying "Make room there"; echoing, too, with the songs of ballad singers—who were often pickpockets, going in couples. While in the quiet of Westover even the flutter of leaves in the breeze was a sound to be noted, a rooster's crow was strident in the stillness, the cawing of crows, a mockingbird singing in the garden, and the sounds of domestic life within and without the house, all punctuated the hours, like the striking of a clock in the quiet of the night.

Writing to a friend in London, Byrd said: "A Library, a Garden, a Grave, and a purling stream are the innocent scenes that divert our leisure." The round of his unending frivolity in London was far away, and the round of plantation life in Virginia was taking its place.

Byrd kept a secret diary of his life at Westover, its meaning wrapped like a mummy in the antique shorthand in which he wrote it, until recently when it was transcribed and edited by Louis B. Wright and Marion Tinling from the original in the Huntington Library, and published in book form in 1941.

The diary records in minute detail Byrd's life at West-over during the first eight years of his marriage. It fills five hundred and eighty-five printed pages, but it can be boiled down to certain items which occur over and over again:

Byrd rises at five, or six, or seven, in the morning. He reads a chapter of Hebrew and several hundred verses of Homer. He says his prayers. He records what he ate for breakfast. He dances his dance. Occasionally he mentions certain slaves who were whipped, and for what faults. He carefully describes the action of his bowels, as does his Boston contemporary, Judge Samuel Sewall in his Journal. He speaks of supervising work on the plantation. He reads law, French, and Italian. He lists what he had for dinner and the friends from neighboring plantations who were received at Westover. He doses himself, his wife and children, his sick servants, his slaves and his neighbors with various medicines, especially with vomits and purges. He threatens this or that servant with a whipping. He returns the visits of his friends. He has been appointed member of the Council, and his official duties take him often to the capital at Williamsburg. He mentions the occasions upon which his wife is "out of humour for nothing," describes his "endeavours to please her again, having consideration for a woman's weakness," and records their reconciliations which usually take that form which produces more Byrds. Pregnancies, miscarriages and births are, of course, duly cited. And perpetuated on the pages of this candid diary are his wife's violent quarrels with her servants and the punishments she had inflicted upon them.

In the evening Byrd is fond of walking about the garden or the plantation, often with his wife. The days close with supper, usually followed by a game of billiards or piquet. And over and over again appears the sentence: "Talked with my people and prayed"—the word "people," thus used in the Virginia of those days, meaning servants or slaves. And finally, Byrd retires remarking, "I had good health, good thoughts, and good humour, thanks be to God Almighty."

Over and over again the diary repeats itself; its variations being the occasions when the dance, or the reading, or the prayers were for some reason omitted, or when the thoughts, the health, and the humor chanced not to be "good."

After the murder of his father-in-law in the Leeward Islands where he was governor, Byrd went to England on business connected with the estate bequeathed his wife by her father. There, he slipped back into the old life of fashion and dalliance, again established in his chambers in Lincoln's Inn. A year later his wife joined him, but within a few months she was dead of smallpox. Byrd mourned, and was gratified that London had admired her.

In an amazingly frank analysis of himself, which he called "Inamorato L'Oiseaux," he declares that "Love broke out upon him before his Beard, and he could distinguish sexes long before he could the difference betwixt good and Evil."

As a *oiseau* thus eternally *inamorato*, his wife was not long dead before he was in pursuit of a second. Among others he passionately courted the "Sabina" to whom many of his letters are addressed. Of Sabina he said: "She has so easy, so regular a shape, that one envies the very girdle that embraces it." In proposing marriage with her he wrote her father: "The estate I have tho it lye so far off as Virginia, is very considerable I have there about 43,000 acres of Land 220 Negros at work upon it." But Sabina reported that to her father "an Estate out of this Island" appeared "little better than an Estate in the moon."

Sabina carried on clandestine correspondence with Byrd in which the postman was called a "varlet" for having shouted her name with such emphasis that she feared the "old gentleman" had heard it. But eventually she married someone else.

With various other ladies he was equally unsuccessful, while at the same time he was greatly disturbed that a baronet fortune hunter was making love to Evelyn, his beautiful sixteen-year-old daughter. And he informed this suitor that he had made a will bequeathing Evelyn "a splendid shilling" if she married without his approval.

Meanwhile Byrd sought for himself political preferment, and attempted to settle to his own advantage his disagreements with Virginia's Governor Spotswood.

And again Byrd was dancing and dining, again he was seen at masquerades and at the theater, again he was attending meetings of the Royal Society, was visiting at the country houses of the aristocracy, was calling upon his various mistresses, was present at divine services at St. Clement Dane's, and was once more an almost daily visitor at Will's coffee-house.

Then he married a certain Maria Taylor, and later returned with his family to Westover.

He now replaced the wooden house at Westover with a handsome Georgian building of red brick. Its main entrance is through great wrought-iron gates between square brick pillars, each surmounted by a life-size spread eagle. But the real face of the house looks out upon James River, across a lawn sloping down to the water. On the right is the lovely garden where William Byrd II loved to walk at the close of day. John Bartram (the Philadelphia Quaker, who was to botany in America what Audubon was to ornithology) visited Byrd at Westover and wrote to his friend, Peter Collinson, in England: "Col. Byrd is very prodigalle . . . in new Gates, gravel Walks, hedges and cedars finely twined and a little green-house with two or three orange trees with fruit on them; in short he hath the finest seat in Virginia."

The garden remains a place of magic, with lofty box hedging its formal squares, with crape myrtle and syringa, calycanthus and wisteria, roses and lilies, violets and peonies.

Within, there is a great hall and a staircase whose mahogany balustrades were imported from England, as were also the wrought-iron entrance gates. At Westover, Byrd accumulated a fine library of four thousand volumes—the largest private library in Britain's American colonies. He hung the walls with portraits of his friends in London; among them a portrait of that Lord Oxford at whose request Thomas Mathew had written his account of Bacon's Rebellion, a portrait of Sir Robert Southwell, who had made Byrd a fellow of the Royal Society, a portrait of the Duke of Argyle, of Sir Wilfrid Lawson, of Lord Edgmont, of Lady Elizabeth Southwell, Lady Betty Cromwell, and of that Charles Boyle, Earl of Orrery, of whose friendship Byrd was so proud.

Through correspondence he tried to maintain his place in London, and he wanted the Earl of Orrery to understand his Virginia life:

"I have a large Family of my own, and my Doors are open to Every Body, yet I have no bills to pay, and half-a-crown will rest undisturbed in my pocket for many Moons together. Like one of the Patriarchs, I have my Flocks and my Herds, my Bond-men and Bond-women and every sort of trade amongst my own Servants, so that I live in a kind of Independence of every one but Providence. However this soart of Life is without expence, yet it is attended with a great deal of trouble. I must take care to keep all my people to their duty, to set all the Springs in motion and make every one draw his equal share to carry the Machine forward. But then 'tis an amusement on this silent Country and a continual Exercise of Patience and Economy. . . . Thus my Lord we are very happy in our Canaans if we could but forget the Onions and Fleshpots of Egypt. There are so many temptations in England to inflame the appetite and charm the senses. . . . They always had, I must own, a strong Influence upon me."

The phrase "in this silent Country" lingers in your mind. It reveals the loneliness that Byrd knew at Westover, writing to the Earl of Orrery in England.

In another letter he thanks the earl for writing. A letter from the earl, he says, can raise his spirits and make him "gay as the Spring." But you feel that the correspondence which meant so much to Byrd in that "silent Country" meant, after all, very little to his London friends.

In writing of his daughters (whom he calls "my young gentlewomen"), Byrd confessed that "they could not get the Plays, the Operas and the Masquerades out of their heads . . . that they may amuse themselves the better, they are every Day up to their Elbows in Housewifery which will qualify them for useful Wives and if they live long enough for Notable Women." Of Evelyn he wrote later that she was become one of the most antique virgins (he spells it "antick") and that "either the young fellows were not smart enough for her, or she too smart for them."

Byrd had hoped that he would again visit England. He even kept for some years his chambers in Lincoln's Inn. And then—he wrote Lord Orrery that the low price of tobacco had prevented him from discharging some engagements that he had the misfortune to lie under, and it was that which made impossible his return to that "enchanted Island" for which he longed.

Gradually Byrd was drawn increasingly into the life of the Virginia colony. He was appointed one of the commissioners to settle the long-disputed matter of the boundary line between Virginia and North Carolina. From a journal kept on that expedition into the wilderness interior, Byrd wrote his *History of the Dividing Line*. Peter Collinson, patron of John Bartram, the botanist, became interested and wanted to see it, but Byrd explained that he had not yet had time to complete it. "I am always engaged," he said, "on some project for improvement of our Infant colony. The present scheme is to found a city at the falls of the James River, and plant a colony of Switzers on my land at Roanoke."

His dream of founding a city at the Falls of the James was realized in 1733, a year after the birth in Virginia of a child christened George Washington. Upon land granted his father by Governor Berkeley, Richmond was founded by

William Byrd II and, because the memory of Richmond on the Thames was still so vividly with him that he saw a resemblance between the two sites, he called his city-that-was-to-be Richmond. His journal records that "we laid the foundation of two large cities, one . . . to be called Richmond . . . the other Petersburg . . . these two places being the uppermost landing of James and Appomattox rivers, are naturally intended for marts where the traffic of the outer inhabitants must centre. Thus we did not build castles only, but cities in the air."

In his London letters Byrd has the affectations of the bewigged man of fashion, and the futility of the psuedo intellectual. His secret diaries are important chiefly in what is to be read between the lines. In themselves they are dull and repetitious; moving almost entirely on the surface of things. But in his account of that survey of the dividing line which took him over much of the old Trading Path into the country of the Catawbas over which his father's caravans used to pass, and in his description of other journeys into what used to be called the "back parts of Virginia," Byrd reveals his powers of observation and his zest for exploration.

Under conditions of primitive discomfort, this London man of fashion found himself "philosopher enough to improve such slender Distresses into Mirth and Good Humour." He slept in tents, in vermin-infested hovels, or under the open sky, in clear weather or in storm. He who had driven about London in his coach-and-six now tramped, always in content, always entertained. Everything interested him: the lay of the land, bogs and creeks and rivers and mountains; vegetation of all sorts; the people he came across—fugitive slaves, debtors and criminals, stoic pioneers with faith in the land; birds and beasts—wild geese and turkeys, pigeons and cranes, deer, elk, buffalo, beaver, wolves, foxes, and rattlesnakes.

In describing all this, Byrd has a piquant gift of phrase which not only draws a picture, but constantly reveals his own nature, always materialistic, inclined to the ribald, ever preoccupied with sex, always without hypocrisy.

In describing the settlement of the British in Virginia, he says: "As it happened some Ages before to be the fashion to Santer to the Holy Land, and go upon other Quixot Adventures, so it was now grown the Humour to take a Trip to America. The Spaniards had lately discovered Rich Mines in their Part of the West Indies, which made their Maritime Neighbours eager to do so too. This Modish Frenzy being still more Inflamed by the Charming account given of Virginia, by the first Adventurers, made many fond of removeing to such a Paradise . . . expecting their Coarsest Utensils, in that happy place, would be of Massy Silver."

Although Byrd himself married two English heiresses, he had ideas about populating the country through marriage between the colonists and the Indians, which he declared would have been the best way to convert the natives to Christianity. "For, after all that can be said, a sprightly Lover is the most prevailing Missionary that can be sent amongst these, or any other Infidels."

The Quakers, he thinks, emigrated to America, "being averse to go to Heaven the same way with the Bishops."

The inhabitants of the back parts of Virginia, he says, "took the trouble to dig abundance of Wolf-Pits, so deep and perpendicular, that when a Wolf is once tempted into them, he can no more scramble out again, than a Husband who has taken the Leap can Scramble out of Matrimony."

In speaking of the food on these expeditions into the Virginia forest, he describes wild turkey and venison stewed together as being so delicious that they "no more tired of it than a man wearies of an engaging wife because of her being a constant dish."

When she was thirty, his daughter Evelyn died. She had been twenty-one when in that letter to the Earl of Orrery her father had spoken of her as "one of the most antick Virgins I am acquainted with." And to the end she remained unmarried. Never to have married seems alien to her nature when you realize that the violent and passionate Lucy Parke, daughter of that "sparkish gentleman," Daniel Parke, was her mother; and that William Byrd II was her father. Comparing her portrait with that of her father you are struck by the astonishing resemblance. Both have dark, heavy, arched eyebrows, the shape and the audacious expression of their eyes is the same, their noses are aristocratic, the carriage of their heads proud and graceful; the weakness in both faces is in their mouths which are tiny Cupid's bows. It is scarcely possible that a girl with Evelyn Byrd's heritage could have been content to live and die a virgin. The tradition is that Westover is haunted by her lovely ghost, the ghost of a girl dying heartbroken because she had not been permitted to marry the lover opposed by her father.

And when you walk about the grounds of Westover, or stroll in its quiet garden, the tradition appears as the truth. In what her father called that "silent Country," in those years beside the "purling" James, there would have been loneliness in which to recall the gaieties of her London life, and to mourn that lover whom her father had commanded that she was "never more to meet, speak, or write to that gentleman, or to give him an opportunity to see, speak or write" to her.

In the University of North Carolina there is a second manuscript diary kept by William Byrd II; also in shorthand, which, translated by Marion Tinling and edited by Maude H. Woodfin, was published in 1942.

Its first entry being in 1739, two years after Evelyn Byrd died, there is no mention of her death, so that it is not possible to know how it affected her father, or whether he ever reproached himself for having parted her from her lover.

This second secret diary continues much as the former one. Its hundred and eighty-three printed pages inform the reader that Byrd continued to rise early, to say his prayers, to read Hebrew, Greek, English, and occasionally French; that almost daily he danced his dance, and that he continued to take and administer purges. Meetings of the Council took

him often to Williamsburg, where he would have a fine dinner at the Raleigh Tavern. He received visits from his neighbors, and returned them. And as before, he loved, when
evening came, to walk in his garden.

Several times he mentions visiting Major John Henry
in Hanover County, in the northern watershed of James
River. At the time of these visits Major Henry's son, Patrick,
was a four-year-old child; it is possible that in his manhood
Patrick Henry could remember the spectacular William Byrd
who used to visit his father.

The Earl of Orrery had died some years before the first
entry in the second secret diary, but Byrd continues to speak
of frequent letters to England. And ships arriving in James
River maintained a direct communication between the colony
and London, their captains a direct and personal link between
the plantations and "home." Plantations had their own docks
where ships came to load tobacco for the London merchants.
In return for the planters' patronage, the captains undertook
a vast amount of shopping in London. Those captains seem
to have been endlessly kind. They looked after women and
children who might be voyaging alone. When colonists sent
birds or squirrels as presents to friends in England, the captains saw that they were cared for aboard ship. News of what
was going on traveled by way of the captains between England and Virginia. To their responsibilities in the matter of
navigation and pirates, they added all this.

Much of the colony's business passed through the firm
of John Norton & Sons, merchants with headquarters in
London and ships plying between Virginia, the West Indies,
and England. Numerous letters were exchanged between the
colonists and John Norton. The correspondence abounds in
personal messages, in items of news and gossip. Everybody
knew everybody else, and many were more-or-less related.
It was a time when handwriting was as fine as copperplate,
when letters and books were profusely splashed with capitals,
and abbreviations were popular. Tobacco appears in these
letters as tobo; hogshead is hhd; Humble Servant is Hble

Servt.; opportunity is oppy; Dear is Dr, and there is much individuality in the matter of spelling and punctuation.

These letter-writers are all, of course, greatly concerned with tobacco:

"Tobo never so plenty since Before I knew the Trade. . . ."

"Sorry to hear from all hands that the Price of Tobo is so low. . . ."

"This serves to convey a Bill of Lading for 6 hhds. of Tobo."

Notices of shipments of tobacco are often accompanied by orders for goods desired from London: medicines, garden seed, tools, lottery tickets, clothing, thoroughbred horses and dogs, elegant sets of table and tea china, decanters and drinking glasses, table silver, painted chariots, music and books—Shakespeare's *Works* in eight volumes, Pope's *Essay on Man,* Locke's *Essay Concerning Human Understanding,* Yorick's sermons in seven volumes, and Sir James Stewart's *Political Economy,* a "Book much celebrated by the Reviewers."

A Mr. William Reynolds sends a bill of lading for eleven hogshead of tobacco, and asks Mr. Norton to send him a tailor, indentured to serve four years. Mr. Reynolds begs that the tailor be not so old, as he has seen some that have "brought their spectacles with them" and were "fitter for a hospital than a shop board."

Catherine Rathell, who has a shop in Fredericksburg, brings her wares over to Williamsburg when the Assembly sits. She is always imploring Mr. Norton to hurry with the goods she orders. Writing in November, she says that the Assembly meets in March. Therefore, she must request "of all things on Earth You will by the very first ship that sails out of London send me these goods."

She has taken a store exactly opposite the Raleigh Tavern, the best situation in Williamsburg. She "piques" herself on having the finest, most fashionable goods in Virginia. In one letter her distress for gentlemen's shoes is very great, and she would call Mr. Norton's attention to the fact that gentlemen now call frequently for shoes with long hind quarters that buckle low on the foot.

And she needs immediately "three dozen sword canes; 6 neat Newest fashioned falling necklaces; 6 nice white silver papered Wedding fans with pierced Ivory Sticks; essence of Pearl for the Teeth; and 3 doz. of thread hair nets such as gentlemen sleep in."

A certain Mrs. Martha Goosley, mother of three ship captains, Cary, George, and William Goosley, writes Mr. Norton that the marriage of one Mr. Cramm "has made a great noise here. But Pray why may not an old Man afflicted with the gout have the pleasure of a fine hand to rub his feet and warm his flannels? Comfortable amusement you will say for a girl of fifteen, but she is to have a chariot and there is to be no Padlock but upon her mind."

Mrs. Goosley expresses herself as glad that Mrs. Norton has grown so fat. "If," she says archly, "you had not told me, it was by Drinking Porter, should have suspected it was owing to some other cause which commonly had that effect upon her in Virginia . . . I Would try the effects upon my thin Carcas. It might perhaps plump my face a little which at Present is almost as sharp as a Hatchet. Am very careful of myself for this spring has been as fatal to old women as to old cows. There is four gone off, within these six weeks."

When Mr. Norton invites her to make a visit to London in a ship of which one of her sons is captain, she replies that she is obliged for his kind invitation and will, someday or other, surprise him. So—she adds—"Pray have the Mill got in order that grinds old women young."

And when these ships out of London or Glasgow were lying in James River their captains would be invited to dine at Westover, or Byrd would be a guest aboard.

On the whole, Byrd's second secret diary resembles the first. But reading the two carefully you see a difference between the aging Byrd and the Byrd of the former diary. No quarrels or passionate reconciliations between himself and his second wife are recorded. The whipping of slaves seems rarely to have occurred. And though he appears still to have been, as he once called himself, the *Inamorato Oiseau,* he confesses to few "Follies" in this later diary. In the year that he was sixty-six the diary remarks: "Played the fool with Marjorie, God forgive me," and twice he says, "Played the fool with Sarah, God forgive me."

But with age he has become a tamer Byrd; resigned now to remaining in Virginia, his interest in the colony deeper than in the days when he dreamed of going once more home to London. The diary comes to an end in August, 1741, when Byrd was sixty-seven.

In 1743 there was born on a tobacco plantation in Albemarle County, also in the northern watershed of James River, a child named Thomas Jefferson. The following year William Byrd was made president of the King's Council, and that same year, at the age of seventy, he died, and was buried in the Westover garden where in the evening he had loved to walk.

The epitaph engraved upon his tombstone is symbolic of those years when England was still home to the Virginia colonists.

It declares that "being born to one of the amplest fortunes in this country, he was early sent to England for his education." It goes on to say that, through Sir Robert Southwell, he was introduced to the acquaintance of many of the "first persons of the age for knowledge, wit, virtue, birth, or high station, and particularly contracted a most intimate and bosom friendship with the learned and illustrious Charles Boyle, Earl of Orrery." It celebrates the facts that in Virginia Byrd was made "Receiver-general of his majesty's revenues . . . was thrice appointed public agent to the court and ministry of England . . . and at last became President of the Council of this Colony." The epitaph concludes by stating that he was "the constant enemy of all exorbitant power and hearty friend of the liberties of his country."

Byrd incarnated the London gentleman of the latter seventeenth century, and the first half of the eighteenth. Byrd is so dated that it would be unfair to judge him out

of his time; while Nathaniel Bacon, who was of the previous
generation, is dated only in the quaintness of his language;
his spirit of rebellion against tyranny is ageless, he would have
been equally at home in the blazing dawn of man's inalienable rights, and today when the world hopes and fights for
wider freedoms. Yesterday, today and tomorrow, Nathaniel
Bacon's marching spirit can never be dated. You never think,
for example, what his dress was, while William Byrd presents
himself before you in his great black curled wig, and his
eighteenth century finery. Only in the wilderness beyond the
Falls did he himself ever forget all that, and reveal the best
that was in him.

❀

Byrd was born to the noisy rushing of James River over
boulders at the Falls; he died with the James flowing deep
and wide and quiet before his doors; he lies buried in his
garden also close to the James, in what he had called "this
silent Country;" the garden where it had been his habit to
walk in the evening.

He was dead, and it was evening in life, as he had known
life. For in the year of his death the birth of a new day was
near. Thomas Jefferson was one year old. Patrick Henry was
eight and learning to read and write at a neighborhood school
in Hanover County, in the northern watershed of James
River. And the twelve-year-old George Washington was
making the most of what opportunities for education came
his way, keeping copybooks in which he set down whatever
appeared to him to be desirable knowledge: geometrical defi-
nitions, the form for a promissory note, for a bill of exchange, a tobacco receipt, a bail bond, a servant's indenture,
a deed of gift, a land lease, a Virginia land patent, a will,
exercises in surveying, and one hundred and ten "Rules of
Civility and Decent Behaviour in Company and Conversation"—all set down in a small, neat, round hand.

Byrd lay dead and Jefferson, Henry, and Washington
were growing up as Virginians, to whom America, and not
England, was to be "home."

The North Fork of
the James at
Buena Vista

CHAPTER SEVEN

The Valley

IN THE YEAR that William Byrd's wife, Lucy, died
of smallpox in London, Virginia's governor, Alexander Spotswood, led an expedition across the Blue Ridge Mountains.
Among the "gentlemen" who accompanied him was the
youth John Fontaine of the famous family of Huguenot
refugees. And John kept a journal.

The expedition, he says, set forth from Williamsburg
at ten o'clock on the morning of August 20, the year being
1716. They crossed York River by ferry, and at six o'clock
in the evening arrived at the house of a friend on the Mattapony River, where they "lay all night and were well entertained." In the morning they crossed the Mattapony, rode
all day, spent the night with that Robert Beverly to whom

poor Ursula Byrd had been married only to die before she was quite seventeen. At Robert Beverly's, Governor Spotswood abandoned his chaise and proceeded, like the rest, on horseback. The next day they advanced to within ten miles of the Falls of the Rappahannock, where they rested their horses and diverted themselves. They were then joined by several other "gentlemen," who had previously arranged to meet them at that point. The expedition took on also four Indian guides and two companies of rangers, each consisting of half a dozen men and an officer; so that the expedition now numbered some fifty persons.

Crossing the Rappahannock, they made ready their tents, and had their horses shod in preparation for the stony mountain trails, so different from the sandy soil of the Tidewater region. Now exploration really began. There were no more plantation houses at which to lie and be well-entertained. They were to sleep in tents upon beds of boughs, they were to be awakened by a trumpet for early morning starts, they were to hunt along the way, living upon venison roasted before their campfire. Several of the party came down with measles, others had fever and dosed themselves with "the bark."

Twelve days after leaving Williamsburg they camped just below the great mountains, beyond which there lay for them a land of mystery. Fontaine says they made camp at what he calls "the head of James River," where, he adds, "a man may jump over it." They climbed a mountain from which they had a fine view, and on the following day they followed the river until they came to the top of the ridge, "to the very head spring"; naming the highest point they reached "Mount George," in honor of the reigning British Majesty. There, Fontaine says, "all drank the King's health in champagne, and fired a volley" . . . the "Princess's health in Burgundy, and fired a volley," and "all the rest of the Royal Family in Claret, and fired a volley" . . . then "the Governor's health, and fired a volley."

In addition to these beverages, Fontaine says that the expedition carried "Virginia red wine and white wine, Irish

usquebaugh, brandy shrub, two sorts of rum, canary punch,
Cider, Etc."

It is not, under those circumstances, singular that Fontaine's geography should have been hazy.

If you have stood on the bank at the headwaters of
the James and watched the Cowpasture flow lazily around
one point of woodland and the Jackson come foaming around
another, to unite and form the James, you realize the absurdity of Fontaine's notion that Spotswood's expedition
encamped "beside the James River where a man may jump
over it."

Neither the Jackson nor the Cowpasture could be
jumped over within many miles of their union; and their
combined waters create a stream wide and swift. The James
has therefore no "very head spring," on the top of the Blue
Ridge, as Fontaine imagined. But drinks so mixed as brandy
and shrub, champagne, two sorts of rum, canary punch,
Burgundy, claret and Irish usquebaugh—to say nothing of
the "etc."—are, after all, a handicap in accurate exploration
of new lands.

Historians have been puzzled to determine just where
Spotswood's expedition did cross the Blue Ridge. It was long
thought to have been at Rockfish Gap, to the southeast of
the present city of Staunton; altogether outside the James
River watershed. Later it seemed to be established that Spotswood crossed the range at Swift Run Gap, also beyond the
northern limit of the James watershed.

But, however vague Fontaine's geography, Spotswood's
expedition actually looked upon the Great Valley of Virginia
enclosed on the west by the Alleghenies and on the east by
the Blue Ridge, with between these two ranges lesser ranges
breaking the Valley into those smaller valleys which were
the open grassy pastures where grazed herds of buffalo
and elk.

Twenty-eight days after leaving Williamsburg the expedition returned, having made a journey of more than four
hundred miles. They brought ecstatic accounts of the beauty

Where the Jackson and
the Cowpasture Meet
the James is Born

shenton

and fertility of the Valley, which appeared to them to be uninhabited, encircled by mountains which they thought "presented almost insurmountable obstacles to savages."

Those hearing this came to think of the Valley as a place of security and of fruitful plenty, and to discuss the possibility of settling there.

Such was the glamour of these travelers' tales, and such was the publicity occasioned by the fact that upon each of the exploring "gentlemen" Governor Spotswood bestowed a Golden Horseshoe, dubbing him a Knight of the Golden Horseshoe, that Spotswood has been often credited with having been the first man to have gazed upon the Valley of Virginia, though he modestly never claimed that distinction for himself; for in 1710 he wrote the London Council that a group of "adventurers" had crossed the Blue Ridge; probably near Balcony Falls on the James. And of course it was well-known in Virginia that forty-seven years before the Spotswood expedition, old Governor Berkeley had commissioned the German, John Lederer, to explore the western wilderness of the colony. Lederer's account of explorations, and his map, had been published in London in 1672, long before Spotswood was Virginia's governor. But Lederer's text is so full of fantastic errors that, though his map does indicate that he reached the top of the Blue Ridge, it is impossible to say with certainty that he did so.

And, after all, first-white-man pretensions are relatively unimportant, and there was the magic of publicity in those Golden Horseshoes, to dramatize a great Valley of opportunity.

The Reverend Hugh Jones, chaplain of the House of Burgesses in Williamsburg, and professor of mathematics in the college, testifies to the fact of the Horseshoes:

"For this expedition they were obliged to provide a great quantity of Horse-Shoes; (Things seldom used in the lower Parts of the County, where there are few Stones:) Upon which Account the Governor upon their Return presented each of his Companions with a Golden Horse-Shoe, (some of which I have seen studded with valuable Stones resembling the Heads of Nails) with this Inscription on the one Side: *Sic juvat transcendere montes:* And on the other is written the tramontane Order."

The Order, according to the Reverend Mr. Jones, was "instituted to encourage Gentlemen to venture backwards and make new Discoveries and New Settlements, any Gentleman being entitled to wear this Golden Shoe that can prove his having drunk his Majesty's Health upon Mount George."

More than a hundred years later, in a letter dated 1841, the venerable Judge Francis Brooke, who had fought under Lafayette in the Revolutionary War, wrote: " . . . I had seen in the possession of the oldest branch of my family, a Golden Horse-Shoe set with garnets, and having inscribed on it the motto: 'Sic juvat transcendere montes,' which from tradition, I always understood was presented by Governor Spotswood, to my Grandfather as one of the many gentlemen who accompanied him across the mountains." In a "Narrative" of his life written for his family, Judge Brooke speaks of this Horseshoe as "a medal . . . worn as a brooch."

And nearly fifty years ago, in 1898, this item appeared in the *William and Mary Quarterly:* "The miniature horseshoe that belonged to Spotswood, according to a descendant of his, the late Mrs. Susan Bott of Petersburg, who had seen it, was small enough to be worn on a watch-chain."

Although, through the years, most careful search has been made to find one of these Golden Horseshoes, it has been in vain. Mrs. Susan Bott remembered having seen one, but Mrs. Bott has been dead for half a century. And these two horseshoes, last seen in the nineteenth century, have mysteriously disappeared.

But certainly beyond question Governor Spotswood and his party crossed the Blue Ridge, and beyond doubt the Tramontane Order and the Golden Horseshoes are established facts.

❀

Meanwhile, in the north of Ireland, men were thinking of America; repeating stories brought back by captains of ships out of Glasgow and London; passing the stories from one to another and another. . . . And there must occasionally have come to them letters giving information at first hand. In the beginning the letters would have been from friends and relatives in Pennsylvania, but later there would have been letters from the great Valley itself.

To Protestants then living in Ireland such a valley in the New World promised escape from endless strife. For when had there not been strife in the north of Ireland? As far back as the Norman conquest, Ireland's native chiefs had been fighting each other. Then the English had fought the chiefs. In the time of Queen Elizabeth, Irish rebellion had been put down with such cruelty that Elizabeth herself had said that nothing would remain for her to rule over except ashes and corpses. Later, in the reign of that decrepit James I for whom the noble James River had been named, rebellion was again plotted; Irish lords of lands in the province of Ulster plotted, failed, and fled. The crown confiscated the vast acreage which they abandoned and settled upon it Protestants from Scotland and England; Londoners founding in Ulster the city of Londonderry. Among those Ulster colonists were vigorous Scotch Highlanders and provident Huguenot refugees. In their hands Ulster prospered, and was briefly tranquil, until Tory High-Church England began a combined religious and commercial persecution of Presbyterian Ulster. Their clergy were not permitted to perform the marriage ceremony, or to bury the dead. Presbyterians might not practice law, or hold office in army or navy, or be elected to Parliament.

Through the years, waves of persecution swept over Ireland. Cromwell exterminated with fire and slaughter the rebellious Catholics. When James II came to power and gave civil and military authority to the native Irish, it was the Catholics' turn to oppress, and Londonderry for three months heroically resisted attack and defied starvation. William of Orange then came to the throne, but the High Church party thwarted his plans to aid the Dissenters, and after his death, when Anne was queen in England, and William Byrd was

driving about London in his coach-and-six, there was despair
in Ulster because of increased persecution, both religious and
commercial.

And in Virginia, Governor Spotswood led that expedition over the crest of the Blue Ridge and down into the
great Valley.

Twelve years later, emigration from Ulster to America
was flowing in a strong tide across the Atlantic, through
Pennsylvania, and into the Valley of Virginia, while at the
same time certain of the more adventurous of the Tidewater
colonists were taking up land in that part of the Valley
drained by the James and its headwater streams.

The Valley appeared to those first settlers to be uninhabited; there were no permanent Indian settlements and the
colonists failed to realize that the Valley was sacred to various
tribes as a game preserve; as much the Indians' own as if
they had cultivated it. At the close of every hunting season
it was their custom to burn the grassy open lands that they
might be perpetuated as feeding grounds for buffalo and elk.
But the colonists saw them as pastures for future sheep,
cattle, and horses.

The herds of buffalo moving from one such grazing
ground to another had worn paths which became roads for
the white men, as did also the Indian trails. The Indian trails
were narrow, for they traveled in single file. Their feet set
down with a straight line from heel to toe, the advancing
foot always on a line with the rear foot; so characteristic a
gait that the colonists called it "Indian file." With the years
these single-file journeys had worn deep narrow trails; passing
through forests, blocked often by fallen trees, and arriving
frequently at the banks of streams where crossing places were
established. In the Valley of the James and its headwaters,
one stream occasionally crosses the mouth of another, and
there bars of sand or mud are formed which provided the
traveling Indians with shallow fords. Over such trails they
moved about the country; fighting, hunting, and to some
degree, trading.

Their Great Road—their warpath—on its way to the

Carolinas came down from the north, crossed the Potomac, passed behind the mountains through the Shenandoah section of the Valley and into the watershed of the James.

The white settlers who took up land in the Valley were chiefly those hardy Scotch Presbyterians who had emigrated from Ulster to start life over again in America. And because the fame of America as a land of opportunity had spread to Europe, some of the Valley colonists were Palatine Germans whose homes in the Rhine valley had been destroyed during the seventeenth century wars between France and Germany. At the same time, men from Tidewater Virginia also were settling west of the Blue Ridge.

These early colonists in the headwaters' region of the James settled along the banks of creeks and rivers. They had been accustomed to the comforts of civilization, but their first homes in the Valley were log cabins, often with earthen floors. Samuel Kercheval, writing in 1833, could remember those primitive cabins, and the plain homemade clothing that people wore; men in coats with skirts halfway to the knees, linsey hunting shirts, leather breeches and leggings; the women in coarse shoes and linsey gowns. Fashionably dressed men from the Tidewater, with sparkling gold or silver knee and shoe buckles, were so rare that Kercheval remembered all his life how, as a child, he had felt "awed in their presence, and viewed them as something more than man."

In the beginning the furniture of these Valley homes was as crude as the cabins: a bed of boards, a table, three-legged stools, all hewn from forest trees. Only the most prosperous had a few pewter dishes and spoons; others used wooden utensils, or managed to get on with only dried gourds. Knives and forks and cooking pots were imported from great distance by pack-horse caravans. Corn-pone bread and "hog and hominy" were the staple foods, but the hunters brought in venison, bear meat, and wild turkey, in the rivers there were perch, mullet, and big catfish, and soon every family had a garden where pumpkins, squash, and potatoes

were raised. The Reverend Joseph Doddridge, in describing
the life of the Valley colonists, recalls the first time he ever
saw a teacup and saucer, or a house that had plastered walls
and ceilings, or was built of stone: "I had no idea that there
was any house in the world which was not made of logs," he
says. Even the churches were log cabins.

At night, in their rude wilderness homes, the settlers
heard what they spoke of as "the awful howling of wolves."
And it was a common thing to see Indians on the warpath
passing up and down the Valley. But they did not at first
molest the whites, who had been in the Valley of the James
some ten years before there was a battle between the two
races.

It happened in December of 1742, when John McDowell,
as captain of the local militia, was sent against a party of
northern Indians who, on their way south to attack their
ancient enemy, the Catawbas, had appropriated property of
the colonists. On North River, not far from where it joins
the James, the militia came upon the marauding Indians, and
in the skirmish McDowell and seven of his men were killed.

That was ominous. But the trouble had been with a
northern tribe on the warpath, and not with the neighboring
tribes. And the colonists returned to the engrossing business
of establishing homes in this fertile lovely Valley. They
sowed fields with corn and wheat, oats, rye, hemp and flax.
Their cattle grazed in the pastures. They built barns, and
mills to grind their grain. And in the autumn and winter
they hunted.

Doddridge remembered how the men "became uneasy at
home . . . the house was too warm, the feather bed too soft,
and even the good wife was not thought for the time being
a proper companion; the mind of the hunter was wholly
occupied with the camp and the chase." At this season
something of the spirit of the forest savage seemed to enter
into the colonists. As hunters they learned to be expert woods-
men, acquiring a knowledge of the habits of every sort of
game, and familiarity with every foot of the land over which
they hunted. By imitative cries they would call to themselves

the wild turkey and the fawn, they could get a response from a pack of wolves, and, thus learning where they were, be on guard against them. Hunting was a serious matter of business, and not a sport.

The settlers prospered and increased. New immigrants came in. Weddings were frolics with plenty of home-brewed whisky, and the dancing of reels and jigs. Then a group of girls would take the bride up the ladder and put her to bed; the young men doing the same for the groom; "placing him," Doddridge says, "snugly by the side of his bride." All night the dance went on, and food and drink would be sent up the ladder to the bridal pair. So was the Valley populated.

Comfortable houses were soon built, trade with Williamsburg was opened, and luxuries to which many of the settlers had once been accustomed were transported on pack horses over routes established through the mountain gaps. Now the Valley colonists had silks and satins for their Sunday best, silver and china for their homes, and good Madeira wine in abundance.

With this prosperity arose increased demand for labor. Negro slaves were always comparatively few in the Valley, but large numbers of indentured white servants were brought in, working out their passage money, and later taking up lands for themselves.

This added ease of living did not soften the austere Presbyterianism of the Valley. Rated among crimes was the singing of profane songs on the Sabbath, and driving wagons on the Sabbath. Housebreaking and horse stealing were listed beside larceny and murder. Punishments were the lash, the pillory, the cropping of ears, and death by hanging.

Children were sternly reared, and in the great Valley a rhyme is still remembered, to the effect that:

> They raised them tough, they raised them well—
> When their feet were set in the paths of hell,
> They put in their heart the fear of God,
> And tanned their hides with a stiff ram-rod.

Meanwhile tribes of Indians passed and repassed through the Valley. Occasionally they paid visits to the colonists. According to an old writer, the Indian would arrive, announcing briefly, "I am come." The food he expected was hospitably offered. The Indian ate, smoked at his leisure, and then remarking, "I am going," departed.

"I am come" and "I am going" . . . quite as though everything was amicable.

The Arsenal and Court House—
Williamsburg

CHAPTER EIGHT

Duke of Gloucester Street

THE EIGHTEENTH CENTURY was young, and Williamsburg was young, when Alexander Spotswood was governor of Virginia. He made Williamsburg beautiful, spending so much money on the governor's mansion that people named it the "Palace." The Reverend Hugh Jones described it as a magnificent structure with a good cupola illuminating most of the town on Royal Birthnights. As for the Virginians themselves, the Reverend Mr. Jones was charmed with their "good diversion and splendid entertainments. Actually," he said, they lived "in the same neat Manner . . . dressed after the same Modes, and behaved themselves exactly as the Gentry of London." And Governor Gooch, who followed some years after Spotswood, boasted that there was not an ill dancer in his government.

Though the little village of Williamsburg was gay the

year round, the season was during the meeting of the Assembly, usually in autumn and spring. The normal population was not more than two thousand, but when the Assembly met the burgesses brought their families in from the plantations. Town houses were opened, taverns crowded, and the streets lively with the coming and going of chariots, coaches, chaises, and horsemen.

By this time there was a theater in Williamsburg, the first in the colonies. Visiting professional companies gave *Othello* and *Romeo and Juliet*, as well as the comedies and drolls of the day. When there were no professionals in town, the gentlemen and ladies of the country put on plays themselves, such as *The Busy Body, The Recruiting Officer,* and *The Lying Valet.*

People were so fond of music that through the open windows of Williamsburg's houses came the sound of harpsichord, harmonica, guitar, German flutes, fortepianos; and voices singing. In the season there were horse races, cockfights, and contests of every description. A number of "brisk young men" would wrestle for silver buckles; dancers would compete for a pair of handsome shoes; fiddlers would enter a contest for a violin; a hat to the value of twenty shillings would be cudgeled for; a pig would be the prize won by whoever succeeded in catching and lifting it by the tail made slippery by soaping; a pair of elegant silk stockings would be awarded to the prettiest young country maid present; and a quire of ballads would be sung for by a number of songsters, all of them provided with "liquor sufficient to clear their Wind Pipes." This was also the profitable season to hold slave auctions and auctions of land, for merchants to bring in their wares, and hairdressers and wigmakers to open shops. And there were, of course, continual balls and dinners, the most brilliant being at the Palace and in the beautiful Apollo Room of Raleigh Tavern.

It was October when a youthful giant rode into Williamsburg, summoned by Virginia's new governor, Robert

Dinwiddie. The young giant's name was George Washington, and he was only twenty-one.

Although he had been to Williamsburg before, he was not a familiar figure in the capital, for his home was on the Potomac. Yet because he was so immensely tall and because, even in a country of fine horsemen, he stood out as a magnificent rider, people must have gazed admiringly, curious perhaps to know who was this young centaur with the frank cheerful face who rode down Duke of Gloucester Street.

The street runs almost due east and west, with the College of William and Mary at its western end, and three-quarters of a mile away, at its eastern end, the Capitol. It is a wide gracious street with a modest dignity all its own. Midway between Capitol and college is Raleigh Tavern, and beyond, on the other side of the Palace Green, Bruton Parish Church lifts a high spire, while facing the green, imposing and stately, the Governor's Palace stands among its gardens.

And since each of us is inseparable from what has gone before, this young man's past rode with him into Williamsburg.

He was only eleven when his father died, and he had early understood that he must rely for support upon his own efforts. Lawrence, his stepbrother, who was the eldest of the family, had, like William Byrd, been sent "home" to England for his education, but there had been no money to give such advantages to young George Washington; not even sufficient money for the college at Williamsburg. If Washington was to have an education he must make the most of every opportunity for schooling that came his way, largely educating himself. Among the "Rules of Civility and Decent Behaviour in Company and Conversation" set down in his boyhood copybooks were maxims later exemplified in the life of the man, George Washington:

"Associate yourself with men of good quality . . . for 'tis better to be alone than in bad company . . . Undertake not what you cannot perform . . . be careful to keep your promise . . . be not hasty to believe flying reports to the disparagement of any . . . Let your recreations be manful

. . . when a man does all he can, though it succeeds not well, blame not him that did it . . . Keep alive in your breast that little spark of celestial fire called conscience."

In his early life Washington spent much time with his stepbrothers, Lawrence and Augustine, on their plantations, and he apprenticed himself to the official surveyor of the county. Lawrence gave him practical experience in surveying his own plantation, which he had named Mount Vernon, in honor of Admiral Vernon under whom he had fought at Cartagena. And when George was sixteen he went with his friend, George Fairfax, into the wilderness beyond the Blue Ridge Mountains, to survey part of that vast track of some five million acres which had descended to Lord Fairfax as a grant made by Charles II to his grandfather. And none of this would have come about but for Lawrence, who was married to a cousin of his lordship. Lawrence gave his brother opportunity; George himself won the friendship of the observant worldly-wise old lord.

Looking back at them across the years, they make a charming picture, the old lord and young George Washington. They were both tall, both with a natural majesty of bearing, both bold horsemen, both devoted to hunting. George was a slender, callow, chestnut-haired youth, with steady blue-grey eyes spaced far apart, and looking at you straight; his lordship, aquiline-nosed, mature, experienced, and the finished product of London society in the eighteenth century. People said Lord Fairfax had come out to Virginia to remain a bachelor through life because of a woman who on the eve of marriage had cast him off for the glittering prospect of a ducal coronet.

This Lord Fairfax was part of George Washington's education, as his brother Lawrence was part of it, and the surveyor with whom he had worked, and the Rules of Civility, and the friends he made when he stayed with Lawrence at Mount Vernon; among them his lordship's Fairfax cousins, living near by on their estate, Belvoir; especially his friend was George Fairfax and the girl he had married—

beautiful gay Sally Cary, whose father had a plantation on the lower James and a house in Williamsburg.

When George Washington was nineteen he went with Lawrence to Barbados. Lawrence had consumption, and a winter in Barbados was recommended. But there George came down with smallpox, while Lawrence realized that for himself death was so near that he was beyond being benefited by climate. And since he must die, he would die in Virginia.

Before George was twenty-one he had inherited Mount Vernon, and had been appointed adjutant general of northern Virginia, with the title of major.

This was the past that rode with him into Williamsburg on the last day of October in the year 1753.

And now, riding down Duke of Gloucester Street, in obedience to that summons from Governor Dinwiddie— George Washington was riding into the future. . . .

There was trouble on Virginia's Ohio frontier. The Ohio Company had been organized to establish settlements in Virginia's western lands, and to develop the immensely profitable fur trade with the Indians. The company opened a road and made ready to send emigrants into the region. But the French, also wanting the fur trade, claimed the same territory as their own, and were preparing to defend it.

Governor Dinwiddie was determined to maintain England's rights: the French must not encroach upon Virginia's possessions; he would send a warning letter to the French commander on the frontier. The messenger who was to carry this letter must bring back a reply; he must also win the friendship of the Indian tribes of the district. The mission involved a journey of at least six hundred miles; in winter, through wilderness country. And stout, red-faced, white-wigged Governor Dinwiddie had sent for young George Washington to convey to the French commander that letter of warning, written in the name of his Majesty, the king.

With these credentials, on October 31st in the year

1753, Washington, with a French and Indian interpreter, set forth from Williamsburg on his dangerous mission.

In January he rode again down Duke of Gloucester Street, to report to Governor Dinwiddie.

He had journeyed through trackless wilderness in freezing rain and snow. When his horse was too exhausted to carry a rider, he had traveled on foot, gun in hand and a pack on his back, adapting himself to forest life, wearing a hunting shirt and moccasins. Along the way he had made speeches to the Indians on behalf of the British king. He had met the savage queen, Aliquipa, winning her with gifts of a matchcoat and a bottle of rum. She preferred the rum. This queen, he said, was "old and fat, as wrinkled as a frosted persimmon. She smoked a pipe and had a tomahawk in her belt . . . I did not think that she would be a comfortable partner in the marriage state."

Washington had made notes and maps of the region, and these he now delivered to the governor in Williamsburg, together with the French commander's letter which stated emphatically that France claimed the Ohio frontier as her own territory, to which the British had no right.

Among the colonists in the Valley of Virginia, it was rumored that Indians had then appeared from beyond the Alleghenies, urging the Valley Indians to abandon their homes and cross the western mountains. It was obvious, the colonists thought, that this was done under the influence of the French.

In April, Dinwiddie again dispatched Washington, this time with a detachment of soldiers with orders to build a fort in the Forks of the Ohio.

Suddenly, suspiciously enough, all Indians left the Valley of Virginia to join the tribes across the Alleghenies. The French were massing their allies for a contest with the British.

At the Ohio Forks they drove off the British party and constructed for themselves Fort Duquesne. There was an encounter and Washington gave the order to fire. Winning in this first skirmish, he hurriedly threw up the stockade which he called Fort Necessity. The French attacked in strength and Washington was compelled to surrender. When he once more rode down Duke of Gloucester Street to report to the governor, he had experienced both victory and defeat.

From New England to Virginia the colonies were alarmed; General Braddock was sent out from England to Virginia with an army of British regulars, and in London General Braddock's frivolous friends were saying that the general's only qualification to conduct a war in America was that his bald head prevented his being scalped. But Braddock believed victory to be certain. The scarlet coats of his regulars were bright, they maneuvered with military precision, scorning to fire, like Indians, from the shelter of tree or rock. Of course, victory was certain; he had no doubt of that. Still, he would take George Washington, as his aide-de-camp: the young man knew the territory and might be of use.

Before his departure for the frontier a dinner was given to General Braddock in Williamsburg. One of the men present wrote of meeting there a certain Major Washington, about twenty-three, "comely and dignified," possessed of "wit, judgment and self-reliance . . . He strikes me as of an extraordinary and exalted character . . . destined, in my opinion, to make no inconsiderable figure in the country."

In early June, 1755, Braddock led his army northwest, and in July, Washington sent to his brother, John, a letter full of the impetuous fire of his twenty-three years. "We have been scandalously beaten by a trifling body of men . . . I had four bullets in my coat, and two horses shot under me, yet escaped unhurt, although death was leveling my companions on every side." And to the governor he wrote that the regulars had stampeded in panic. Their "dastardly behaviour exposed their officers and all who tried to do their duty to almost certain death." But their officers had fought "with incomparable bravery" and the Virginia companies had "behaved like men and died like soldiers . . . of three companies scarce thirty left alive" . . . and General Braddock had been shot through the lung and had died in three days' time.

As always, when reading Washington's own words, the strange sanctimonious haze in which others—never himself—have sometimes enveloped him dissolves, and he stands forth so masculine that he comes to you with the smell of freshly turned earth, with the odor of a gun just fired, with the scent of the moist feathers of the bird which a dog brings in his mouth to the hunter. You smell wet wood, smoldering over a forest campfire, or breathe the new-mown fragrance which a horse exhales in warm summer air.

In his own uncensored speech, Washington emerges a man of dynamic vigor. At the beginning he had to work over his spelling. You see his mastery of it, from the time of that first journal of a surveying expedition when he wrote that they started on "Fryday" and at night they slept under a "thread bear blanket with double its weight of vermin." Now and then his spelling reveals his pronunciation, as when he speaks of watching the Indians "daunce."

The simple, stately dignity of style characteristic of him becomes, when necessary, vehement. There was that "dastardly" behavior of the oysterman at his landing; and the man whom he calls "a thorough pac'd Rascall." Of another he says that "a damneder scoundrel God Almighty never permitted to disgrace humanity." And "How in God's name did my brother Samuel get himself so enormously in debt?" (That his brother Samuel was five times married may explain it.) A sum of money appropriated in wartime, Washington describes as "but a flea-bite," compared with what was needed.

An editor of Washington's collected writings, with good but mistaken intentions, cut out such words as he thought unworthy of the colorless paragon he would have this forceful human Washington appear. Washington's "but a flea-bite" he altered to read "totally inadequate." "Rid" the editor changed to "rode," and so on. In the process Washington was denatured. But now that the diaries and letters have been printed as they were written, the man is at last unveiled.

He is not subtle; his humor is rather a sense of fun than of humor; his mind does not flash, it moves with a slow certainty; "the honestest man, I believe that ever adorned human nature," was the opinion of one who knew him well. And he was always human; loving intercourse with people, dancing, hunting, playing cards and billiards, devoted to the theater, and with a nice taste for dress; a man of gusto, with an immense zest for living, yet with a realization of values which made excess impossible. Rarely does a man know himself as Washington did: understanding the strength of his passions, the violence of which he was capable, the necessity for control of his emotions.

But for all that he knew of himself, Washington had no notion that he was a great man; for his greatness was as the greatness of a mountain, or of the sea—a greatness unaware of itself. Without consciousness of self he performed whatever duty was assigned him. When Braddock's defeat left the whole western frontier at the mercy of Indian raids, Washington undertook the building and manning of a chain of defensive blockhouses, stockades, and forts, on James River, Jackson's, the Bullpasture, Cowpasture, and Calfpasture rivers. He was moved by "the sorrowful condition of the settlers" in the great Valley, living as they did in constant peril; he was indignant at the "worthlessness of the militia," and undaunted by the "scarcity of tools," and "want of contractors," needed in constructing forts, and by the lack of men for garrisons. Superintending this defense of the frontier, Washington traveled up and down the Valley. As you travel about the valley today, you say to yourself: "There was a fort here . . . a fort there. Washington directed their building."

Finally, exhausted by anxiety and exposure, he comes in the autumn of 1757 to Mount Vernon, and from there he sends a messenger with a letter to his neighbor, Sally Fairfax. He has been three months seriously ill, and he writes to borrow her receipt book that he may instruct his servants to prepare such food as the doctor has ordered; and he would be grateful, too, for materials to make jellies, for a pound of tea, and a bottle or two of wine. It is a touching letter, from a man alone in his illness.

In the early spring he is able to ride down to Williamsburg. He breaks the journey by spending the night with his friends, the Chamberlynes, near York River Ferry. The Chamberlynes happen to have a house guest: the young widow, Martha Custis. Of course, George Washington knows who Martha Custis is: "Martha Dandridge that was," as the Virginians quaintly express it. But Mr. Custis having died, Martha was left a wealthy widow, with two small children. And Martha, like everyone in Virginia, knew about George Washington: that he had had two horses shot under him, and four bullets in his coat; and that, though he was only twenty-six, he'd been made a commander in chief of all the forces in Virginia.

He must have appeared hugely tall on that spring day when he was presented to the little widow Custis at the Chamberlynes' house; tall in his uniform and his laurels; and she a tiny creature. In a portrait of the times she wears her hair combed back from an oddly childish face. It is hard to believe she is a few months older than Washington; hard to believe that she had had four children and, had known the sorrow of burying two of them in Bruton churchyard.

So they met—Washington and Martha Custis—in an hour of mutual need, the lonely soldier and the little widow. People said it was love at first sight. Certainly it was need at first sight.

George Washington stayed the night at Chamberlynes' and rode the next day to Williamsburg.

On his way back to the frontier where he was determined to plant the British flag, removing forever the banner of France, he visited his little widow in her own home—the White House on the Pamunkey River; and when he resumed his journey, soldier and widow were engaged to be married.

Along the way he sent her a letter:

"We have begun our march for the Ohio. A courier is starting for Williamsburg and I embrace the opportunity to send a few lines to one whose life is now inseparable from mine. Since that happy hour when we made our pledges to each other my thoughts have been continually going to you as to another Self. That an allpowerful Providence may keep us both in safety is the prayer of your ever faithful and affectionate friend."

He is engaged to this little widow Custis. She is vivacious, pretty, and vastly affectionate; Martha, his "dear Patsy," who needs a man to look after her. They have not one financial care, he and Martha; for Lawrence has left him Mount Vernon, and since he was sixteen he has earned a living at his trade as surveyor; to that he has now added military distinction. As for Martha Custis, she is in her own right one of the richest women in Virginia.

His thoughts go continually to Martha, "as to another Self" . . . her life is now "inseparable" from his.

And that year Colonel Washington led a strong expedition against Fort Duquesne. And that year, the French commander fled.

❖

George and Martha were married in January of the year 1759, in the bride's home, on the Pamunkey River.

Martha wore white brocaded silk into which was woven a glistening silver thread. The brocade was draped to show an embroidered satin petticoat. Her feet were in purple slippers trimmed with silver lace, and for jewels she wore necklace and earrings and bracelets of pearls. Colonel Washington was in citizen's dress of blue cloth, with an embroidered waistcoat of white satin. There were gold buckles at his knees and on his shoes; his hair was powdered, and he carried a dress sword.

And as you look upon them—the majestic bridegroom and his pretty little bride in her wedding furbelows—you are convinced that she will be happy in her new life; for a woman —or a nation—might trustfully give her hand into the keeping of George Washington, confident of contentment and security.

The couple went to Williamsburg to spend their honey-moon in Martha's town house.

And when the House of Burgesses convened in the spring, Washington was among its members, elected from the county of Fairfax. When he first took his place in the Capitol at the eastern end of Duke of Gloucester Street, the speaker of the House announced the gratitude of the Assembly to Colonel George Washington "for his brave and steady behaviour, from the first Encroachments and Hostilities of the French and their Indians, to his Resignation after the happy Reduction of Fort Duquesne."

And those who were present say that when Washington rose to acknowledge the honor, he so blushed and stammered that the speaker considerately came to his relief: "Sit down, Mr. Washington, your modesty is equal to your valour; and that surpasses the power of any language I possess."

Where Looney's Creek enters the James

CHAPTER NINE

Looney's Ferry

LOONEY'S CREEK flows up from the south and pours its waters into James River, opposite Purgatory Mountain and fertile Cherry Tree Bottom; only a few miles from Natural Bridge.

Cherry Tree Bottom was early chosen for himself by James Patton, a North of Ireland man from County Londonderry. In the beginning he had settled on the land known as Beverley's Manor, adjoining, on the north, Benjamin Borden's vast James River grant. Patton married Borden's daughter, and took up in his own name additional land along the banks of the James, both north and south, until he became one of the greatest landholders in that part of the valley. He was spoken of everywhere as a man with a fine head for business. People said he had once served in the Royal Navy, and that later, as a ship captain, he had crossed the Atlantic more than a score of times, bringing "redemptioners" to Tidewater Virginia. Everything Patton did appeared to succeed, and when his daughter married John Buchanan, the three biggest land barons in the James River valley were linked by marriage.

Robert Looney was certainly wise in establishing himself near men like Patton and Buchanan. He built his house on the point of land between James River and the creek from the south. He planted an orchard, cleared pasturage for his cattle and fields for grain. He built a mill, and people began to call the creek Looney's Mill Creek.

The great Indian warpath from the north to the Carolinas, coming down through the Valley behind the Blue Ridge, crossed the James at the mouth of Looney's Creek, where the river might be forded when the water was low. The colonists blazed a wagon road, following the general direction of the warpath, and James Patton obtained the license for a ferry across the James at the eddy just above the mouth of Looney's Creek, and he commissioned Looney to operate it. And it was known as Looney's Ferry. Looney had plenty of sons to share with him the work of farming, cattle raising, operating the mill and the ferry.

The villages of Buchanan and Pattonsburg grew up on the banks of the James. There was constant coming and going of new settlers taking up land, and of established colonists bringing their grain to be ground at Looney's mill. All this made abundant traffic for the ferry.

Among the colonists who took up land in the neighborhood of Patton, Buchanan, and Looney, there was Josiah Dennis and his young wife, Hannah. Hannah Dennis came to have a place in history, and when a young woman becomes a tradition she becomes invariably beautiful as well as young.

At that time there was, as a rule, peace in the Valley. The Indians paid their phlegmatic calls upon the settlers.

Hospitable themselves, they expected and received from the colonists generous entertainment. Thomas Walker, exploring western Virginia and impressed with the openhanded hospitality of the colonists, remarked that they would be better off if the Indians did not take so much from them.

Then had come that ominous disappearance of the Indians across the Alleghenies. "They have gone to join up with the French," people said, apprehensive. And it was true. War soon broke out between the French and the British, and the Indians fought beside the French.

Looney's son Robert was among the first killed. Peter Looney, a sergeant at Fort Vause, was captured when the fort fell, and carried off by the Indians. Perhaps he would never again be seen at Looney's Ferry; for you never knew what would happen to prisoners taken by the Indians. Sometimes the tribe would adopt a captive, and in that case they showed him affection. Children had been adopted and loved, becoming so completely Indian that they refused to return to white civilization. Or the Indians would take a child and dash its brains out against a tree. Incomprehensible people! You never knew what they would do. And it was always feared that captives would be tortured; a thing more to be dreaded than death and scalping. They brought up their own children to smile under torture. The various tribes were constantly at war, and if taken prisoner, torture was to be expected. The braver, the stronger the man captured, the more fiendish would be the torture devised for him.

The colonists at Looney's Ferry understood this; and were sick with fear for those of their number who were carried off by Indians.

Peter Looney, whom they all knew, Peter who had often poled them across the James at Looney's Ferry, what was Peter's fate? Was he being roasted over live coals, removed now and then so that his anguish might be prolonged? Or had the savages stuck sharpened pieces of wood into his body

and set fire to them, watching them burn to his bone?
Or—Peter being a brave young fellow of the sort they honored with especial torture—had they torn the flesh from him
with red-hot pincers?

The colonists knew how the Indians danced yelling and
laughing around their victims. Under such torture an Indian
would feel disgraced if he so much as uttered a groan.

And now that there was war, and the Indians allied
with the French against the English, anything could happen
to those taken captive.

In the year of young Robert Looney's death, James
Patton also was killed by Indians. It happened on a Sunday,
the day before the French defeated General Braddock and
his red-coated "regulars." Patton had delivered a supply of
powder and lead to a frontier settlement, and was sitting
writing at a table, with his broadsword lying before him;
for a man must ever have a weapon close at hand. Suddenly
the room was full of Shawnee Indians. Patton, seizing his
sword, felled two of them, but others fired and killed him.
In that attack the entire settlement perished.

At Looney's Ferry it was hard to believe that James
Patton was dead. He had been a man of such physical power,
such energy; a huge man standing six feet four. And, though
he had behind him years of activity, yet he was making
plans for the future; planning to erect a home on his Cherry
Tree Bottom property. A contractor had been engaged to
build the house and Patton had ordered from Robert Looney
eight thousand rail.

After Braddock's defeat, Governor Dinwiddie sent
George Washington to direct the construction of a chain of
forts across Virginia's western frontier. And Washington's
letters to the governor show the condition in which he found
the Valley.

"The supplicating tears of the women," he wrote, "and
the moving petitions from the men melt me into such deadly
sorrow, that I solemnly declare, if I know my own mind,
I could offer myself a willing sacrifice to the butchering

enemy, provided that would contribute to the people's ease.
. . . Not an hour, nay scarcely a minute, passes that does
not produce fresh alarms . . . so that I am distracted what
to do! . . ."

He lacked money, he lacked provisions, he lacked men
to defend adequately the forts he was building. He wrote
over and over again to the governor, emphasizing the danger.
He explained that five hundred Indians excelled ten times
that number of regular soldiers. He said that the Indians
were tireless, that they had almost superhuman endurance
under sufferings, and that they were unequaled in cunning
and craft. "They prowl about like wolves, and, like them,
do their mischief by stealth."

Washington wanted men with whom to scour the woods
and all suspected places in the mountains and the valleys of
the frontier.

The Buchanans had come to live at Cherry Tree Bottom,
which they had inherited from James Patton. Washington
visited Buchanan there, to beg aid in getting the necessary
number of men. But Buchanan himself had attempted, some
days before, to raise men for the defense of a fort in the
neighborhood, and had failed.

"I am distracted," Washington repeated.

But before he was recalled to Williamsburg to take command of forces to be sent against the French at Fort Duquesne, Washington had done much to organize defense on
the frontier.

The winter passed, and summer came to the Valley.
Peter Looney had come back from his long captivity, in
which he had been taken as far north as Detroit. He had
suffered much hardship, but he was alive and had come home
to Looney's Ferry, publicly commended for bravery during
the Indian attack upon Fort Vause.

Then, upon a summer night, sixty Shawnee warriors
crossed Purgatory Mountain through Bowen's Gap, descending on the far side where they could not be seen from the
fort at the mouth of Looney's Creek. It was the Shawnees'

boast that in warfare they excelled all other Indians, and that they had inflicted more punishment upon the Long Knives, as they called the white men, than had any other Indian tribe.

Now they had come to raid the James River settlements in the vicinity of Looney's Ferry. The raid was carried out with such stealth and speed that there had been no time to give the alarm. So that none of the settlers had "forted"— their word for taking refuge. They had not "forted," so that the Shawnees expeditiously scalped a number of men, and carried off a group of captive women and children Among the captives was Hannah. Her husband, Josiah Dennis, and her young child were both murdered.

The Indians separated into two groups, and Hannah found herself alone, her friends being taken off in a different direction. Her captors marched her out of the Valley, over the Alleghenies to their distant home near Chillicothe. The wall of the Alleghenies and many miles of wearying travel now stood between her and her James River home. Her husband had been murdered and scalped, and her little child murdered. . . .

But Hannah Dennis, undaunted, laid her plans.

In order that she might communicate with her captors she set herself at once to learn their language. If she was ever again to see the boat at Looney's Ferry gliding across the James opposite Purgatory Mountain, or the place she had called home, she must carry out the plan. The Indians must be convinced that she had become one of them; no longer Hannah Dennis, a woman of the hated Long Knives, but a squaw of the Shawnee tribe. She painted her body as the squaws did, and performed the hard labor exacted of squaws. Coming to understand Indian superstitions, she played upon them; with ever in her mind the determination to find her way back, over the western mountains to the Valley, and home. She persuaded the Indians that she was possessed of powers of healing. She spent much time in the woods collecting herbs from which she compounded medicines. She saw that the savages began to hold her in awe, and she did not deny that she had the gift of prophecy, predicting by signs in smoke and fire. She cast spells in which she feigned to converse with their dead. And she made a habit of whispering into the ears of animals.

It came about that she was first accepted as a loyal squaw, then revered as a witch, and finally honored as a queen.

Then at last, after years of patient preparation, she felt the hour to have come when she must risk everything.

Without suspicion, the Indians saw her go into the woods to gather herbs, as they had seen her do a thousand times before. She knew that she could count on a head start before they had any notion that she was escaping.

When the alarm was finally raised and the Indians had set out in pursuit, Hannah was miles away. She had crossed the Scioto River before they caught sight of her. When she heard their guns go off, she knew that it was a matter only of minutes before they, too, would have forded the river and come upon her.

But when they reached the opposite bank Hannah had vanished. They searched the woods along the river, but she was nowhere visible. They had been close upon her, but she was now nowhere visible. They sat down, recalling to each other how she had often admitted to them that she had supernatural powers. Here was proof. Which way should they turn to seek a vanished witch?

Darkness fell and they built a fire. In its flickering light they watched all night, and talked: recollecting the years of Hannah's life among them. Her simplest healing now appeared a miracle. Animals had understood what she said when she whispered in their ears. She could look into the future, she could talk with the dead. Now she had passed from the seen into the unseen. They might have expected that one day this would happen. It was merely another of her miracles.

Morning came and with it the decision to abandon search for her. They might as well go home. They would never again see Hannah Dennis.

When she felt that they must be out of sight, Hannah crept painfully out of the hollow trunk of a fallen sycamore in which she had lain hidden throughout the night. She had no dread of the Indians' return, understanding how completely they were convinced that she was gone to the spirit world. In her flight she had cut her foot on a stone, and she now remained some days calmly where she was, giving it time to recover before she started on her long journey.

For greater safety from any wandering groups of Indians, she then traveled at night, resting by day, in a cave if she could find one or concealed under the branches of a tree; she had chosen the summer for her desperate attempt, that she might count upon the protection of foliage, and upon finding wild fruits to eat.

She crossed the Ohio on a drifting log, and marched for twenty nights. But her strength was ebbing, for roots, green grapes and herbs were poor fare, and finally the day came when, weakened by hunger and exhaustion, she knew that she could not go on.

A pioneer colonist came upon her, despairing, sitting on a riverbank waiting for death. He took her to the nearest white settlement, where she rested and was fed, until strong enough to be put on the back of a horse and taken to Fort Young on Jackson's River, where the city of Covington now stands. Then, following the course of the Jackson, and the James, they took her to Looney's Ferry at the foot of Purgatory Mountain, where she had lived—ever so long ago—as the young wife of Josiah Dennis, one of those murdered in the Shawnee raid at Looney's Ferry.

Her husband was dead, her child dead, some of her friends murdered, others carried off in captivity: like Mrs. Renick and her five children, and the white servant girl, Sally Jew. Mr. Renick had been murdered. And poor Mrs. Renick expecting a baby . . . what had become of her!

Only the dear familiarity of the place remained the

same; the hills unchanged, and at Looney's Ferry, when there were customers, the boat was still poled, as before, across James River.

You may go to the James River Valley, and relive this story where it happened. You may walk over what was in the long ago Looney's farm, on the south bank of the James and the west bank of the creek; walking across heavy plowed fields toward the line of trees which overhang James River, with on your right a similar line of trees where Looney's Creek ought to be. All about are tumbled green hills, and in the distance the mountain range which so well deserves its name—the Blue Ridge.

Arriving finally at the point for which you have aimed —James River where it is joined by Looney's Creek, flowing up from the south—you will see, as it was in the beginning, the river and the creek, though there is no longer a ferry, for at Buchanan a modern bridge crosses the James. But the farm is still cultivated: you have walked across plowed fields, in a pasture cattle have stared at you, and there was smoke curling up from the chimney of a farmhouse.

You may sit upon a fallen tree beside the river. Birds will twitter in the branches overhead. Perhaps a big yellow butterfly, marked with black, will drift in and out of shadow and light, low over the water. You can hear the cows lowing back in the pasture, and the far-off crow of a cock. Opposite, on the north bank of the James, Purgatory Mountain rises, a sheer cone. And there is Cherry Tree Bottom, with Purgatory Creek flowing down to James River from the north.

Looney's Creek, Purgatory Mountain, Purgatory Creek, there they are, exactly where history has placed them. There is the eddy in James River, and just above it was once Looney's Ferry.

Monticello

CHAPTER TEN

New Rights

THOMAS JEFFERSON decided to send himself to college; one of his reasons being that at home there was so much company that it interfered with his studies. He lived with his widowed mother at Shadwell, a plantation on the road to Williamsburg; and people on the way to and from the capital always stopped at Shadwell. Since Jefferson's father was dead, it fell upon him as the eldest son to act as host, and at the same time more or less to bring himself up. Now, at seventeen, he decided to go to college. Study there would not be interrupted by the constant demands of hospitality. Also, he thought, at college he would make "a more universal acquaintance."

So it happened that, some twelve months after George and Martha Washington's honeymoon in Williamsburg, gawky young Jefferson came to Duke of Gloucester Street and entered himself as a student at the College of William

and Mary. It does not seem to have occurred to him—or to
his mother—that he should go to England for his education.

On his way from Shadwell to Williamsburg, he had
stopped to spend the Christmas holidays in Hanover at the
home of Colonel Dandridge. And he met there a strange man
who was neighbor to the colonel: a gaunt shabby man, with
brilliant eyes deep-set in a thin shallow face. People were
never able to agree on the color of these eyes; one saying
they were light blue, another calling them hazel, another
grey.

The passion of this man's life, as Jefferson saw him on
that Christmas holiday, appeared to be for fiddling, dancing,
and pleasantry. Jefferson liked all that too, and as a youth
of seventeen, he and Patrick Henry, a man some seven years
older, immediately became friends. Patrick Henry was in
fact the gay heart of the party. His was a spirit that could
rise above personal disaster; he happened to be bankrupt at
the time, but what place had bankruptcy at a party?

The small country store in which Henry's father had
set him up had failed. Then he had tried farming, working
in the fields beside a couple of Negro slaves. He made another
attempt at storekeeping. People said the store went bankrupt
because Henry could not resist giving credit to anybody who
wanted it. And what with bad debts, and what with his
running off all the time to fish or hunt, how could he have
expected to succeed? Henry, they said, seemed to love idle-
ness for its own sake. It was too bad; no man was fonder
of his wife and children than Patrick Henry, but there were
times when he could not seem to stick to his work. People
talked of how he would lie all day in the shade of a tree
overhanging the river. True, he had a fishing rod, but it
seemed to make no difference to him whether or not there
was a nibble at his line; it seemed enough for him just to
be idle. And "his great delight was to put on his hunting-
shirt, collect a parcel of overseers and such like people, and
spend weeks together hunting in the 'piney' woods, camping
at night, and cracking jokes round a light-wood fire."

In the store, Henry was more interested in talking to

customers than in selling them goods. He loved to listen and he loved to talk, to make people laugh or cry, to make their blood "run cold or their hair to stand on end." It was as if the human heart was an instrument on which he played, making it express whatever emotion he liked.

People would come to the store just to hear Patrick Henry tell stories in the deep strong voice which unerringly stirred their emotions.

In that country store, Henry acquired little by little the gift of speaking in such a way as could not fail to reach the simplest heart.

Yes, everybody liked "Pahtrick" Henry; so in those days did Virginians pronounce his name.

Thomas Jefferson had reasoned that in going to college he would make a "more universal acquaintance." And already, even before he arrived in Williamsburg, he had made a friend in Patrick Henry. Henry had confided to Jefferson that he thought he'd be a lawyer. He'd teach himself law; when he felt he was ready for his examination he'd be coming to Williamsburg, and then he'd see Jefferson, he'd look him up. His previous education had been the local grammar school; instruction under his father at home, reading; and that invaluable education in the understanding of human beings which he had received from the customers in a country store.

The second of Jefferson's new friends was Dr. Small, the Scotch professor of mathematics at William and Mary. This man, Jefferson always said, "fixed the destinies of my life." Dr. Small was cultivated, broad-minded, and of aristocratic manner. He was at once attracted by his brilliant young pupil and made him his close friend. Through Dr. Small, Jefferson met George Wythe, the great lawyer, and Governor Fauquier, a man distinguished in mind and manner.

These men were young Jefferson's intimate friends, for, like George Washington, he had the power of attracting the best always, and the wisdom to absorb what the best had to teach.

Jefferson was popular with the young people of Williamsburg, as well as with older men. He became infatuated with pretty Rebecca Burwell, christening her Belinda; and when that lady married someone else, he set down in his "commonplace book" the cynical quotation: "O Zeus, why hast thou established women, a curse deceiving men in the light of the sun?" He was convinced that his disappointed springtime love was an eternal matter from which he would never recover.

But Belinda did not move him so deeply as to interfere with study, or with reading; for he worked hard and he consumed books like a devouring flame: Tully and Seneca, Epictetus, Euripides, Socrates, Milton, Homer, Shakespeare, Swift, Cervantes, Locke. . . .

He graduated from William and Mary and began the study of law under his friend, George Wythe. For exercise and amusement he was fond of horseback, or at dusk he would lay down his books and run a mile. Then there was always dancing. Young and old danced. When there were balls in Williamsburg everybody went and everybody danced. The fiddlers played; such pieces as "Kiss Me Early," "Money Musk," and "The Buff Coat." The dances were courtly minuets, gavottes, the Virginia reel, the hearty jig, and the hornpipe. And the candlelight flickered upon men as gorgeous in color and elegant brocade as their women.

Meanwhile Patrick Henry had come to Williamsburg, won admission to the bar, and gone home with a license to practice.

❀

In May iris and roses, mock oranges and magnolias bloom in the gardens along Duke of Gloucester Street. And it was in May of 1765 that news of Parliament's passing the Stamp Act came to the burgesses in session in the Capitol at Williamsburg.

The Stamp Act would tax practically every business transaction. No will or deed, no insurance policy, no ship's clearance papers, would be legal without bearing the new stamps. Even newspapers and advertisements must carry them. The object was to raise money to pay for the costly French and Indian War and to support an armed British force in America.

The Stamp Act was, of course, discussed in the House of Burgesses; among those present were Colonel Washington, Richard Henry Lee, Pendleton, Randolph and Richard Bland, who, because of his knowledge of history, was called the Antiquary. And sitting for the first time was the new member, Patrick Henry, known now as the brilliant lawyer of Hanover County, but still a shabby ungainly figure, conspicuous among the other burgesses in the richly spectacular costume of their day.

Standing in the doorway listening to the debate was a lanky carrotheaded young man named Thomas Jefferson. And so it happened that Jefferson heard Patrick Henry make his famous speech.

The Stamp Act, Henry thundered, was tyranny: "Caesar had his Brutus; Charles the First, his Cromwell; and George the Third—"

"Treason!" certain of the burgesses shouted, at such mention of the king's name. "Treason!"

"George the Third"—Henry paused—"may profit by their example. If this be treason, make the most of it."

He spoke, Jefferson said, as Homer wrote. And the flame of his oratory swept men off their feet.

Today, overfamiliarity has blunted our reaction to this, as to so many of history's big scenes; the pages which record them appear mere wilted words. If we believe, it is now with the mind and not, as Jefferson did, with the heart. Or perhaps we think skeptically that none of it really happened, but is merely a fabrication, like George Washington's legendary cherry tree. Certainly Henry's great speech in the House of Burgesses has become for most people devitalized by textbook repetition.

But in seeking the authority for it, the scene suddenly comes to life.

"Did it actually happen in just that way?" Thomas

Jefferson was asked. He had at the time been standing in the doorway, so he ought to know and Jefferson replied: "I remember the cry of treason, the pause of Mr. Henry at the name of George III and the presence of mind with which he closed his sentence, and baffled the charge vociferated."

Henry had come to Williamsburg to protest against the Stamp Act, and now that was done he would go home to Hanover. That same afternoon he was seen on Duke of Gloucester Street. He was dressed in rough buckskin breeches, he carried his saddlebags over his arm, and he was leading his horse; walking slowly as he talked to a friend who strolled beside him.

The friend who walked down Duke of Gloucester Street beside Patrick Henry, as he was leaving Williamsburg after that historic speech, was Paul Carrington, a member of the Burgesses, and he later confirmed in writing the incident as Jefferson related it.

Tyler, in telling the story, spoke of how he had been impressed by the poor coarseness of Henry's dress, in contrast to the elegance and fashion of the others.

Then there is the manuscript journal of a French traveler who happened to be present at the famous debate, and to record Henry's speech, with its interrupted comparison of George III with Caesar and Charles I.

And none who heard Henry speak ever forgot what one called "the rugged might and majesty of his eloquence."

It was now 1774, and again it was spring and again the Virginia Assembly met in the Capitol at Williamsburg. They appointed the first of June as a day of fasting and prayer to express sympathy for Boston. England, indignant at the famous "tea party," had ordered the port closed. Governor Dunmore retaliated by dissolving Virginia's Assembly, which again moved serenely over to the Apollo Room of gay Raleigh Tavern.

An attack upon one of the colonies, it declared, was an attack upon all. The colonies decided to call a Continental Congress, to meet in Philadelphia, for the purpose of con-

sidering their position. A convention was summoned to Williamsburg to elect delegates.

Roger Atkinson, from his home south of the James,
wrote his brother-in-law, describing those delegates chosen
to represent Virginia in that first Continental Congress:

"Richard Henry Lee," he said, is "as true a trout as ever
swam, as staunch a hound as ever ran."

Peyton Randolph has "knowledge and experience. . . .
Above all things a man of integrity and the Roman spirit."

Benjamin Harrison was not described, because so well
known to the brother-in-law.

Edmund Pendleton, "a humble religious man . . . also
a very pretty smooth-tongued speaker."

Patrick Henry, "in religious matters a Saint, but the
very Devil in Politicks—a son of Thunder . . . stern and
steady in his country's cause."

Richard Bland, "staunch and tough as whitleather"
with "something of the look of musty old Parchments which
he handleth and studieth much."

Colonel Washington, "a modest man but sensible and
speaks little—in action cool, like a Bishop at his Prayers."

Roger Atkinson, writing freely and familiarly to his
brother-in-law, said no word of whether a man was of wealth
or of birth. What he thought important was that a man be
true, stanch, stern and steady, learned and modest; that he
possess good sense, judgment, experience, and above all,
integrity.

And because these qualities were honored in the young
New World they were produced; which is not to say that
there was no dishonesty, for then as now, mankind was mankind. But it is to say that in every age and place that which
is most reverenced comes always into existence; where there
is demand for "true trout," there always will be true trout.

Normally Patrick Henry's figure slouched, his shoulders
stooped, but as he spoke he gradually became erect. His face

shone, and his eyes. What color were his eyes—green or blue, grey or hazel? Men never agreed upon their color. As for his voice, it was always magic in its effect on those who heard it.

So it was when Patrick Henry spoke at the convention in old St. John's Church in the city of Richmond, high on the hill above the rushing falls in James River.

It happened in the month of March, following the famous First Continental Congress. That Congress had sent to George III a Declaration of Colonial Rights, insisting upon freedom to manage their own affairs; a thing no colony in the world had ever before demanded. Now in Richmond, Patrick Henry was speaking in St. John's Church; a church built upon land given for the purpose by William Byrd II, to whom England had always been "home." The tolling bell which had summoned those who crowded the church was silent, and Patrick Henry was speaking:

"The war is inevitable! . . . let it come! . . . Is life so dear or peace so sweet as to be purchased at the price of chains and slavery? Forbid it, Almighty God! I know not what course others may take, but as for me, give me liberty or give me death!"

There was deep silence when he sat down. Then the cry rose: "To arms!"

Three months later, the Congress in Philadelphia named George Washington commander in chief of all the Continental forces. In accepting, he said: "I beg it be remembered by every gentleman in this room that I this day declare with the utmost sincerity, that I do not consider myself equal to the command I am honoured with."

A year passed and in June of the famous year 1776 Virginia voted herself a free and independent country, electing Patrick Henry her first governor. George Mason presented his immortal Bill of Rights, which was unanimously accepted, and in that same month Virginia adopted a constitution, and sent orders to her delegates at the second Continental Congress in Philadelphia, instructing them to introduce a resolution which would declare all the colonies free and independent.

Between the meeting of the first and second Congresses something had happened in the minds of men. America had begun by fighting for the rights of colonies; now America wanted independence based upon a right new in the world: the right of man to equality of opportunity in the pursuit of happiness.

Richard Henry Lee—he who was described "as true a trout as ever swam"—presented to this Philadelphia Congress the resolution of independence which had been suggested by Virginia.

John Adams, of Massachusetts, seconded it. But, although all favored independence, still might it not be wiser to delay a little? Was it prudent to go so fast? For some weeks the Congress considered and debated.

Then, on the second of July, the resolution was passed.

Already a committee, headed by Thomas Jefferson of that part of Virginia drained by the James River system, had been appointed to prepare a declaration of this independence.

The first three sections of the Declaration, Jefferson based upon George Mason's Bill of Rights—that new right of man to life, liberty, and the pursuit of happiness.

In the second section, Jefferson stated America's charges against the British king; not against the Parliament but against the king, George III.

Among the pages of these charges against the crown, this stands out:

"he has waged cruel war against human nature itself, violating the most sacred rights of life and liberty in the persons of a distant people, who never offended him, captivating and carrying them into slavery in another hemisphere, or to incur miserable death in their transportation thither, this piratical warfare, the opprobrium of infidel powers, is the warfare of the Christian king of Great Britain, determined to keep open a market where Men should be bought

and sold, he has prostituted his negative for suppressing every legislative attempt to prohibit or restrain this execrable commerce. . . ."

The section stating America's charges against the British king was followed by Richard Henry Lee's resolution that the colonies "solemnly publish and declare" that they "are and of Right ought to be Free and Independent States . . . absolved from all allegiance to the British crown."

The document closed with the pledge: "And for the support of this declaration . . . we mutually pledge to each other our lives, our fortunes and our sacred honour."

In the debate on the Declaration which Jefferson had presented, that important sentence was stricken out in which the British king was charged with "violating the most sacred rights of life and liberty in the persons of a distant people who never offended him, captivating and carrying them into slavery" . . . suppressing "every legislative attempt to prohibit or restrain the execrable commerce."

Over and over again, ever since 1699, Virginia had tried to put a stop to the importing of slaves, petitioning the throne, begging permission to check this trade of "great inhumanity."

And the first clause of Virginia's constitution listed the king's protection of the slave trade as one of the reasons for separating from Great Britain.

But, to placate American shipping interests engaged in importing slaves, and certain colonies of the Far South, both of which opposed abolition of the traffic, a similar clause was ruled out by the Congress at Philadelphia, leaving the question to be settled at a future date.

In its final form, the Declaration of Independence was put to the vote of the delegates, John Adams, of Massachusetts, pleading eloquently in its favor. And on the evening of July fourth the Congress adopted the document, which in solemn, beautiful cadence expressed what then filled men's hearts. All over the land it was proclaimed with the firing of cannon and the ringing of bells.

Men who had been fighting for "life, liberty, and property" would now fight for "life, liberty, and the pursuit of
happiness."

With the Declaration of Independence a great light had
dawned upon the earth: the light of the New World was
risen. And nothing would ever again be as it had been. Men
would grope still, and stumble, but they could never again
be blind, for they had recognized that man possessed "inalienable rights." And that one of them was happiness.

Jefferson once said of the Declaration that his aim had
been to express in words what was in the heart of the people.

Twenty-five years later there was published in London
a book titled *Travels Of Four Years And A Half In The
United States Of America During 1798, 1799, 1800, 1801,
1802,* and "Dedicated by Permission to Thomas Jefferson."
Its author, an Englishman named John Davis, had opened
what he says "some called an Academy, and others an Old
Field School." The school was established in a log cabin on
Pohoke plantation, within sight, Davis says, of the Blue
Ridge. His book contains this provocative sentence: "The
higher Virginians seem to venerate themselves as men . . ."
Not as individuals, but as men.

Letting your mind run back over old Roger Atkinson's
concise estimate of the Virginia delegates to the First Continental Congress, you are impressed with the integrity, courage, wisdom, stanchness, faith, and humility, upon which
this veneration of man as Man was based.

Veneration for man's potentialities was part of Thomas
Jefferson's creed. Writing to John Adams in 1813, from the
contemplative peace of his beloved Monticello, Jefferson, after
spurning what he called "false aristocracy," said: "I agree
with you that there is a natural aristocracy among men. The
grounds of this are virtue, and talents. . . . The natural aristocracy I consider as the most precious gift of nature for
the instruction, the trusts, and government of society. . . .
May we not even say that that form of government is the

best which provides the most effectually for a pure selection of these natural *aristo* into the offices of government?"

The veneration of such values is the answer we seek in the troubled year 1945. With new rights there must be also new veneration, leading to a new and higher goal. And only those who venerate man as Man can be equal to the stupendous responsibilities which tower before us.

Kerr's Creek

CHAPTER ELEVEN

At the Foot of the Lighthouse

THERE IS an old proverb to the effect that "it is dark at the foot of the lighthouse." Those who have lit the light in the tower know that there is a light, but have, as a rule, only a humble understanding of its magnitude. While at the foot of the lighthouse, the perspective of time has not yet revealed how great a thing has happened in the world.

Records of domestic affairs in periods of vast moment to civilization reflect a current of daily human living which has seldom any notion that future men and women will look back with wonder upon the light of which they are but dimly aware.

Old letters and diaries, and an occasional newspaper,

come down to us, quaint and faded, from eighteenth century Virginia. They are largely concerned with the trivial, yet in their way significant, details of the day-by-day life of what we now know to have been an immortal epoch.

The *Virginia Gazette,* printed in Williamsburg, was a weekly representing itself as containing the "Freshest Advices Foreign and Domestic." It recorded facts like these:

A young gentleman "of fine Estate is wed to a young Lady of Beauty." A gentleman of twenty-three marries a "Sprightly old Tit of eighty-five, possessed of a fortune of three thousand pounds." A grey bobtailed horse, branded on one buttock "XX" and on the other "R" has disappeared, and along with him a white flea-bitten mare, with switch tail and long mane. Runaway slaves and fugitive indentured servants are advertised, with reward offered for their recovery.

A group of such indentured servants escapes in a longboat; among them a man wearing a dark wig, "a red Daffil coat and blue cloth breeches; a lusty fat Englishwoman in gold-laced hat and brown Holland gown." There is missing also a convict servant man, bowlegged, with the "Picture of our Saviour on the Cross" tattooed on one of his arms. This man's apparel is said to be uncertain, as he has stolen various sorts of clothing. His name, too, is uncertain, since he has the habit of changing it. Also he is a "sly subtle fellow who pretends to be a Scotchman, but *is* an Irishman."

Among the missing slaves is a Negro called Cajar, a man with a "downcast look and a voice that sounds as if coming out of a tree." And there is an "outlandish negro named George who plays exceedingly on the banjo." There are occasionally also eloping wives, whose husbands place announcements in the *Gazette* to the effect that said husbands will pay no debts of said wives' contracting.

The owners of stallions advertise largely in the *Gazette,* for Virginia is interested in the breeding of horses. One such notice reads: "Merry Tom stands at my house, and covers mares at a guinea the leap, or five pounds the season." Turning the pages, you see these advertisements appearing over and over; then suddenly ceasing. And you wonder . . . was that servant man, of uncertain name and clothing who pretended to be a Scotchman but was really an Irishman, caught and returned to his master, and the man with the picture of Christ on the Cross tattooed on his arm? And what happened to the longboat in which the lusty fat Englishwoman was escaping? And that white flea-bitten mare with the switch tail, what became of her? The Negro whose voice sounded as if coming from a tree? The outlandish George who played exceedingly on the banjo? And how many pedigreed colts were sired by Merry Tom?

The advertisements appear, reappear in several issues of the paper, and then are seen no more.

It records also the passage of laws, and the meting out of punishment for crime: hanging being the penalty for housebreaking, horse stealing, and murder; for felony men and women are burnt in the hand. And it lists arriving and departing ships; sometimes a sinister slave ship has come from Guinea, or a sloop from the West Indies, with a cargo of rum, sugar, and tropical fruits.

In the columns of the *Gazette* you read, too, the disasters of the day: how, in the absence of the master of a house, three Indians came and killed his wife and children and set fire to his home. You read of the loss of ships at sea. Poor Catherine Rathell, who piqued herself on carrying goods of the newest taste, sailed for England upon a ship which never reached its haven.

Personal letters from Williamsburg to friends and relations in England are concerned about smallpox, so prevalent in London. It is too bad that Aunt Turner is suffering from "St. Anthony's Fire," and what a misfortune that Colonel Tucker's six warehouses and his wharf were struck by lightning and burnt down. Occasionally the letters contain good wishes on the occasion of a marriage: there is a comment that "A virtuous woman is ever a blessing to a Man. Others are nothing better than a Moth in a garment."

In many of these letters there is talk of taxes, especially

of the hated Stamp Act; and there is comment upon William Pitt and Edmund Burke's defense of the American colonies.

The letters never forget the perils of the sea. Bills of lading declare so many hogsheads of tobacco, "Shipped by the Grace of God." Captains are listed as "Master under God for this present Voyage . . . bound by God's Grace for the port of London." The documents conclude, "And so God send the good ship to her desired port in Safety. Amen."

In this latter half of the eighteenth century, a young divinity student—Philip Fithian—came from New Jersey to act as tutor to the children of Robert Carter, of Nomini Hall, one of Tidewater Virginia's great estates. Fithian was an earnest, observant young man and in his leisure hours kept a journal; purely for his own pleasure, with no idea of publication; not, however, a secret journal in stenographic cipher like that of William Byrd, but a diary which gives a fresh, intimate impression of a river plantation in the Tidewater Virginia of that time.

Fithian is far from home—a seven days' journey on horseback. His diary is his companion; he sets down his memories of home, his devotion to the absent girl whom he calls "lovely Laura," and he records every detail of life on Robert Carter's plantation as it appeared in his theologian's eyes.

He is shocked that Sunday should be a day of diversion as well as of churchgoing. Actually everyone is in a happy mood, and by Saturday night the faces of the slaves shine already with festive smiles. Sometimes Fithian comes upon them fighting cocks in the stable. There is a strange air of jollity about Sunday to which Mr. Fithian is not accustomed. The river is alive with sailboats and canoes. True, some are going and coming from church; but others are fishing. And church itself has the genial air of a club. Horses and carriages stand under the trees; beaux buzz about the local belles; older men gather in groups discussing politics and farming, actually until the service begins, when the men enter the church in a body.

Conviviality thus extends even to worship; a thing most surprising to Mr. Fithian. And he himself begins to thaw, recording not only the text of a sermon, but the dinner which follows, the invited guests, and the elegance of the food—beef and greens, roast pig, oysters, fine boiled rockfish, puddings and cheeses and fruits, and brandy toddy, in which they drink to the king and queen, the royal family, the governor, and finally to the young ladies of their acquaintance.

Among the sermons Fithian records one preached from the text, "He that walketh uprightly walketh wisely." And slowly, as he comes to know these people, at first so alien to him, he seems to realize that they, too, endeavor to walk uprightly. His friends had warned him of the danger of going to live among a people exceedingly wicked and profane. "You'll have no Calvinistic books to read," they said, "and hear no Presbyterian sermons, and you must keep much company."

Now, little by little, the pages of his journal warm, as though the life in which Fithian finds himself cast upon them a faint rosy flush.

Nomini Hall appears to the young tutor majestic and agreeable: looking down the avenue of poplars—an avenue three hundred yards long—the house seems most romantic, gleaming white through the trees, its many windows catching the light; a truly elegant building, with stately white columns on its south side.

Mr. Carter, whom he had been prepared to find a wicked and bitterly swearing person, he analyzes as "sensible and judicious, given to much retirement and study" . . . law is this gentleman's chief study; music is his "darling among amusements"; and he and his children are constantly practicing on a great variety of instruments. Mr. Carter has a "vastly delicate ear," his conversation is "always profitable," and nowhere is swearing so excessive as Mr. Fithian had feared.

The Carters take their tutor to visit other plantations, and he becomes familiar with talk of breeding horses and dogs, talk of fox hunting and horse racing. Occasionally, with a certain reluctance, he is persuaded to go to a ball. There is a ball at Squire Lee's that lasts four days. The ladies "dress gay and splendid"; when they dance their skirts and brocades rustle and trail behind them.

But Mr. Fithian does not forget the beautiful "Laura" he has left behind him in Jersey. "Keep her, kind Heaven," he prays, "and in her friendship, make me happy. . . . Good and benevolent Laura" for whom he has the "highest esteem." You feel this girl's presence on every page of the journal, yet happily for us Mr. Fithian has an eye for the plantation young ladies, describing their clothes, their persons, and their characters.

Miss Jenny Washington impresses him with her propriety and her easy, winning behavior. When she dances a reel or a country dance it is without any "flirts or vulgar capers." She dresses richly and in good taste: her light-brown hair is "craped" high with two rolls on each side, and topping the whole a small cap of beautiful gauze and lace into which is woven an artificial flower.

Little Miss Priscilla Carter—one of his own pupils—he praises for her sweet obliging temper, for the fact that she never swears, that she dances finely and plays well on keyed instruments.

Miss Betsey Lee sits erect, placing her feet with great propriety, and letting her hands lie carelessly in her lap, never moving them but to adjust her dress or to perform some exercise of her fan. Brilliant earrings sparkle in her ears. Her dress is rich and fashionable, but Mr. Fithian, divinity student, finds her "pinched up rather too near in a long pair of new-fashioned stays," which, he comments, "I think are a nuisance both to us and themselves. For the late importation of stays, said to be most fashionable in London, are produced upwards so high that we can have scarce any view at all of the Ladies Snowy Bosoms; and are extended down so low that Walking must cause a disagreeable friction on some parts of the Body."

As for the gentlemen, the great wigs of William Byrd's day had gone out of style, for the time is just before the Revolution. Shorter wigs have come in and men are beginning once more to wear their own hair, but powdering it and combing it back into a queue which is tied with a black bow, or confined in a black silk bag. They are still wearing knee breeches, clocked silk stockings, lace ruffles, and gold and silver laced cocked hats. Breeches, coats, and waistcoats are of plush and satin and broadcloth, in black or blue, green, scarlet, or peach color.

And Fithian finds it "beautiful to admiration to see a number of such persons set off by dress to the best advantage, moving easily to the sound of well-performed music."

"Blow high, Blow low," he exclaims, "these Virginians will dance or die!" He himself, of course, cannot dance, but he can play a game called Button, and in redeeming his pawns he has several kisses from ladies.

The country as a whole he declares delightful, and the Virginians so sociable, "so kind, one can scarce know how to dispense with, or indeed accept their kindness."

You feel that Mr. Fithian is melting; actually, when expected letters do not arrive from his Laura, he speaks of her as "that vixen, Laura." He may yet know the contentment of the middle way, of a reasonable balance between the gay and the serious.

He has seen that those Virginia girls, so bewitchingly and sinfully frivolous, marry early, bear huge families, bring up their children well, manage the complicated domestic machinery of big plantations, and yet at a moment's notice gaily throw on a scarlet cloak, tie a crimson kerchief over their hair, mount a horse and gallop off to a neighbor to dance all night. He has noticed to his amazement the planters' understanding of agriculture and of the many industries practiced on estates, maintaining their own blacksmiths, brickmakers, masons and carpenters, breeding livestock, training horses for the races and dogs for the hunt. It is a life vigorous and zestful, beyond anything Fithian had known before.

❖

The letters of Lucinda Lee to her friend, Polly Brent, reflect the same sort of existence described in Philip Fithian's journal.

Lucinda Lee's letters were found, torn and discolored, lying forgotten in an old desk. Ninety years passed between their writing and their publication. Reading them today, more than a hundred and fifty years since Lucinda sat down to write to Polly, you marvel that anyone could ever have been so young, or so feminine.

Lucinda is paying a visit to her plantation kin, and in odd moments writing to tell Polly Brent all about it:

Lucinda has just come in from a ride on a hard-going horse. There is company for dinner and she must smart herself. She has to have her hair "craped," which, she thinks, is of all things the most disagreeable. The house is full of guests. Two new beaux have come. One is homely but is a mighty worthy man. There is going to be dancing. She has met a Mrs. Pinkard—the best creature about lending you anything. Really she is among the finest women Lucinda has ever seen, and is thought very handsome. She always chooses which headdress Lucinda shall wear.

It is September and a quantity of delicious peaches are ripe. The garden is the most beautiful place. Lucinda walks there with Nancy and Milly Washington. Milly is a thousand times prettier than Lucinda at first thought. They all cut thistles to try their sweethearts. One of the gentlemen catches them at it, and "you can't conceive how he plagued us."

Cousin Hannah wears a blue lutestring habit, with a "taffety" apron and the most "butiful little hat you ever saw on the side of her head." When Hannah's young husband is away in Fredericksburg the poor girl is dejected, and rejoices when he returns. "You may depend on it, Polly, this said Matrimony alters us Mightily, I am afraid it alienates us from everyone else. It is I fear the bane of Female Friend-ship. Let it not be with us Polly, if we should ever marry."

On another day Lucinda writes all about a great frolic:

"After we went to our room we took a large dish of bacon and beef; after that, a bowl of sago cream, and after that apple-pye. While we were eating the apple-pye in bed— God bless you, making a great noise—in came Mr. W. dressed in Hannah's short gown and .petticoat, and seized me and kissed me twenty times in spite of all the resistance I could make; and then Cousin Molly. Hannah soon followed wear-ing his coat. They joined us in eating the apple-pye, and then went out.

"After this we took it into our heads to want to eat oysters. We got up, put on our rappers and went down to the cellar to get them; do you think Mr. W. did not follow us and scear us just to death. We went up tho, and eat our oysters. We slept in the old lady's room too, and she sat laughing fit to kill herself at us."

Lucinda is reading Lady Julia Mandeville. "The stile is beautiful but the tale is horrid. . . . I think I never cried more in my life reading a novel." She reckons that Polly must have read it. Lucinda confesses herself too fond of novels but in reading other books she is becoming less so. All one morning she is entertained by reading Telemachus; really delightful and very improving.

Frequently she mourns being separated from Polly's dear company, but such, she says, "is the fate of Mortals . . . never to be perfectly happy." But it must be right, "else the Supreme Disposer of all things would have not permitted it. . . ."

So in eighteenth century Virginia, they ate and drank, were merry, danced and rode, had their hair "craped" . . . and did not forget the "Supreme Disposer of all things."

Philip Fithian had married his "Laura" and gone as an itinerant preacher to the Valley of Virginia. His journal and his letters now contrast Virginia frontier life with that of a Tidewater plantation.

Fithian traveled by the Great Road from Philadelphia down into the James River Valley; preaching in churches on the James, the Jackson, the North, the Bull and the Cowpasture.

He describes the Valley as watered with many large streams running into the main stream—the James, whose "waters are very light and rapid."

But it was winter, and cakes of ice "rattling and creaking" float with the current. Snow was falling on the tops of the mountains. A cold wind "hummed in the leaves of the pines," and in the evening he often heard the dismal howling of wolves. The roads were frozen and nearly impassable, but Fithian found the Valley beautiful, the narrows of the North River branch of the James he thought "prodigiously romantic." And he was impressed with the prosperity of the Valley, exclaiming at the plenty of the bread, at the abundance of cheese and butter, the venison, pork, potatoes, turnips and cabbage "beyond your askin'." There were fine orchards, cider and peach brandy.

In fact, he says, "with the plenty of Cyder and perpetual Good-Humour, should I continue to live here a month I should surely fatten. . . . The very air of Virginia seems to inspire all the inhabitants with Hospitality."

Fithian loved comfort, and was less philosophical a traveler than the fashionable William Byrd, who explored the Virginia wilderness when it really was a wilderness. When Fithian happened to run into primitive conditions he had much to say of "fleas biting; bugs crawling!"

But the many whom he considered "genteel" consoled him. A certain Colonel Dickinson, a long-experienced soldier in the Indian service, Fithian found living in "fullness and elegance." This Colonel Dickinson and his wife, like all the Valley people, were, Fithian says, "very taleful of the Indian Wars" and their sufferings from savage cruelty.

How could any of them forget what they had seen and heard? They had heard Hannah Dennis describe the long preparation for her escape from the Shawnees, and her painful journey, alone through the forest and over the mountains.

Everyone in the Valley had had relatives or friends murdered, or carried into captivity by the Indians, from which few ever came back.

But Hannah Dennis and Peter Looney—they had come back. And after the British had won the French and Indian War, and the Indians had lost their French allies, the English had succeeded in ransoming some of the captives. Mrs. Renick, stolen near Looney's Ferry on the same morning that Hannah Dennis was carried off, was later ransomed with two of her sons; her daughter had died, and her son, Joshua, had taken an Indian wife, and become a chief in the tribe of the Miamis.

But other captives had gone, never to be heard of again.

As for the Kerr's Creek massacres, they were a horror haunting every man and woman whom Fithian met on his journey from church to church in the Valley of the James.

Not long after Hannah Dennis had come home, a party of Shawnees had crossed Mill Mountain, and North Mountain, not many miles from Lexington. They had burned the Kerr's Creek settlement, tomahawked and scalped, and taken captives, not one of whom had returned; nor had there been any news of their fate.

The second massacre had come some years later. The Shawnees, led by Cornstalk, their chief, had again come over North Mountain. Their tracks had been found in a field, and the alarm given. The colonists with their women and the children had gathered at Big Spring, and there the savages had rushed yelling upon them; the desperate whites crying out for mercy, running crazily in every direction. The Indians had pursued, always yelling. From sixty to eighty whites had been killed, even the children. Twenty-five to thirty had been led away captive.

The Valley could not forget. Naturally Fithian found people "very taleful of the Indian Wars."

Among his friends in the Valley, Fithian was especially taken with the family of the pastor of Timber Ridge Church; his wife a woman of "ideas extensive and distinct," who "speaks slow—something on the Scotch accent . . . more than elegant and classical . . . it is peculiarly forceable." Her daughter, Miss Betsey Brown, "young, sprightly and robust . . . born in this distant and unimproved country . . . few young women may be compared with her in the most excellent of all accomplishments the Ornaments of her Mind. . . . She has read many English Authors and several of the Latin classics."

And, like her mother, Miss Betsey was extremely "chatful."

Fithian found the Valley churches only log houses, small, open, damp, and so intolerably cold that he once preached only a few minutes, "and later held a service by Candlelight at Colonel Dickinson's." And "in these woods," Fithian says, "where sermons are seldom heard I find more attention and deeper solemnity than where it is set forth weekly in its brightest glories."

Men from the Valley were at that time away, fighting with the forces under Washington, and recruits were being assembled, yet the Revolution seemed far off, and little news of it reached Fithian. There is an entry in his journal, in which he mourns: "Boston is yet the property of tyrannizing Britain." And another in which he celebrates the news that "Boston is taken by the brave American Army under the Command of Immortal Washington."

It was in July of that year that the Congress in Philadelphia adopted the Declaration of Independence. And in October, Fithian, as chaplain with Washington's forces, died of fever on Long Island, not yet twenty-nine years old.

The light was lit in the lighthouse, though not Fithian, nor any then alive—not even Jefferson and Adams, who lived through the first quarter of the nineteenth century—could dream how far that light was to shine in the world.

Yorktown

CHAPTER TWELVE

Goody Bull and Her Daughter

I T HAD BEEN years since he was in Tidewater Virginia and now at last he was returning.

"It's General Washington . . . and his army."

And they wondered where the battle was to be.

But the passing soldiers could say nothing of the general's plans, for they themselves did not know. Actually they had been kept in such complete ignorance that there had been high betting on whether the general planned a siege of New York or whether he would lead them to Virginia. Yet their trust in him was so implicit that wherever he led they would follow. They had been marched from New York across New Jersey and down into Virginia. At the same time, Count Rochambeau was conducting the French forces, also down into Virginia. Perhaps they were all going to Yorktown, where the British commander, Cornwallis, had established his army. Perhaps General Washington, Rochambeau, and Lafayette would unite against Cornwallis.

Those who watched the marching men did not yet know that de Grasse was bringing up a fleet of twenty-eight French ships from the West Indies to Chesapeake Bay. For only bit by bit was Washington's scheme unfolded. Deep secrecy was necessary in order that de Grasse might block off any aid to Cornwallis by water, while the combined armies joined in attacking him by land.

If this succeeded . . . But it must succeed!

Then—it was Washington's hope soon to go home, to return to the pastoral plantation life which he so loved.

There would be no more the heartbreaking sight of Hessians, fat, well-fed mercenaries putting to the bayonet his ragged, hungry troops; there would be no more treason; and no longer the ordeal of that propaganda by which the Tories had tried to poison the North against the South, forging letters containing insults to New England; letters hinting at a personal scandal so foul that Washington could not stoop to defend himself. Every charge could be proved false, was one day to be proved false; yet the whispering campaign had continued.

In accepting the command of the American forces Washington had insisted upon serving without pay. And once, in the torment of what he had been made to suffer, he had exclaimed that not for fifty thousand pounds would he again subject himself to such an experience.

Yet he had gone on with a courage constant under every adversity, a man incapable, people said, of fear; "in action cool, like a Bishop at his Prayers," just as Roger Atkinson had written of him to his brother-in-law.

But when independence was won, how Washington would rejoice to return to the tranquillity of Mount Vernon; where he would ride through his fields, wearing a big straw hat, and carrying an umbrella tied to his saddle; riding over his lands from daybreak to dark; superintending every detail of the plantation, making improvements, and trying experiments in agriculture. For, like all Virginians, he had an almost mystic devotion to the soil; the plantation was to them the very heart of life.

They loved the land because it was their own
And scorned to give aught other reason why.

In the peace of that yearned-for retirement to domestic
life, Washington would never forget the great hour when
news came that France had recognized the independence of
the United States, and had signed the treaty of alliance: he
would remember Lafayette, the eager, redheaded, blue-eyed
boy, not yet twenty, who, leaving his home and his young
wife had bought and fitted up a ship, that he might go to
the aid of America; explaining, "The moment I heard of
America, I loved her. The moment I heard she was fighting
for freedom, I burnt with a desire to bleed for her."

In the tranquillity of Mount Vernon, Washington would
not forget that every year when the army went into winter
quarters his wife—his "dear Patsy"—had come to cheer him
with talk of Mount Vernon, and of Jack Custis's wife and
babies; sitting placidly knitting while she talked; knitting
socks for his brave, barefoot soldiers. And memory of these
soldiers would never pass; ragged hungry regiments, with
"Liberty or Death" embroidered on the hunting shirts which
were their uniform, and on their banners the device of a
coiled rattlesnake and above it the words "Don't Tread
on Me."

These would be Washington's memories when victory
was won, and he might return to the meditative peace of
Mount Vernon.

Now, on his way to Yorktown, he marched through
a land laid waste by the enemy.

Virginia's manhood had been fighting with the armies
in the North and in the Carolinas. And how they had fought,
how they could shoot, those men bred on the plantations and
the frontiers of Virginia. They had left Virginia defenseless
when they went to join Washington's army. The British had
found her thus helpless when they sailed up James River to
Westover, and thence proceeded overland to Richmond,
burning and raiding as they went.

Jefferson had followed Patrick Henry as Virginia's governor, and because Richmond, seated upon the navigable James River, was more central, more easily defended than Williamsburg, the capital had been moved to that city. But, with the British invasion, the government had been forced to flee temporarily to Charlottesville, and then from Charlottsville to Staunton. And Richmond had been burned, as formerly Dunmore had burned Norfolk.

At last Lafayette had been sent to the protection of the stricken state. "The boy cannot escape me," Cornwallis said, marching fast upon his heels, and as he marched he also ravaged the land. And here was General Washington himself. "It's General Washington!" people cried as he passed.

Since the Americans had taken the British "Yankee Doodle" for their own, making up verses which told the tale of the Revolution as it progressed, the British had abandoned it for a song called "The World's Turned Upside Down." The words describe a quarrel between Goody Bull and her daughter. "Goody" was the name for a housewife, whose rank was not high enough to entitle her to be "Madam." And Goody Bull was, of course, England; her daughter represented the revolted American colonies.

> Goody Bull and her daughter together fell out.
> Both squabbled and wrangled and made a—rout.
> The daughter was sulky and wouldn't come to,
> And pray what in this case could the old woman do?

Now to the rhythm of drum and fife the American troops marched swiftly through Virginia to Williamsburg. And "Yankee Doodle" was their tune:

> Cornwallis, too, when he approached
> Virginia's Old Dominion,
> Thought he would soon her conqueror be;
> And so was North's opinion.

Yankee Doodle, keep it up,
Yankee Doodle, Dandy. . . .

. . . .

But our allies, to his surprise,
The Chesapeake had entered
And now, too late, he cursed his fate,
And wished he ne'er had ventured.

At last all knew that de Grasse had arrived with his fleet in the Chesapeake, blocking the entrance to York River. The general's plans were working out. When the allied forces marched from Williamsburg to Yorktown they outnumbered Cornwallis two to one, and there was no escape for him by water. He had fortified Yorktown, but it would not be possible for him to hold out long.

And now too late he cursed his fate
And wished he ne'er had ventured.

The drums and fifes were jubilant. The combined troops surrounded Yorktown. Silently in the dark of night the soldiers threw up breastworks. At dawn they were cannonaded from the town, but with each day they moved nearer.

Within the little town there was smallpox and fever. Cornwallis lacked fodder for the horses, which as the days passed were led one by one into the river and shot, their carcasses drifting down the stream. And steadily the American line advanced; finally to within six hundred yards. When they were ready to begin the bombardment General Washington himself set off the first gun. Then for eight days and nights Yorktown was besieged.

Thacker described the scene as he saw it from the trenches: "Bombshells were incessantly crossing each other's path in the air . . . clearly visible in the form of a black ball in the day, but in the night, each like a fiery meteor with a blazing tail . . . brilliant, ascending majestically from the mortar to a certain altitude, and gradually descending to the spot where they were destined to execute their work of de-

struction." Some of them "over-reaching the town fall into
the river, throwing up columns of water like spouting mon-
sters of the deep." Four British ships lying there were set on
fire, their flames lighting the dark night.

At length Cornwallis sent out a white flag requesting
a parley.

It was very quiet now that the delirium of bombardment had ceased. In this quiet Cornwallis prepared the terms
of his surrender. And on the morning of October nineteenth,
Washington submitted those to which he would agree; on
condition that they were signed by eleven o'clock, and that
by two o'clock the garrison was surrendered.

In an avenue of men a mile long the allies waited, the
French on one side, the Americans on the other; General
Washington on horseback heading the Americans; Count
Rochambeau heading the French. With the Americans were
those three young men so loved and trusted by Washington—
Lafayette, Hamilton, and Light-Horse Harry Lee.

Washington named General Lincoln to receive the surrender. At two o'clock the garrison came out, with General
O'Hara at its head, representing Cornwallis, who was said
to be ill. The procession moved slowly with colors furled
and cased; marching to the time of the familiar song whose
words told the story of how Goody Bull and her daughter
fell out. . . .

And you recall that when Washington accepted the post
of commander in chief of the Revolutionary forces, he said
to the Philadelphia Congress: "I beg it be remembered by
every gentleman in this room that I this day declare with
the utmost sincerity, that I do not consider myself equal to
the command I am honoured with."

And now at Yorktown the British were surrendering
to this modest General George Washington.

In Samuel Kercheval's old book—*History of the Valley
of Virginia*—there is this footnote: "Sending things to

England, was, in the phrase of the times, termed sending things home. This mode of expression, 'going home or sending home' was in use within the recollection of the author. In truth, the term 'going or sending home,' was never abandoned till after the war of the revolution."

Michie Tavern

CHAPTER THIRTEEN

Union

I<small>T HAPPENED</small> in a long drought which had parched and killed the young tobacco plants. The day was Sunday, the first of June; a hot bright day. The delegates who were to debate the Federal Constitution arrived in Richmond thickly powdered with the dust which their horses' hoofs had raised in clouds along the way. The dust was white, grey, or red, according to the section of Virginia from which the men had come. All day they had been arriving; on horseback, in gigs, or in phætons.

One of those who had journeyed by gig came up from south of the James. He was driving himself, and this man, they say, was dressed in the homespun of his own loom, and the dust which covered him was brick-red. They say, too, that as he drove his tall spare figure leaned forward in the gig, and that he seemed worn with travel; perhaps also worn with the anxiety concerning that battle which he was come to fight.

At the same time, from north of the James, another man was approaching, driven in a well-turned-out phæton, and the dust which lay upon this man, upon his vehicle and his horse, was grey. Even before the phæton stopped at the steps of Swan Tavern, and the traveler got out, you could see that he was lame, for he had crutches beside him. He was a tall man but his body was shrunken with age. Yet neither his age nor the fall from a horse which left him a cripple had taken from him the distinction of his bearing.

It was a little before sundown when these two men arrived at Swan Tavern, and on its steps met and greeted each other. The man who had arrived in the gig was Patrick Henry, the "Son of Thunder," come to oppose the Constitution. The man helped out of the phæton and assisted up the steps was Edmund Pendleton, its ardent supporter.

Ever since Henry's speech against the Stamp Act, both he and Pendleton had played a great part in the momentous history of their time. Now they were come to Richmond as delegates to the convention which was to decide whether Virginia would accept the Constitution which would change the United States from a mere league of independent states to a union.

Before the Revolution the American colonies had been isolated, one from another. The war had temporarily related them, and they had then formed themselves into a confederation of separate states. But their league had been a ship without a captain, for the confederation had no president and no real power. It could make laws but could not enforce them. It was helpless before the problems which crowded upon it. The states must pay off their debts, must establish credit, must have treaty relations with the rest of the world. Without any central authority this was impossible, and in many parts of the country liberty had become license. Europe laughed at the chaos in America. "Let us act as a nation!" George Washington had cried. "Let us have a government by which our lives, liberties and properties will be secured."

In this crisis a Congress met in Philadelphia to discuss how the new states might be saved from ruin.

The difficulties of the Congress were great; opinion in the various states was divided. There was the question of abolishing the slave trade. Washington had long said he was "principled against slavery," that he wanted to see it abolished, but that the "one proper and effectual mode by which this can be accomplished is by legislative authority." George Mason, author of Virginia's Bill of Rights, called it a "diabolical trade . . . a disgraceful thing in America." Virginia delegates to the Congress voted the immediate abolition of foreign slave trade. New Jersey, Pennsylvania, and Delaware voted with her. The other states all voted no. In order to get consent to the Constitution there had to be compromise. At any cost the new system must quickly be adopted, for the captainless ship was headed for the rocks. The compromise was made: "The Migration or Importation of such Persons as any of the States now existing shall think proper to admit, shall not be prohibited by the Congress prior to the year one thousand eight hundred and eight . . ." Importation of slaves might, therefore, continue for twenty years more. This contented the rice and cotton planters of the deep South and those New England shippers engaged in importing slaves from Africa.

But of all the difficulties before the Congress, the most troublesome had been the problem of combining States' Rights with a strong central government.

Now at last the work was done. The Constitution was in process of being submitted to the states. Eight had already accepted it, though in Massachusetts it had won by a narrow margin. One more state was necessary for ratification. And in that June when on the Virginia plantations drought was killing the young tobacco plants, New York, New Hampshire, and Virginia were to debate on the Constitution and to make their decision.

Patrick Henry, though his affection and regard for Washington were "unalterable," was determined to fight with all the power in him against this system of government which Washington thought held the only salvation for the states. When Henry had gone home to Hanover after the First Continental Congress, the neighbors had crowded about, asking who was the greatest man at the Congress, and Henry had replied that for wisdom and solid judgment George Washington was the greatest man on the floor. Yet now Henry could not follow the judgment of this man whom he so admired.

Of the Virginians who had been delegates to that first Congress, Peyton Randolph, of the "Roman spirit," and Richard Bland, the "Antiquary," were dead. Of that group who had ridden up to Philadelphia to represent Virginia at the First Continental Congress, three more did not appear at the Convention in Richmond which was to vote on the new Constitution. Jefferson was in Europe. Richard Lee remained on his plantation, and Washington awaited the result at Mount Vernon. Of the original company only Henry, Pendleton, and Harrison were in Richmond now, but the great lawyers, George Wythe and John Marshall, were present, as were George Mason, Light-Horse Harry Lee, and two young men—James Madison and James Monroe.

The Constitution was debated in Richmond for three weeks. Patrick Henry spoke almost every day; often two or three times a day.

"I am but a poor individual," he said, "but I speak the language of thousands." To Henry's mind the new system would rob the states of their rights. "You will sip sorrow," he said, "if you give away your rights. . . . It is said that this Constitution has beautiful features, but . . . they appear to me horrible, frightful. Among other deformities is an awful squinting. It squints toward monarchy. Your president may easily become king . . . He will be a man of ambition and abilities, how easy for him to render himself absolute . . . we shall have a king . . . " Yes, the Constitution "squints toward monarchy."

During this speech Henry's eyes, sweeping the crowded hall, fell upon his son. Henry knew that he must have come with news from home, and he paused to ask a friend seated near him to take the boy out and question him. The boy's news was that his father's second wife had just given birth to a son. The cradle, as Hugh Grigsby has said, began to rock in Henry's house when he was eighteen; it continued rocking until his death at the age of sixty-three. So this latest birth was not startling news to Patrick Henry, and he continued his impassioned plea to "preserve the poor commonwealth of Virginia . . . to preserve," he told his audience, "your liberty and mine."

Day after day the debate went on. George Mason and James Monroe backed Henry. Madison, Marshall, Wythe, Light-Horse Harry Lee, and Edmund Pendleton argued for the Constitution.

And Washington waited at Mount Vernon. It was a choice, he felt, between anarchy and a "union under one federal head." The people must choose "whether they will be respectable and prosperous, or contemptible and miserable as a nation."

There came the last day of the debate before the vote was to be taken.

"The gentleman," Henry said, speaking of Madison, whose part in the drafting of the Constitution had been great, "the gentleman has told you of the numerous blessings which he imagines will be the result of this system. I see the awful immensity of the dangers with which it is pregnant. I see it. I feel it. When I see beyond the horizon that bounds human eyes . . . and see those intelligent beings which inhabit the ethereal mansions . . . I am led to believe that much will depend on what we now decide . . ."

A violent storm, ending the long drought, broke into Henry's speech. One who was present says that it shook the whole building, and that the spirits Henry had called seemed to come at his bidding. "It grew dark. The doors came to with a rebound like a peal of musketry. The windows rattled. The huge wood structure rocked. The rain fell from the eaves in torrents which were dashed against the window panes. The thunder roared, the lightning flashed."

But the "Son of Thunder" did not pause in his eloquent pleading. . . .

The next day the vote was taken. Henry had spoken with all his old magic. He had carried men on the tide of his profound sincere feeling. But he had been answered. And over the Convention there had hovered the spirit of the man who waited at Mount Vernon.

"We are either a united people, or we are not," Washington had insisted. "If the former, let us in all matters of general concern act as a nation which has a national character to support."

When the vote of the Richmond Convention was counted, the majority was not large; it was only ten. But that majority agreed with Washington that the world must not think that "we are a nation to-day, and thirteen States to-morrow. For who would treat with us on such terms?"

Patrick Henry, for the first time, had lost. But now that it was settled, he said, all must cherish the Constitution and give it a fair chance.

Yet he had not really lost. For certain amendments safeguarding the liberty of the individual states were to be added. And Virginia had still further qualified her vote by declaring the right to secede if ever she should feel her liberty to be threatened.

Pendleton, rising on his crutches, dissolved the Convention, in a voice tremulous with emotion. "We are brothers," he said, "we are Virginians. Our common object is the good of the country. . . ."

So, at Richmond beside the rushing waters of James River, Virginia voted for the Constitution and the Union.

Negro cabin near Buchanan

CHAPTER FOURTEEN

Bondage

UNDER WASHINGTON a group of loosely confederated states had been fused into a nation, and a standard raised to which, as he used to say, "the wise and honest might repair."

He had twice been president of this new nation, setting an example of integrity in high office. He had led the way in development of the great West. Yet one problem which had long disturbed him was unsolved when he died: slavery remained, and the traffic with Africa continued; its abolition having been postponed by the Constitution until the year 1808.

During Thomas Jefferson's second term as president, at last the law abolishing forever all importation of slaves was enacted, to go into effect on the first day of 1808, the year in which the constitutional restriction was to expire.

Now that slavery has receded into the mists of vanished things, the word itself—slavery—stirs in the mind of today certain pictures, become so legendary that they are accepted without conscious thought:

A dear old black mammy, very fat, wearing a starched white apron, and a bright bandana head-handkerchief. Probably she is putting a white child to sleep, crooning softly, "Swing low, sweet chariot." Or the swift image which the word "slavery" brings into focus may be some faithful old black Joe, mourning that "Massa's in de cold, cold ground." And the "massa" is always white.

Such pictures slide into view down the easy ways of tradition.

Yet Negroes owned slaves too; not only in Africa, but in America.

There was, to give an example, the Negro who called himself Patrick Henry. In the year 1774 Thomas Jefferson had purchased from George III (to whom it could hardly have belonged!) that great wonder of the world, Virginia's Natural Bridge, in the Valley of the James. Jefferson built a cabin near the top of the Bridge and installed this black Patrick Henry as watchman. Patrick proceeded to buy himself a woman slave, Louisa, then the property of a Mr. Darst, living in the neighborhood of the Bridge. It was not unusual for free Negroes to buy slaves; but this Patrick Henry being apparently himself a slave, the transaction was unique. It is not known how he acquired the money for such a purchase; perhaps by collecting gratuities for showing the Bridge to visitors. But however he contrived the purchase, (according to J. Lee Davis and E. P. Tompkins, coauthors of *The Natural Bridge and Its Historical Surroundings*), there exists in the legal records of Rockbridge County, Louisa's document of emancipation; obviously drawn up for Patrick by someone familiar with legal vocabulary. It is quoted verbatim from the records:

"Be it known to all to whom these presents may come, that I, Patrick Henry of the county of Rockbridge and state of Virginia, having in the year of our Lord One thousand Eight Hundred and Fifteen, purchased from Benjamin Darst of the town of Lexington, a female slave Known as Louisa, and since then known by the name of Louisa Henry:

"Now, for and in consideration of her extraordinary meritorious zeal in the prosecution of my interest, her constant probity and exemplary deportment subsequent to her being recognized as my wife, together with divers other good and substantial reasons, I have this day in open court in the county aforesaid, by this my public Deed of Manumission determined to enfranchise, set free, and admit her to a participation in all and every privilege, advantage, and immunity that free persons of colour are capacited, enabled or permitted to enjoy in conformity with the laws and provisions of the Commonwealth, in such cases made and provided.

"And by these presents I do emancipate, manumit, set free, and disenthrall the said Louisa, alias Louisa Henry, from the shackles of slavery and bondage forever. . . ."

To this document the Negro, Patrick Henry, set his hand and affixed his seal on December 2, 1816.

The legend that the master was always white cannot therefore stand in the evidence of Virginia court records.

While of course it is unquestioned that the source of Negro slaves was the African jungle, yet illogically, in the instant of flashing reaction to the thought of bondage, those slaves of the long ago appear transported from the Dark Continent as thousands of white-aproned mammies and devoted black Joes. Unless the mind pauses to reason, it does not immediately visualize a cargo of jungle savages, from a land where slavery was a common thing; where men often sold, or pawned, their wives and children, where victorious tribes enslaved, or executed, those they captured; and where, when a chief or the head of a family died, many of his wives and slaves were sacrificed.

Yet it was from such as these that the affectionate mammies and the black Joes were evolved; it was from such material that the slaveowners made cooks and nursery maids, seamstresses, field laborers, bricklayers, carpenters, masons, gardeners, coachmen, and butlers.

And slavery was the most tremendous human experiment the world has ever seen. Primitive savages in vast numbers were picked up, transported across the sea, and set down in a strange land, among an alien people who had over them a complete control. It was an amazing experiment. But no one then saw it as an experiment: the whole thing was unconscious. Slavery had its beginning in this country because the tobacco, cotton, and rice plantations needed labor, and the African was better adapted to such work under a southern sun than was any other race. The demand for this labor was supplied by traders who found a fortune in buying slaves in Africa for the paltry price of watered rum or lengths of calico; and then selling them at fat profits to the plantations.

All this began in a period when men were less sensitive to human rights than they are now. If it is to be judged, it should be by the standards of the time; remembering that in those days witches were burned and drowned; gossiping women were punished in the ducking stool; hanging was the penalty for a long list of crimes, and severe flogging was considered necessary in the proper rearing of children.

But why, after all, judge slavery now that it is past and done with? It is enough to say that the slave traders of old England and of New England share the blame with the slaveowners.

It is as a vast experiment in the influence of two races, one upon the other, that slavery in America is a subject so important that the impressions of those who saw the strange experiment in operation must always be of interest.

Some seventeen years after that December day when the Negro, Patrick Henry, emancipated his slave-wife, Louisa, an

English novelist, Miss Harriet Martineau, paid a visit to the South. She came with so great a horror of human bondage that she had a nervous dread of the moment when she would look upon a slave for the first time.

But when finally she became familiar with slavery, she declares that nothing has struck her more than the patience of slaveowners. "In this virtue," she thinks, "they probably surpass the whole Christian world; I mean in their patience with their slaves . . . when I consider how they loved to be called 'fiery Southerners,' I could but marvel at their mild forbearance under the hourly provocations to which they are subject in their homes."

Miss Martineau goes one Sunday with her hostess to dine on a neighboring plantation. The carriage is ordered to come back for them at eight o'clock. To their concern it arrives at six; the slave-coachman saying that his master has sent him to say that they must return directly. But when they reach home, the "master" is much surprised. The coachman, it appears, has invented the message in order that he may have the evening to himself. And Miss Martineau is astonished that her host and hostess merely laugh.

"Patience," she explains, in that degree in which she constantly sees it, "can be obtained only by long habit. Persons from New England, France or England, becoming slaveholders, are found to be the most severe masters and mistresses, however good their tempers previously." They cannot "sit waiting half an hour for the second course, or see everything done in the worst possible manner, their property wasted . . . their plans frustrated . . . themselves deluded by artifices—they cannot, like the native proprietor, endure all this unruffled."

Reading Miss Martineau, you remember Washington's struggle with slave labor. Since he was so much away from Mount Vernon, as general and as president, his correspondence with his overseers reveals this struggle. He writes that it is his foremost desire that the overseer be particularly attentive to the Negroes in sickness; they are never to work when unfit for it, and should then be taken care of. He has a doctor

engaged to look after them by the year. If they are ill they
must have wine when necessary.

Wine when necessary . . . Then what increase of sickness! "I find by the reports," Washington writes, "that Sam
is in a manner always returned sick; Doll at the Ferry and
several of the spinners frequently so, and Ditcher Charles
. . . what sort of lameness is Dick's and what kind of sickness is Betty Davis's? And is there anything particular in the
cases of Ruth, Hannah and Pegg that they have been returned
sick for several weeks together?"

He goes on to say that he cannot conceive how it is
possible that six thousand twelvepenny nails could have been
used in building the cornhouse, and that he believes it would
take a week for his carpenters all working together to build
a chicken coop. In four years, even with the aid of fifty
thousand dollars from the sale of land, his plantations have
just managed to keep out of debt.

Six thousand twelvepenny nails to build a cornhouse
. . . Yes, it was patience that most impressed Miss Harriet
Martineau, visitor from England.

Nineteen years after Miss Martineau's visit to America,
Thackeray, in 1853, writes from Richmond on the James, to
a friend in England:

"There's beautiful affection in this country, immense
tenderness, romantic personal enthusiasm, and a general kind-
liness and good nature which is very pleasant and curious for
us folks at home who are mostly ashamed of our best emotions. . . . " And, in the same letter, writing of slavery as
he saw it in Richmond, Thackeray said: "The happiness of
these niggers is quite a curiosity to witness. The little niggers
are trotting and grinning about the streets, the women are
fat and in good case . . . The great plenty in this country
insures every one enough to eat . . . I wish you could see
that waiter in our hotel with 5 gold medals in his shirt, 2
gold chains and a gold ring. . . . I don't mean to say that
slavery is right but that if you want to move your bowels
with compassion for human unhappiness, that sort of aperient

is to be found in such plenty at home that it's a wonder people won't seek it there. . . . The rule [here] is kindness, the exception no doubt may be cruelty. . . . Of course we feel the cruelty of flogging and enslaving a negro—of course they feel here the cruelty of starving an English laborer, or driving an English child to a mine—Brother, Brother, we are kin."

In the year following Thackeray's visit to Richmond, the Reverend Nehemiah Adams of Boston is forced to spend three months in the South on account of his health. He is a zealous abolitionist and confesses that he comes with feelings of dread and curiosity—with anticipation of the groans and the clanking chains which he has so often heard described.

It is in the harbor of a southern seaport town that he first sees slavery. He goes ashore and slaves are all about him. He is astonished. They are all in a good humor. The delivery of every trunk on shore, he says, is the occasion of some bit of repartee. "I began to like those slaves. I began to laugh with them. It was irresistible. Who could have convinced me an hour before, that slaves could have any other effect upon me than to make me feel sad?"

In the streets, the Reverend Nehemiah finds it difficult to pass the slaves without smiling; they have a singular effect upon his spirits; he says that he has never seen a happier, better looking, more courteous set of people.

On Sunday he is amazed at the dress of the slaves on the street: well-fitting broadcloth suits, polished boots, white Marseilles vests, brooches in their shirt bosoms, gold chains, elegant sticks; the women dressed with taste and refinement. On the way to church a little girl about eight years old trips along ahead of the Reverend Nehemiah. He admires the profuse flounces on her dress, her light-colored boots, her mohair mitts, her sunshade. He approves the hymnbook in her hand. Then, when the child happens to turn her head, he sees that she is black.

When he observes all this he says that he cannot help remembering the thousand paupers on Deer Island near Boston.

Ten years later, Frederick Olmsted, also from the North, travels in the South. In contrast to Miss Martineau and Thackeray, the British novelists, and to the abolitionist, Reverend Nehemiah Adams, Mr. Olmsted is a practical man of affairs, observing Negro bondage from the economic angle. He calculates that the cost of getting anything done under slavery is double the cost with free labor; that it requires four times as many people and takes four times as long. He watches slaves at work and reports that they appear to him to go through the motions of labor without putting strength into them.

Mr. Olmsted visits a James River plantation. In the three hours that he spends with the owner, he says that not more than ten minutes pass without interruption by slaves, coming with childlike confidence and dependence, asking help or direction of some sort. The planter has to leave the dinner table three times to attend to their various demands.

"You see," the planter explains to Mr. Olmsted, "the trouble and responsibility of properly taking care of your negroes. You see how constantly I am called upon . . . The slaves are careless and wasteful. To make anything of farming a man has got to live a hard life . . ." But "they are interesting creatures, Sir, and with all their faults have many beautiful traits. I can't help being attached to them and I am sure they love us."

And Mr. Olmsted, in the course of his southern travels, makes the discovery that gangs of Irishmen are employed at the hardest labor, such as draining the land. "But why not slaves?" he asks. "Oh, it's dangerous work. A negro's life is too valuable to be risked. If a negro dies it's a considerable loss you know."

Mr. Olmsted notes how greatly slaves have to be humored to get them to work. He and the Reverend Mr. Adams both describe the method of tasking slaves: setting as a day's work an average stint, and paying the slave for whatever he does above that amount. They also describe the custom of giving each slave a plot of ground, where he can raise pigs, poultry, and garden produce, which he may sell or use for himself. Not having to consider old age or sickness, his daily living provided, a slave's personal money may be spent upon the "foppish finery" which so impresses Mr. Olmsted in Richmond; or such money may be used by the slave to buy his own freedom. All this is very surprising to Nehemiah Adams and to Mr. Olmsted. Free Negroes themselves owning slaves are astonishing to an abolitionist; and what is he to think of a Negro woman owning her husband, and when he displeases her, threatening to sell him downriver?

Looking through the eyes of these long-ago visitors to the South, it is plain that slavery was not a one-way matter. In a very real sense the slave owned the master, as in another sense the master owned the slave. Property is always possessive, especially when that property is alive—when it is human.

Practical Mr. Olmsted realizes that the slave may in a thousand ways retaliate upon an unfair master, or upon one he dislikes. In the most innocent manner in the world he may destroy tools, neglect cattle and horses and mules, sham sickness, or run away. These are his punishments for punishment. The master may, of course, sell him, but everybody well knows that he who sells must almost invariably sell at a sacrifice. The owner cannot simply discharge an unsatisfactory slave; he is held legally responsible for him; he must make the best of one who is troublesome; he can get rid of him only by selling him; or by taking the loss of freeing him.

But the Negro slave had a stronger hold upon his master than any power of retaliation. He was so touchingly responsive to affection, so engagingly playful and childlike, so impulsive, so without bitterness, that he created a new relationship between employer and employed. Only the utterly heartless could be indifferent.

When Miss Martineau asks herself what are the morals of the society which is subject to slavery, her answer is that the most obvious is Mercy. "Nowhere, perhaps, can more touching exercise of mercy be seen than here. I saw endless manifestations of mercy, as well as of its opposite. The thoughtfulness of masters and mistresses and their children, not only in the comforts, but the indulgence of their slaves, was a frequent subject of admiration with me."

But not Miss Martineau, nor Thackeray, nor the Reverend Nehemiah Adams, nor Frederick Olmsted, for a moment condoned slavery as an institution; but they honestly reported the life as they saw it; though never changing their conviction that fundamentally slavery was evil.

For, no matter how benign the form of slavery, and it has been conceded to be nowhere more benign than in Virginia, still . . . nothing could alter the fact that it *was* slavery; a thing in itself "diabolical," as the author of Virginia's Bill of Rights described it.

However benevolent the master, every form of slavery is alien to the human spirit. The Englishman, John Davis (who in the last years of the eighteenth century, and the first year of the nineteenth, kept the "Old Field School" on Pohoke plantation within sight of the Blue Ridge), unconsciously dramatizes man's inherent craving for freedom. Davis, in describing the absence of discipline under slavery as he saw it in Virginia, cites as an example the case of a runaway slave. A neighbor recognizing this fugitive Negro, brought him back to his master. With no thought of any punishment, Davis says, the master merely wanted to know why the man had run away.

The answer was simple:

"I was born to travel," the man said.

And the essence of the indictment lies in that naïve sentence; though, at the time that it was uttered, few men could see its implications. To them the anecdote testified to a master's benevolence. To us, in the year 1945, the man who feels himself "born to travel" has the "inalienable right" to achieve that for himself.

But even in that long ago, those men of plantation Virginia, who had so large a part in the winning of American independence and in the creation of a United States, under-

stood how serious the slavery question was. Washington
wished from his soul that the legislatures of the various
states could see the policy of its gradual abolition. Jefferson
prophesied that nothing was more certainly written in the
book of Fate than that this people would one day be free.

But how was it to be brought about with justice both
to the owner and to the slave? What, for instance, was to
become of the enormous numbers of Negroes who would be
set adrift by freedom? Such Negroes as had already been
freed by their masters, or who had bought their own freedom, did not have an easy time. They were not welcome in
the free states.

Mr. Olmsted tells the story of a Negro who purchased
his freedom and went to Philadelphia. A few weeks later he
was back in Virginia. "Oh, I don't like dat Philadelphy," he
explained. "Ain't no chance fo' colored folks dere. 'Spec'
if I'd been a runaway de white folks dere would of took care
o' me. But I couldn't git anythin' to do. So I jes' borrow ten
dollar of my brudder, an' come back to old Virginny."

The free Negro was a perplexing problem. People
thought that colonization, perhaps in Africa, would be the
only solution.

For nearly two hundred years Africa flowed, a black
river of life, westward across the sea, across that dreadful
"Middle Passage," into the South. For nearly two hundred
years slave ships from Guinea came to anchor in James River.
Africa thus poured into British America; the great experiment constantly supplied with fresh material, with "New
Negroes," as they were then called.

And as the bondage was a mutual thing, so the experiment was also.

In America, the African curse of witchcraft slowly disappeared: the sacrifice of wives and slaves on the death of
their lords was no more; the power of vengeful gods, who
must ever be appeased, faded; medical care and sanitation

lowered the death rate; of the evils of Africa only slavery remained.

In his new world the African slave found a new language and a new religion. His emotional soul had a genius for worship, and into the Christian religion he poured all his heart, his history, his drama, his humor, his unique musical rhythms. He made of it a warmly passionate thing. The Negro spirituals are African psalms, set to African music:

Their thought is often very humble:

Keep a inchin' along.
Massa Jesus comin' bime-by
Keep a inchin' along like a po' inch-worm.
Massa Jesus comin' bime-by
Massa Jesus comin' bime-by.

Side by side with this humility there is the Negro's shrewd, picturesque analysis of character:

Hypo-crite an' de concubine,
Livin' among de swine,
Dey run to God wid de lips an' tongue,
An' leave all de heart behind.

Sometimes these songs call upon those forces of nature, feared and adored on the great Dark Continent:

O hear dat lumberin' thunder,
A' roll from do' to do',
A' callin' de people home to God.
Dey'll git home bime-by.

O see dat forked lightnin'
A' jump from cloud to cloud.
a' pickin' up God's chillen,
Dey'll git home bime-by.

The Negro takes the crucifixion and makes it break your heart:

Were you dere when dey crucified my Lord?
Were you dere?
O—sometimes it causes me to tremble, tremble! . . .

Were you dere when dey nailed him to a tree?
O—sometimes it causes me to tremble, tremble. . . .
Were you dere when dey pierced him in de side?
O—sometimes it causes me to tremble, tremble. . . .

In many of these songs you hear the cry of slavery:

Lord, have mercy, mercy! Lord, have mercy.
Lord, have mercy over me, over me!
An' befo' I'll be a slave, I'll be buried in my grave
An' go home to my father an' be free . . .
Lord, have mercy . . .

There are songs, too, of triumph, when all God's chillen will shout all over God's heaven; when all will have a robe, a crown, shoes, a harp, a song and wings; and thus will shout and walk and play and sing and fly all over God's heaven.

And in none of their songs is there ever to be found one single word of bitterness.

Out of the great experiment there was given to America, not only these immortal spirituals, but there was given also a new laughter, the rhythm of new dancing, a new awareness of the invisible world, and a new intimacy with all living creatures; with Br'er Rabbit, and Sis' Goose, Sis' Cow, and Br'er Turkey Buzzard.

The great accidental experiment had brought the African Negro thus far. And as it was not a one-way bondage, so it was not a one-way experiment; for the genius that is Africa crossed in the slave ships and entered permanently into the life of America.

But whatever mitigations one may concede, slavery of the white man and of the black was the horror of the seventeenth and eighteenth centuries all over the world. The pity is that in our own United States it lived beyond its time; lived over into the nineteenth century, a disgrace to be shared alike by the slaveowners of the South and by the shipping interests of New England who made fortunes from the slave traffic with Africa.

Two years after the Negro, Patrick Henry, at Natural Bridge, "emancipated, manumitted, set free, and disenthralled" his Louisa from "the shackles of slavery and bondage forever," the territory of Missouri petitioned to be admitted into the Union as a state: a slave state.

And after violent debate the Missouri Compromise was proposed and passed; providing that Missouri should be admitted with slavery, but that in all the remaining territory west of the Mississippi, and north of the southern boundary of Missouri, "slavery should be forever prohibited."

Long ago, as a young man, Jefferson, in writing of slavery, had said: "Indeed I tremble for my country when I reflect that God is just; that his justice cannot sleep forever." Before the Constitutional Convention he had said: "Nothing is more certainly written in the book of fate than that these people are to be free. . . . " As author of the Declaration of Independence, as governor of Virginia, as president of the United States, he had urged Negro emancipation.

Now, at Monticello, in the northern watershed of James River, on the occasion of the passage of the Missouri Compromise, six years before his death, Jefferson was writing to a friend: "This momentous question, like a fire-bell in the night awakened and filled me with terror. . . ."

Old Canal Lock at Balcony Falls

CHAPTER FIFTEEN

"It Was Not Lonesome on the River in Those Days"

BEFORE the canal there were the bateaux: great flat barges fifty to ninety feet long, propelled by a crew of three Negroes; two to pole and one to steer. Between Richmond and Lynchburg there were as many as five hundred bateaux on James River; to say nothing of those on the upper James. Most of them were owned by the plantations, and in their day were the only freight service up and down the river; the largest could bring downriver eighty barrels of flour, or twelve hogsheads of tobacco, and carry up abundant quantities of general supplies: coffee, sugar, salt, molasses, whisky, and all sorts of merchandise. It took a week to get

206

from Lynchburg to Richmond and ten days to get back. Time was unimportant.

Out of my study of transportation on the James there stands forth this sentence: "It was not lonesome on the river in those days."

The era of the bateaux, and later of the canal, is long vanished. Railroad tracks, laid on what was once the towpath, lie close to the riverbank; but the traffic which year after year passes over them comes and is swiftly gone: it has no contact with the river. And it is lonely now on the James. No one is left alive who can remember when the bateaux animated the river.

The bateaux traveled generally in groups of three; each with its captain, the senior captain of the group ranking as the commodore of the little fleet. The life of the bateaux crew was a water life, spent almost entirely upon the river. By day they made stops to take on freight at wharves stationed several miles apart; on the stretches of the river the boatmen poled over the shallows, and where the water was deep used long sweeps, guided always by the steersman with a powerful oar. The crews all knew one another, and passing on the river they shouted greetings, hurled jesting taunts, laughed, or, resting on their sweeps, exchanged gossip and charged each other with messages to friends.

It is fortunate that, before he died, George W. Bagby, whose home was in Lynchburg, remembering the bateaux as he saw them when a child, recorded his recollection of them:

"If ever a man gloried in his calling—the negro batteau-man was that man. His was a high calling, demanding skill, courage and strength in high degree. I can see him now striding the plank that ran along the gunwale to afford him footing, his long iron-shod pole trailing in the water behind him. Now he turns, and after one or two ineffectual efforts to get his pole fixed in the rocky bottom of the river, secures his purchase, adjusts the upper part of the pole to the pad at his shoulder, bends to his task, and the long, but not ungraceful bark mounts the rapids like a sea bird breasting the storm. His companion on the other side plies the pole with equal ardor, and between the two the boat bravely surmounts every obstacle, be it rocks, rapids, quicksands, hammocks, what not. A third negro at the stern held the mighty oar that served as a rudder."

At night the bateaux would tie up at the bank, often in groups of twenty or thirty. The crews built fires and cooked their supper: corn pone, of course, fried bacon, fish from the river, chickens, and eggs. When supper was over fiddles and banjos were brought out, and men danced the buck and wing, as lively as though they had not navigated great loaded bateaux all day. They would dance, and then they would sing; passing from mood to mood; singing as savage men sing upon a jungle river, or merrily with the laughter and humour characteristic of their race, or with a profound religious faith, in which were combined sorrow and exaltation.

But when their voices were stilled in sleep, and the fire had flickered out, even though it then became quiet on the river, it was not lonesome.

From the time that young George Washington was sent by Governor Dinwiddie across Virginia's western mountains on a mission to the French commander, he was impressed with the importance of linking the East with the West. He dreamed of waterways which would unite such eastward-flowing streams as the Potomac and the James with westward-flowing rivers beyond the mountains which led to the Ohio, and down the Ohio to the Mississippi.

If James River could be opened for navigation, it would not only provide a waterway, crossing Virginia from east to west, but by means of a turnpike over the Alleghenies, connection from the highest point of possible navigation on the Jackson—James River's main branch—might be made with the westward-flowing Kanawha, and so to the Ohio.

As early as 1774 Washington put the idea before the Virginia House of Burgesses, but it was not until 1785 that the James River Company was organized, to open the river for navigation above Richmond. Washington was made the company's president, with Edmund Randolph as director and acting president. Washington advised him to "press the execution of the survey between the James River and the navigable waters of the Kanawha," adding that he was convinced that such a waterway to the West would be "productive of great political consequences to the country."

No work needed to be done on the Tidewater James, but it was necessary to build a canal around the Falls from Richmond to Westham, a distance of seven miles; and the river channel had to be cleared all the way from Westham to the mouth of Looney's Creek, more than two hundred miles distant.

For the first twenty years the James River Company was a discouraging investment for its stockholders, but then it began to pay large dividends, causing much public complaint of high profits and inferior service; and in 1820 the state purchased the canal rights, though retaining the company as manager. In 1835 the enterprise was reorganized as the James River and Kanawha Company, to carry forward the dream of linking East and West.

In 1840, one hundred and forty-six miles of canal between Richmond and Lynchburg were completed and opened for service; reducing the time from ten days by bateaux to a little more than thirty hours by canal. Packet boats now plied three times a week between the two cities. In 1851 the section between Lynchburg and Buchanan was finished and in operation; adding fifty more navigable miles, of which thirty-six were by slack water. In 1854 there were one hundred and ninety-five freight boats between Richmond and Buchanan. There was daily passenger boat service, except Sunday, between Richmond and Lynchburg; the extension from Buchanan to Covington was begun; four years later navigation was in operation for a distance of twenty miles up the North River branch of the James, to a point six miles southeast of Lexington, where stage connection to Lexington was made. By 1860 the Canal passenger business had doubled,

and packet boats were providing forty-four-hour service
from Richmond to Lexington, and forty-seven-hour service
to Buchanan.

In the years of its history the James River and Kanawha
Company had not only to conquer the engineering obstacles
presented by the river, but it had to overcome financial
panics and such disasters as the occasional floods which
broke the banks of the Canal, and wrecked its locks and towpaths. Then came the War Between the States and the collapse of ambitious dreams for linking James River with
the Kanawha and the Ohio and the Mississippi.

The packet boats were drawn by three horses which,
being changed every twelve miles, were able to keep up a
speed of four miles an hour. The horses were driven tandem,
the driver mounted on the rear horse. Newspaper advertisements of the time described the boats as "affording luxurious
accommodations and polite Society." They were long narrow
boats with a deck above a main cabin, a dining cabin, a
galley, and "a small bar for gentlemen." The main cabin
was by day the lounge, but at night was converted into
sleeping compartments by the simple expedient of suspend-
ing a heavy curtain to separate the quarters for men from
those for women; and then making up berths in the two compartments; one above another, three deep: a lower, a middle
and an upper.

As a child George W. Bagby heard the blasting of rock
on what he was told was the "Jeems and Kanawha Canell,"
and as a schoolboy he made his first canal trip, traveling from
Richmond to Lynchburg. Bagby, remembering that trip,
described how "mournfully" the packet horn sounded in the
night as the boat approached a lock, and how in the early
morning, with a big tin dipper provided for the purpose,
each dipped from the river water for his morning "ablution."
Bagby never forgot the rosy light on the wooded hills of the

James, nor the dewy vines and bushes growing along the banks of the canal, nor the fresh purity of the morning air. "In fine summer weather," he said, "the passengers stayed most of the time on deck, where there was a great deal to interest and naught to mar the happiness, except the oft-repeated warning, '*braidge!* low braidge!' No well-regulated packet-hand was ever allowed to say plain 'bridge'; that was an etymological crime in canal ethics. For the men, this on-deck existence was especially delightful; "it is such a comfort," Mr. Bagby said, "to spit plump into the water without the trouble of feeling around with your head, in the midst of a political discussion for the spittoon."

He recalled with nostalgia the enchantment of the scenery, and then commented that "all the scenery in the world . . . all the facilities for spitting that earth affords avail not to keep a Virginian away from a julep on a hot summer day." He himself was "then in the lemonade stage of boyhood" and could only "watch the Virginians at their juleps: 'Gentlemen, your very good health'; 'Colonel, my respects to you'; 'My regards, Judge. When shall I see you again at my house? Can't you stop now and stay a little while, if it is only a week or two?' 'Sam', (to the barkeeper) 'duplicate these drinks.'

"How they smacked their lips: how hot the talk on politics became. . . . "

Certainly in those days it was not lonesome on the river.

North River enters the James just above Balcony Falls. There the James makes sharp turns around steep thickly wooded hills, where masses of dark conifers give the impression of deep shadows lying on the hillsides among the paler trees. At Balcony Falls the James dashes foaming and roaring over great boulders; the river here cutting its way through the Blue Ridge range, and at the same time the river drops two hundred feet in a distance of four miles. And along the banks of North and James rivers runs a depression that was

Through the Mountains, River and
Canal wound their lonely way

once the James River Canal; with at intervals what remains of old canal locks.

In this rugged, beautiful setting, nearly a hundred years ago, the Negro slave, Frank Padget lost his life. It happened in 1854, when nearly two hundred freight boats were plying between Richmond and Buchanan, and there was regular packet boat passenger service all the way from Richmond, at the head of the Tidewater James, to Buchanan, near Natural Bridge and the mouth of Looney's Creek, a distance of more than two hundred miles. Four hundred horses were then employed in the operation of the canal, and nine hundred men.

And of these nine hundred men, it is the Negro, Frank Padget, who must be remembered.

In the Library of Washington and Lee University at Lexington there are old files of the Lexington *Gazette*. The issue of Thursday morning, January 26, 1854, contains a letter to the editor, dated, "Mouth of North River, Saturday, January 21st." It is printed beneath the headline: *Canal Boat Lost in the Mountain!*

"Mr. Editor: We have just passed through a day of the most thrilling and awfully melancholy scenes and adventures that it has ever been my lot to witness. For several days the water courses have been quite fresh, and the heavy rain of last night raised North River several feet higher than it was the evening previous. This morning the Canal boat *Clinton*, Captain Wood having on board some 34 negro hands, and several white hands who were on their way to the Central Railroad to work for Messrs. Coleman, Morris & Co., besides four or five young gentlemen, and the boat hands, five in number, attempted to pass on up the river to Buchanan. . . . The towline broke, and the boat drifted at the mercy of the water down James River towards the Mountain dam—the water being too deep to touch bottom with poles. About 100 yards before she reached the dam at the Cement Kilns, seven persons jumped off and attempted to swim ashore, four reached the shore safely . . . three went over the dam and perished. . . . The Captain of the

Boat held the Tiller and called to those on the bank to enquire what he had best do. He was told to straighten up his
boat and let her run, but to stick to her. He therefore exerted
himself manfully, succeeded in getting down her stern to
prevent her from going over broadside, and over she went
riding the waves, like a thing of life. No lives were lost in
this leap, but now came the awful crisis . . . to run through
the White Rock, the Little Balcony, the Great Balcony falls
and the Tobacco Hills, places that formerly made the boldest
hearts quake, and the strongest nerves give way under favorable circumstances, now the scene became most thrilling and
exciting to observe, the boat crowded with human beings,
hurried on, as it were, by the boiling waters with the speed
of a race horse, down the river, as we all supposed, into
the very jaws of destruction. On she speeded, and as she
passed within a foot of the White Rock, which, if she
had struck, she must have gone to pieces—the Captain and
four or five persons jumped from her on the rock, and there
they were out in the middle of James River on a naked rock,
the raging waters roaring around them—on went the boat
. . . We all thought she must ineviably go to pieces, but
a kind of 'Providence' determined to have a hand in the
matter . . . and she missed every rock until she reached the
head of the Tobacco Hills where she hung lightly on a
rock in the middle of the river. Then came the question,
can these people be saved, then came the response, 'We'll
try' and off some of us dashed to get a batteau and some
skilful watermen who were willing to peril their lives in the
humane effort. . . . Some hands were collected who dragged
the boat over the towpath and launched her in James River
below the Cement Kilns. No time was to be lost, the river
was still rising, and the wind by this time was blowing
a perfect hurricane through the gap of the mountain, making the adventure the next thing to madness. But the
question was propounded, 'Boys, who will go?' When out
stepped some half dozen or more brave hearts, among them
an old boatman named Frank Padget, upon whose skill we
felt rested our main dependence to rescue those who were

in such imminent peril. Frank was requested to take the head
of the boat and select such men as he wanted to man and
manage her. This he did with the accurate judgment usual
with him in such matters. He said he wanted but two
assistants and selected Sam and Bob, two negroes, out of a
half dozen others. A Mr. Wm. Mathews and a Mr. McCol-
logan, two gentlemen in the employ of the James River
and Kanawha Company, volunteered to go along and assist
also. Those five jumped aboard, pushed out from shore, and
pulled manfully for the off shore, to get into a current
that would take them near the White Rock. They had
scarcely reached the middle of the stream when a heavy
squall struck the boat and drove them back to the same
shore they started from. Their brave resolve was not to be
shaken by this catspaw, so up the river they rowed and
out they again shot into the angry stream, and on they
flew towards the White Rock, they approached it. Frank is
heard to give some direction, the men get ready, a towline is thrown to the men on the Rock who caught and
clung to it with all their energy. Frank skilfully shoots the
head of his boat into the eddy under the Rock. He is heard
to call out 'down with your stern,' the boat comes up
beautifully to the Rock just below. Hurrah they are
saved. . . . But half their work was not done, to take them
aboard, to pull across and land the poor fellows took less
time than to write it. Then to make a few more preparations
to cut out and fly down the stream through the fearful
Balcony Gorge to the rescue of the rest was the work of
a few minutes only—while engaged in saving those above,
the water had risen enough to start the Canal boat off again,
and away she went headlong through the Tobacco Hills, and
hung just below in the small timber of a small island, then
mostly covered with water. On her passage one of the negroes
on board had jumped off on a flat rock near the Velvet
rock, and . . . stood there without his coat, wet with spray,
shivering in the cold, imploring help, but the boat could not
then be gotten to him, and it flew to the assistance of those
who remained still on the Canal boat. Many persons on

the shore were affected to tears. . . . The Canal boat was reached in safety and all hands taken off and brought in safety to shore. Then . . . 'Frank, can the poor man on the rock be saved.' He replied 'Yes Sir, I think so.' 'Then let us lose no time.'

"The boat was gotten in the Canal at the rope ferry and towed back above the falls and pulled again over the tow-path. The same noble fellows . . . again volunteered, and two others, one a white man and one a negro consented also to go. The situation was dangerous in the highest degree. Away they fly, the man on the rock is motioned to jump into the boat as she passes . . . He fixes himself so as to jump. The boat arrives, he jumps into her. . . . But Oh God! Horror of horrors! the boat has struck. The stern swings around. The water washes over the gunnal, and in the twinkling of an eye she is wrapped around the rock, crushed like an eggshell. Five of those on board have just time to leap upon the rock, three are in the water, the brave Frank, the courageous Bob and the poor man they had gone to rescue. Bob clung to the stern oar, drifted ashore on the opposite side. Frank struggled manfully for a minute, and went down to rise no more . . . with the poor creature he was trying to save. No one can describe the feelings we all experienced. . . .

"Now there were five brave hearts on that rock to save, and no time to be lost for night was approaching. The water was sloshing over the rocks and covering them with spray. The weather freezing. To send off for another headman . . . to send another messenger for the waterman to get out another bateau, and collect together hands to throw her over the tow-path occupied but a few minutes. We reached proper place, pulled the boat out, and were just starting her over the bank, when awful to tell the negro let her get away and she went out, with all our efforts to prevent—beyond our reach in the river, and broke to pieces below on the rocks. . . . It was now fully dark [and we were] obliged to wait until the morning.

"By daylight we collected what hands we could and

commenced work and got her launched in the river below the dam. Placed the old mountain ferryman, Sam Evans, in command and sent him with six volunteers. . . . The river had risen some in the night. . . . but the men still alive and still on the rock. . . . The five poor fellows . . . all escape with their lives."

That account was written for the Lexington *Gazette* by a Captain Edward Echols, who himself played a tireless part in the efforts to rescue the men of the Canal freighter *Clinton* on that January day in the year 1854. And Captain Echols was so deeply moved by the heroism of the Negro slave, Frank Padget, that he erected a monument to honor his memory; placing it below Balcony Falls, on the left bank of the James, at a spot where green hills rise sheer on both sides of the river. The monument is a granite slab, and carved upon it are the words:

In Memory of
Frank Padget
A colored slave who during a freshet in James River in 1854 Ventured and lost his life by drowning in the noble effort to save some of his fellow creatures who were in the midst of the flood, from death.

The monument stands in a lonely and lovely spot; so shut off by precipitous hills rising almost from the river's edge that it may be reached only by walking along the tracks of the Chesapeake and Ohio Railroad, which lie close to the riverbank upon what was the towpath of the canal in the time of Frank Padget.

There you feel yourself alone with the James and with the hills of the Blue Ridge; for the infrequent trains rush through and you are a couple of miles in both directions from a station.

The voice of the river is in your ears, and it is a river from which has vanished the busy human life of bateaux, canal freighters and packet boats. Only the towpath, the depression where once stood the waters of the canal, and the remains of the old locks speak to you of days when it was not lonesome on the river.

A train rushes noisily past Frank Padget's monument, and is gone. Again there is no sound but the voice of the river, the James on its way from that union of the Cowpasture and the Jackson, flowing eastward to the sea.

The train has gone, and in the complete tranquillity of hills and lonely river you may reread the words carved upon the monument:

In Memory of Frank Padget, A colored slave who during a freshet in James River in 1854 Ventured and lost his life in the noble effort to save some of his fellow creatures who were in the midst of the flood, from death.

From the inscription you may re-create that moment in the history of the river: Raging waters. A freezing wind. Fear. Peril. Death.

In the words of that account in the Lexington *Gazette:*

"A day of the most thrilling and awfully melancholy scenes and adventures that it has been my lot to witness. Three went over the dam and perished. Into the jaws of destruction. Men . . . in the middle of James River on a naked rock. Raging waters roaring about them. The wind . . . a hurricane through the gaps of the mountain. *Boys, who will go?* Five brave hearts. . . . Among them an old boatman, Frank Padget . . . a Negro slave. Two other Negroes. Two white men. Men on rock . . . saved. Men remaining on the canal freighter . . . saved. But there is a Negro . . . alone on the rock to which he has leaped. He begs help. The boat goes to him. He jumps in. . . . But, Oh God! . . . The boat is crushed on a rock—like an eggshell. . . . And Frank Padget sinks . . . goes down with the Negro they had tried to rescue. . . ."

The monument stands just where Captain Echols had it placed. It must always stand there. In their book, *The Natural Bridge and its Historical Surroundings,* Dr. E. P. Tompkins and J. Lee Davis say that "When the canal property passed into the hands of the Richmond and Allegheny

Railroad Company, a stipulation was entered in the contract that the monument is never to be disturbed; and when the Chesapeake and Ohio Company acquired the former road it convenanted to keep the monument intact, and it has faithfully carried out its agreement."

George W. Bagby lived through the era of the James River Canal, from the moment when, as a seven-year-old child, he had been startled by the blasting of rock on what thev told him was the "Jeems and Kanawha Canell." He lived through the years of the canal's prosperity, through the later years of decline, and its final surrender to the railroad.

"Well," Bagby said of the canal, "let it go. . . . But I can't help feeling sorry for the bull-frogs. . . . What will become of them, I wonder? They will follow their predecessors, the batteaux; and their pale, green ghosts seated on the prows of shadowy barges, will be heard piping the roundalays of long-departed joys. . . . Farewell canal, frogs, muskrats, mules, packet-horns and all. . . ."

CHAPTER SIXTEEN

Robert and Edgar

"ROBERT was always good."

So his father, Light-Horse Harry Lee, wrote from wandering exile in the West Indies. It had been four years since he had seen Robert, and the child had then been not more than five years old. Yet, writing from those faraway islands under the wind, he took comfort in little Robert's goodness. There was poison in almost every other memory.

When he thought of his courtship of Robert's mother he must have remembered how he would gallop down the long driveway that led to Shirley. There was no more lovely place on James River than Shirley. There was dignity in the rhythm of its white columns, and in the repetition of its many-paned windows; in the tawny red of its mellowed brick there was a tender warmth, and the carved white pineapple on its roof was the symbol of its hospitality. And Ann Carter was like the house. Not every girl of twenty would have known how to appreciate, as she did, a man of Harry Lee's fame and achievement. Most girls would have thought

221

only of the seventeen years' difference in their ages. But
Ann had valued his experience and delighted in his talk.
She was proud that Lafayette and Washington were his
friends, she gloried in his record in the Revolution, and in
the fact that he had been three times governor of Virginia;
loving him for these things as well as for the fact that he
was dashing, handsome Light-Horse Harry.

But to think of Ann and of Shirley was to realize that
she no longer owned any interest in the place. There was pain
in the memory of that day when she had set out in a ram-
shackle carriage to drive across country to her old home.
She had looked so ill. Three babies had come fast; already
another was soon expected. And Harry Lee knew that he
was ruined; bankrupt by ill-judged speculation in land.
Therefore Ann must travel in a broken-down open carriage,
exposed to the cold winds of late autumn. And how ill she
was! Unfit for the shock of finding her father dead; and
for discovering that he had left her only the income from
a trust, carefully safeguarded so that Light-Horse Harry
might not touch it. Perhaps, but for this humiliation to her
husband, Ann might have stayed on at Shirley until her
baby was born.

But of what use to say perhaps? Nothing now could
alter the fact that creditors had beat upon their door, and
that Robert had been born to a mother so anxious, so griev-
ing. And what could ever erase from Ann's heart the disgrace
of a husband jailed for debt?

In the little brick house in Alexandria, to which he had
moved them when he was freed from jail, they might have
lived in a frugal peace on the income that Ann had from
her father, if only that dreadful thing had not happened
in Baltimore. . . .

Still, could he blame himself for that?

He had not believed it wise again to wage war with
England; and it had seemed right to go to Baltimore to the
support of an editor whose paper was opposing the war. A
man ought to stand by his convictions.

Now his mutilated face, his shattered nerves, would not

let him forget the terror of that war-crazed mob which had attacked him at the office of the pacifist paper.

Thus he sailed the Caribbean, seeking health and the peace he might never find. He wrote to Carter, his eldest son, warning him against speculation and debt. But for Robert he felt no anxiety: "Robert was always good."

A year later Light-Horse Harry Lee died, on his way home to be united once more to his family.

Of his children, Robert was then eleven years old, Carter away at college, Smith a midshipman in the Navy, Ann in delicate health, and Mildred only eight. Their mother had become a chronic invalid. Many duties now fell upon Robert. He became his mother's nurse and housekeeper; yet found time for school, for hunting, for swimming with the boys in the river, and every year for a gay visit to his relatives at Shirley.

Robert was happy and never knew that he was good.

Meanwhile, in Richmond, Frances Allan was delighting to set on little Edgar Poe's dark curls a purple cap with a gilt tassel, to put upon his feet pumps with shiny buckles, and to dress him in voluminous trousers of yellow silk. Then together they would drive about Richmond paying calls.

Sing for the ladies, Edgar. . . . Dance for the ladies. . . . Recite one of your pretty pieces for the ladies.

Everyone agreed that Edgar was remarkable. Even John Allan began to take pleasure in the social triumphs of his little foster son; though he could not quite get over the fact that the boy's parents had belonged to the wicked profession of the stage. Allan, implacable toward any fault in a woman, saw something certainly ugly in the fact that Elizabeth Poe did not know what had become of her husband. As star of a touring theatrical company she had arrived in Richmond with a baby daughter and three-year-old Edgar; but without a husband.

Edgar got the impression very early that there was some-

thing disgraceful in his life, something unhappy that made
him different from other children. He knew that his mother
had died . . . died in the furnished room back of Mrs. Phillips's
millinery shop in that part of the town known as the Bird-
in-Hand, because of an inn of that name; famous for its
spitted mutton. And he understood that as a homeless orphan
he must be grateful for the good home Mr. Allan gave him.

Edgar was taught to call Mr. Allan "Pa" and Mrs. Allan
"Ma," but little by little he came to know that he only
called them by those names, that it wasn't real, because "Pa"
wouldn't agree to adopt him legally. Not to be legally
adopted must be a dreadful thing, since "Ma" was so unhappy about it. But "Pa" said, wasn't he providing a home,
and didn't he plan to give the child as good an education as
any boy in Richmond?

From his own mother Edgar had nothing but the miniature of herself, which was all there was to leave him. The
miniature fixed her image in his mind. "Ma" was beautiful,
with dark hair piled on her head, and dresses that made her
look as stately as a statue; but his mother, the girl that looked
out of the miniature, had long dark curls falling to shoulders
childishly frail, and she had enormous eyes, wide-apart eyes,
very big eyes.

Of course, he couldn't actually remember her; he had
been only three when she died, and childless Frances Allan
had taken him home to be the son of her heart. He couldn't
actually remember, yet neither could he forget. Nothing
seemed real—not even his own mother.

In the autumn of 1824 a serene old man visited the
United States. Thirty-five years ago he had fought beside
Washington in the Revolution: he had been present at the
surrender of Yorktown. Now he had come back, and no
man ever received so great and joyous a welcome in a foreign
land. For General Lafayette was more even than the brave
soldier who had made America's struggle his own; he was
the very spirit of the New World. "I have always loved
liberty," he said; "I have loved it with the enthusiasm of

a religious man, with the passion of a lover, and with the conviction of a geometrician."

The United States went wild over this gallant white-haired figure out of its past, dressed still in the outmoded fashion of his youth, with cocked hat, knee breeches, swansdown waistcoat, and blue coat with gilt buttons.

In Alexandria, in tribute to the memory of his old friend, brilliant Light-Horse Harry, Lafayette paid a call upon the widow in the little brick house. Of course, Robert shone in the glory of General Lafayette's visit.

Upon Edgar, too, the great Lafayette left an impression. Perhaps in all his life Edgar never knew a prouder, happier day. Artillery thundered in salute and bands played as the steamer from Norfolk brought Lafayette up James River to Richmond. Four white horses drew the hero's carriage through streets packed with cheering crowds. And in the procession marched Edgar himself. The press of the day states that in the parade there was a "pretty looking company of small boys dressed in hunting shirts, and styling themselves the 'Morgan Legion.' " Of this "Legion," sixteen-year-old Edgar was the lieutenant, handsome and erect, fair-skinned and brown-haired, with grey eyes veiled by astonishingly long lashes.

In that same year John Allan inherited a fortune from a rich uncle, and the Allans moved into an imposing dwelling which Frances Allan filled with extravagant furnishings. And Edgar was the son of the house. Yes, but was he really? The house was his home, that was true. He had been accustomed by the Allans to luxurious living. But how secure could he feel? Actually, he did not belong anywhere. "I am a Virginian," he would say; but even that was only partly true, for he had been born in Boston.

This was the year that he fell in love with little Elmira Royster; and she had given him her promise. He would soon be gone to the university; but, of course, Elmira would write; they would have each other's letters. In the year that the University of Virginia was opened, Frances Allan herself drove with Edgar to Charlottesville, entered him and left him for the first time in his life free from all restraint.

Thomas Jefferson had been all his life interested in public education. He was convinced that the success of democracy rested upon the education of the citizen. "No other sure foundation," he said, "can be devised for the preservation of freedom and happiness."

Through the years Jefferson had been evolving a system of education; with the great object of founding a university which would be the most eminent in the United States, drawing to itself the youth of every state. Education, he said, had been his earliest public concern. It became the dominant interest of his last years.

A site for the University was secured near Charlottesville; on the northern limit of the James River watershed, and four miles from Jefferson's home at Monticello. He was seventy-seven when the University Charter was granted, and he could begin to carry out his vision. His plan was "not one magnificent building, but an academical village. . . ." Jefferson designed the campus and was the architect of the buildings; all as he had dreamed it. And he personally supervised every detail of the construction.

The University, as it stands in gracious dignity today, is the embodiment of Jefferson's dream. He was the most widely cultivated man of his day in America, and the University course as he planned it added to the classics the study of modern languages and of all the sciences. He selected a group of able professors, five of them from England, and became himself the first head of the University. He was past eighty when it opened its doors to receive students.

Jefferson, passionately believing in democracy, considered that students should govern themselves, that professors should teach, but should not discipline. "We studiously avoid too much government," he wrote to a friend, and a year later he said of the students: "They committed some irregularities at first, until they learned the lawful length of their tether."

It is said that the merchants of Charlottesville exploited
for their own ends this new freedom for youth. They offered
limitless credit; whatever the young gentlemen wanted was
theirs. In due time their fathers would receive the bills.

And young Edgar Allan Poe, only seventeen, unaccus-
tomed to liberty, and wondering why, though he wrote again
and again to Elmira imploring a word from her, there was
only silence. In his trouble he began to gamble.

It was in July and the heat heavy in Charlottesville.
Thomas Jefferson was now eighty-three. And in the shimmering heat he felt death lay hands upon him. Unworried
about the hereafter, he made ready to go. He talked of the
University, the hopes he had for it, and his confidence in
its future. So the second and the third of July passed. From
time to time he fell asleep, but when he roused his mind was
alert. On the evening of July third he seemed to have drifted
into a coma, but suddenly he spoke to the doctor sitting
at his bedside:

"Ah, doctor, are you still there?"

His voice was faint, as though coming from far away.
The doctor assured him of his presence. Then the voice questioned: "Is it the Fourth?" These were the last earthly words
of Thomas Jefferson, author of the Declaration of Independence.

Morning came, and at one o'clock on the afternoon of
the great anniversary of the Declaration, Thomas Jefferson
quietly ceased to live.

And in Massachusetts, on that same day, John Adams
sat muttering unintelligibly in his chair, a palsied old man
whose time could not be long. Through the open windows
there came the noisy explosion of rockets and firecrackers.

Suddenly, then, the meaningless mumble of old John
Adams cleared. "Thomas Jefferson," he said, "still lives." And
with those words he died; not knowing that Jefferson had
preceded him by an hour.

Jefferson and Adams, signers of the Declaration of Independence, had died on the Fourth of July.

Many wondered if there was some portentous, awful meaning in their passing together on that day.

Poe dressed in black, his black frock coat buttoned up to his black stock, without a vestige of white anywhere, except for his abnormally pale face. His figure was held erect with an air of immaculate distinction; his step was light and quick.

The ancient peoples of Guatemala believed that each human being had his counterpart in an individual creature of the animal world: it might be any animal—a hummingbird or a jaguar or an armadillo. They thought that the life of some particular animal was identical with that of every human being; that it shared his joys and sorrows, lived as he lived, and died when he died.

The raven of Poe's creation seems in this mystic sense to be identified with him.

It was in December that he came home to Richmond from the University at Charlottesville, and Frances Allan was giving a Christmas party to celebrate his return. Would Elmira be there? But Elmira, they told him, was not in Richmond. She had gone away on a visit, and people were saying that she was to marry a certain Mr. Shelton, a prosperous middle-aged bachelor. But Poe had a thousand sweet proofs of Elmira's love, and she had given him her promise. Why should she marry anyone else? As John Allan's adopted son, there was nothing he could not give Elmira. But perhaps, since Mr. Allan had not legally adopted him, Elmira's father did not look upon him as the son of the house. Was he, after all, only a charity boy, saying "Pa" and "Ma," not to parents, but merely to patrons? Was that why, now that he was come home, Elmira had been sent away? And why had she not answered his letters?

In "The Raven" that hour wrote itself into the lines:

Ah, distinctly I remember it was in the bleak December,
And each separate dying ember wrought its ghost upon
  the floor.
Eagerly I wished the morrow;—vainly I had sought to borrow
From my books surcease of sorrow—sorrow for the lost
  Lenore—

That was a troubled winter in John Allan's fine new
house. Elmira remained away, and silent. Edgar could not
return to the University unless Mr. Allan would pay off his
angry creditors. This Mr. Allan refused to do. Poe confessed
his ambition to be a writer; but that was crazy nonsense
to which Mr. Allan would not agree. And Frances Allan,
so loved by her adopted son that it was his habit to speak
of her as "dear Ma"—Frances Allan was ill and sad.

Perhaps gossip brought to Poe's ears a reason for her
sadness. Perhaps he could accept no guidance from John Allan
because he thought him a hypocrite. At any rate, a few weeks
after that "bleak December" he and Mr. Allan quarreled,
and Poe flung himself out of the house, into a future darkly
uncertain.

Frances Allan, distracted with grief, tried to prevent
Poe's leaving Richmond, but the small boat by which he
journeyed to Norfolk slipped away unobserved from the
tobacco-scented wharves at the foot of the hill. He had no
definite plan. He was not yet twenty, and his mood of
"strange, impending doom" came only in occasional night-
mares; it had not yet fastened itself upon him. There was
hope in his heart. The lovely James River houses stood in
tranquil dignity upon the banks—Shirley and Westover,
Carter's Grove, Claremont and Brandon, among their shel-
tering trees. Surely one day the quarrel with "Pa" would be
made up, and he would go back home, to fall asleep at night
to the sound of the old Jeems rushing over the falls at
Richmond.

Meanwhile, under an assumed name, he enlisted as a
private in the army, and was sent to Sullivan's Island off

the coast of South Carolina. He did not see Virginia again until the end of the year, when he was ordered to Fortress Monroe. Then Frances Allan was dying, imploring to see Edgar once more. But Mr. Allan was convinced of Edgar's "black heart," of his "deep ingratitude"; considering him "alike destitute of honor and principle."

Frances Allan, growing ever weaker, begged that if she should die before Edgar came, they would not bury her until he arrived, for she would have her darling boy look once more upon her.

But while Poe was returning by stagecoach from Norfolk to Richmond, she died; forcing from her husband the promise not to abandon Edgar. She was buried the day before the stagecoach rattled into Richmond.

Then beside her grave Poe let his heart break.

Frances Allan was gone . . . and in Richmond he learned that Elmira was married.

And of the raven he wrote that it was

Caught from some unhappy master whom unmerciful Disaster
Followed fast and followed faster till his songs one burden
    bore—
Till the dirges of his Hope that melancholy burden bore
Of "Never—nevermore."

John Allan had promised not to abandon him, but he would keep only the letter of that pledge. He arranged the discharge from the army which Poe wanted; his record had been good and the discharge easily managed. Also Allan used his influence to get Poe admitted to West Point. But it was not long before, restless and unhappy, he deliberately got himself expelled, and went to Baltimore to his aunt Maria Clemm, his father's sister, a widow, earning as seamstress an uncertain living for herself and an eleven-year-old daughter.

From time to time he sent appealing letters to Mr. Allan. He could never accept the fact that Mr. Allan was no longer "Pa" and Richmond no longer home. "I am a Virginian," he would say, and then add, "at least I call myself that."

Memory of the luxurious home in Richmond appears in "The Raven" in the "silken rustling" of the curtains, in the "sculptured bust of Pallas," and in the "cushioned velvet lining that the lamplight gloated o'er." And Poe had described himself in that "stately raven with mien of lord or lady," that "fowl with fiery eyes"; garbed, like Poe himself, in the simple elegance of black. And Poe's appeals by letter to Mr. Allan were not unlike the tapping of the raven at the door.

Now and then Poe sold a tale or a poem, but not sufficiently often and not for enough money to give him any sense of security. Mr. Allan had written plainly that he was to expect nothing either then or as a legacy. But Poe seemed unable to believe that he and Mr. Allan did not belong to each other. Even after John Allan married again and became a father, he still thought of him as "Pa."

"For God's sake," he wrote, "pity me and save me from destruction." That was his last letter to Mr. Allan. It was never answered, and when Mr. Allan died his will revealed illegitimate children for whom he made some small provision, but Edgar Poe was not mentioned.

Increasingly now he sought escape from a reality in which he felt he had no place, until he became a stranger in the actual world, living more and more in the abnormal world of his fancy, a place whose fantastic horror dwarfed the sordid facts of his actual existence. His stories and verses carry you into that alien world of his creation. And when not even the imagination provided release, there were drink and drugs. In a society which drank in genial good-fellowship, Poe drank seeking only escape.

"I have absolutely no pleasure," he said, "in the stimulants in which I sometimes so madly indulge. It has not been in the pursuit of pleasure that I have periled life and reputation and reason. It has been in the desperate attempt to escape from torturing memories—from a sense of insupportable loneliness and a dread of some strange impending doom."

In "The Raven" all this is to be found, and the end predicted:

"Prophet!" said I, "thing of evil!—prophet still, if bird or
    devil! . . .
Is there—is there balm in Gilead?—tell me—tell me, I implore!
Quoth the Raven, 'Nevermore.' "

  .   .   .   .   .

And the lamplight o'er him streaming throws his shadow on
    the floor;
And my soul from out that shadow that lies floating on the
    floor
Shall be lifted—Nevermore!

Graduated with honors from West Point, and stationed
at Fortress Monroe, at the mouth of James River, Robert E.
Lee married Mary Custis of Arlington, great-granddaughter
of Martha Washington.

They had a merry wedding. The company laughed and
danced, with no presentiment of Appomattox to dim the
future. Lee, people said, was bound to rise in the army; his
very looks, his handsome distinguished presence surely guar-
anteed him success. Something set him apart from other men.
Everyone was aware of it—everyone but himself. As for
Mary Custis, she was a sensitive, quickly responsive girl, with
the gift of making people happy. And the many relics of
George Washington which made Arlington so sacred to
Lee seemed to grant benediction upon this marriage. In
Mary's father—George Washington Parke Custis—there was
a living link with Mount Vernon. And among the servants
at Arlington was a woman who had been Martha Wash-
ington's maid. She had been in the room, standing near the
door, on the night Washington died; and now she saw Mary
Custis married to Robert Lee, whose father, Light-Horse
Harry, had been Washington's friend.

At Fortress Monroe the young Lees were soon absorbed
into the life of an army station, preoccupied with promo-

tions and transfers, flirtations and marriages, births, servants, and parties, and what is good for croup or teething.

Then suddenly news had come of a slave uprising; a bloody uprising in eastern Virginia.

People, terrified, remembered what had happened in Haiti; how the black emperor, Dessalines, had commanded his soldiers to seek out the whites; to seek in the cane fields, under the thatch of roofs, among the branches of trees, even in the great ovens. The soldiers were to bring those they found to a place outside the town. Then, when Dessalines should give the signal by striking three times on his snuffbox, the massacre was to begin. All were to be butchered, with mercy for none. Dessalines had boasted that his horse would paw the ground in blood from one end of Haiti to the other. In revenge for the cruelty of French masters, he would have his horse paw the ground in blood. There were refugees in Richmond who had fled from those atrocities.

Could such things happen in Virginia? But Virginia slavery had never been like that of the French islands. Dreadful things had taken place in the French islands. But, even while people thus argued, the insurrection had been put down, and Fortress Monroe slipped gradually back into its customary routine; this one had been transferred, another promoted; Mrs. Lee was expecting a baby and going home to Arlington for its birth.

There must have been talk also of England's freeing of slaves in her West Indian possessions, for it occurred at about this time. It had cost England twenty million dollars; for the slaveholders had been paid for the eight hundred thousand Negroes in bondage to them. There must have been discussion of this in Virginia, for there were many anti-slavery societies in the state and everyone was interested in the free colony of Liberia, whose capital—Monrovia—was named for James Monroe. Yet the momentous question, of which Jefferson had said that "like a fire-bell in the night," it had awakened him and filled him "with terror," remained still unsettled.

From Fortress Monroe, Lee was assigned to duty in Washington, and after that was sent to survey the boundary between Michigan and Ohio territories. Babies came to the Lees through the years, as regularly as the striking of a clock; more regularly unfortunately than army promotions. Lee was in the Engineer Corps, where advancement was particularly slow. And Mrs. Lee had fallen into ill-health, spending much time at Arlington with her parents.

Without Mary and the children Lee was always lonely. "I am the father of children," he said, "so entwined around my heart that I feel them at every pulsation." On his long absences they were always in his thoughts.

In his every scheme of happiness he looked forward to retiring to a farm in some quiet corner among the hills of Virginia. He desired promotion only as a means of caring for his family; he seems never to have thought of it as recognition, or found in it a personal gratification.

His instinct was to send his roots deep into the soil he loved, there in peace to live and at length to die. Once he said that all he wanted in the world was a Virginia plantation, no end of cream, fresh butter, and fried chicken; not one fried chicken, or two—but unlimited fried chicken.

All day on his plantation he would be busy; roads and fences would have to be kept up, buildings would need repair, livestock would require continued care, and always there would be the cycle of sowing and reaping. For companionship he would need only Mary and the children. Could anything be more delightful, he thought, than romping with little children? They were never too young to be your friends. Then, as they grew older, it was important that his boys should be taught to ride properly, sitting the "dragoon" seat, and never rising in the saddle. Mary would see that all the children knew their Bible, and that the girls learned to sew. It would be his part to help with the other lessons.

But he had chosen the army as his profession.

War with Mexico over the Texas boundary question sent Lee into active military service. In his first battle he won

the title of major; his perilous crossing of the Pedregal, alone
at night, brought him the brevet of lieutenant colonel, and
soon after he won the brevet of colonel. During this war
he was repeatedly cited for gallantry, for intrepid coolness
under heavy fire, for daring and soundness of judgment. He
constructed roads and bridges over which the army might
pass; he brought forward guns and conducted columns under
hot fire. General Scott called him the very best soldier he
ever saw in the field.

Yet his heart was that of a man of peace. "You have
no idea," he said, "how horrible a sight a field of battle is."
And he wrote home describing how one day, near Jalapa,
he had come upon a drummerboy with a shattered arm, who
was unable to move because a dying soldier lay on the injured
arm. A little girl, with tears pouring from big dark eyes,
stood helpless over them. She was a barefoot creature, her
slender brown arms crossed on her breast, her hair hanging
to her waist in a long black braid, her tears streaming.

"The plaintive tone," Lee said, "of her *Mille gracias,
Señor*,' as I had the dying man lifted off the boy, and both
carried to the hospital, still lingers in my ear."

A River in the Sea

Winds and Currents

Y OUNG MATTHEW MAURY rode over the mountains from Tennessee into Virginia. A neighbor had provided him with a horse, a grey mare named Fanny. At the end of the journey Fanny was to be sold and whatever price she brought sent back to her owner. In his pocket Maury had thirty dollars for Fanny's expenses and his along the way. He had earned the money doing some teaching at the local academy. Now he had Fanny and thirty dollars, and, best of all, he had his appointment as midshipman in the navy; he had Sam Houston of the Valley of the James, to thank for that. Maury's father had contributed nothing. Sons were valuable in a pioneer farmer's family; an older son had gone into the navy, and had died of yellow fever aboard his ship as she was "standing in" to Norfolk. So, at the moment of Matthew Maury's riding away, his father had turned from him in mute sorrow.

But the life of the road blurs the edges of the past for

those who travel, and Maury's bright blue eyes looked eagerly
into the future. When spring sunlight shimmers over a road,
dreaming youth may summon the image of ambition to
appear in the quivering light.

Yet riding over the mountains into Virginia he could
not have foreseen the value of the work he was to do in the
world. It was not revealed to him that he was one day to be
called the "Humboldt of America" the "Pathfinder of the
Sea"—and that the great Humboldt himself was to say that
Matthew Maury had founded a new science.

These achievements and honors could not have appeared
to Maury in the sunlight dancing on the road: it was enough
for him to know that at last he had his appointment as
midshipman in the navy, and that now anything might
happen.

Certain events in his life had combined to shape his
destiny. There was the cobbler who made the family shoes.
The cobbler had the habit, as he worked, of covering the
soles of shoes with odd little *y*'s and *x*'s. When Maury came
to know what they meant he found them to be a fascinating
puzzle called algebra. The cobbler had introduced Maury
to the mathematical universe. Then when he was twelve years
old he had been helped to an education by the accident of
falling from a tree.

Had it not been for that his labor on the farm would
have prevented his getting much more than the fundamentals
of reading and writing and figuring; but the fall, which was
from a great height, had so injured him that hard physical
work was for a time impossible. So it happened that he was
sent to the academy to get what learning it could furnish.
By that time pioneer life had already shaped his body; not
tall and slim, but stocky, with sturdy muscles.

Far back in his childhood, even before the family had
migrated from Virginia to the Tennessee frontier, his brother
John's going into the navy had established a connection for
Matthew with the great wide world. Now, as he journeyed,
he resolved that he would *make everything bend to his
profession*.

Meanwhile the grey mare, Fanny, was taking him over the mountains into Virginia where he had been born.

More than a hundred years ago his father's people had come to James River, Huguenots fleeing from persecution in France. And the Virginia of his mother's Cavalier forebears had welcomed the fugitives. His very name—Matthew Fontaine Maury—was woven into James River history. The Reverend Peter Fontaine had been chaplain on William Byrd's famous Boundary Line Commission. The Reverend Francis Fontaine had been professor at William and Mary. John Fontaine was one of those knights of the Golden Horseshoe who had accompanied Governor Spotswood on his fabulous expedition into the mountains. Anne Fontaine had married Matthew Maury, and their son, James Maury, had moved to Albemarle County and established a school. Jefferson, Madison, and Monroe had been his pupils.

It was therefore to the home of his ancestors that young Matthew Fontaine Maury journeyed on his borrowed mare.

He found in Virginia living kin, as well as departed ancestors, to welcome him; among them little Ann Herndon, young enough to look up to her new cousin, for she was only thirteen, and he a man of nineteen with an appointment as midshipman in the navy. Ann was a pretty thing; her eyes as blue as his own, her hair auburn, and her voice so musical that it echoed in his mind. Relatives were truly a delightful discovery. One of them bought Fanny, which made it possible to discharge the debt to Maury's frontier neighbor.

When Maury was assigned to the new frigate *Brandywine,* of course the kin were delighted with his good fortune, for the *Brandywine* was to carry General Lafayette back to France. And the papers were saying that in "elegance and efficiency" the frigate had never been surpassed by any ship clearing from an American port.

General Lafayette took a fatherly interest in the young midshipman aboard the *Brandywine;* he had many talks with the ruddy, brown-haired, blue-eyed youth who, while he walked the deck, studied problems in spherical trigonometry which he sketched in chalk where he could see them as he paced back and forth. Maury was conspicuous, too, as a man able to joke no matter how seasick he was, and he was very seasick. Lafayette, a poor sailor himself, naturally had a fellow feeling for similar sufferers.

As for Maury—to have sailed with Lafayette on the *Brandywine*, actually to have talked with him—no youth could ever forget that.

It was in the following June, some three weeks before Poe heard in Charlottesville the tolling bell which marked the death of Thomas Jefferson, that Maury again sailed out of the harbor of Norfolk, this time aboard the frigate *Macedonian*, with orders to proceed to South America . . . bound once more for the future, with Rio de Janeiro the first port of call.

He said that when standing his watch he felt "God's voice in every wave that claps its hands, and in every breeze that blows." The ocean appeared to him as a "face upon which time writes nothing," and of the clouds moving across the sky, he said, "they have commandments to fulfill." He saw the beauty of an everlasting wisdom in the universe of sky and sea, and longed to understand that wisdom.

He noted winds and currents, and meditated.

Sixty-two days out from the bay into which James River pours its tawny water, there was Rio, with the breath-taking beauty of its green hills rising from the blue harbor; with the tragedy of slave ships anchored there, and in the streets an emperor's gilded chariot drawn by six mules magnificent in gilt trappings. Then Rio slid into memory; the host of albatross which hover about Cape Horn joined the company of remembered things, and the west coast came into the focus of the present. The waves broke now upon that long, arid strip of land which is Peru, with the Andes towering, snow-crowned, above it.

When the frigate *Vincennes* arrived in the harbor of Callao bound for the Orient, he asked to be transferred; he must see more of the world's oceans, he must observe new currents and new winds.

He sailed to the Marquesas, to China, Manila, Java, Sumatra, down the coast of Africa, around the Cape of Good Hope. And slowly a dream was taking shape within him. He dreamed of a time when the mariner could accurately map his course. To that end he set himself to study the ocean.

When he finally returned to Virginia he had been gone four years. Blue-eyed Ann Herndon was no longer a child, and almost his first act ashore was to fall in love with her. And Ann Herndon told him that when she first saw him, long ago when he was newly arrived from the wild frontier, he had seemed to her "like young David, fresh from his sheep."

In the year after Maury had married "charming Nannie, his first and only love," Poe came again to Richmond; that city haunted for him by memory of the dead mother who lived only in her miniature, by memory of "Pa" Allan and "dear Ma," of himself as lieutenant of a company of boys escorting the great Lafayette, and of Elmira Royster who had kissed and promised.

He returned to the familiar city as editor of the *Southern Literary Messenger;* to be remembered because Poe was its editor, and because it published Maury's important "Harry Bluff" articles. Poe's tale of the "Manuscript Found in a Bottle" had been winner in a prize contest, and through that he had made contacts which obtained for him this editorship. He brought with him to Richmond his child-wife, Virginia Clemm, daughter of his aunt Maria, his father's sister. Poe was then twenty-four and Virginia not yet fourteen; "Sis" was the little name by which he tenderly called her.

As editor Poe immediately made a reputation for savage book criticisms. Maury must have anxiously wondered what the *Messenger* would say of his book on navigation, his first book. Would Poe flay it? But the review was favorable;

"here," it announced, "is a work that strongly commands notice."

With Poe's editorship and the success of Maury's book, the married life of the Poes and the Maurys started off with a cheerful flourish. Incomes were, to be sure, tiny, but hopes might well be vast.

Mrs. Clemm came over from Baltimore to keep house for Poe and the young little wife who was her daughter. When Poe was up late writing, Mrs. Clemm sat quietly beside him, every hour or so serving him a cup of hot coffee. She kept his clothes mended and brushed and cleaned. Virginia helped in household matters as a child might help. Poe adored her, and almost equally adored his mother-in-law, who so worshiped them both that they made up for her the universe.

The circulation of the *Messenger* multiplied with Poe as editor. On the surface the future promised happiness. But more and more Poe felt an alien in the normal world, belonging nowhere. Only he himself, Virginia, and Mrs. Clemm had reality; all else appeared to him a fantastic mirage, while in the strange imagined world of his creation he saw actuality. In its terror and its abnormality he felt at home.

It was a world where "black draperies shut out the moon, the lurid stars, and the peopleless streets—but the boding and the memory of Evil, they would not be so excluded." In the atmosphere was "a sense of suffocation . . . yet we laughed and were merry in our proper way—which was hysterical; and sang the songs of Anacreon—which are madness; and drank deeply, although the purple wine reminded us of blood." And then in that weird world "there came forth a dark and undefined shadow . . . but it was the shadow neither of men, nor of God, nor of any familiar thing."

Such was Poe's world, while for Maury flowers and babies bloomed, and ships roved the seas.

Then Poe ceased to edit the *Messenger*. Its owner appreciated his brilliant mind, and regretted! . . . If only Poe would keep away from liquor!

And again Poe explained sadly: "I have not been driven to insanity by drink, it is insanity that has driven me to drink."

He lost his place on the *Messenger,* and the tide of his fate carried him away from Richmond. Occasionally he found other editorial work, but he was never able to keep it. He had won literary reputation; he wrote and gave lectures; but these irregular earnings were not enough. From poverty he slipped into destitution. And Virginia was slowly dying of consumption.

The years passed, and at last Poe returned once more to Richmond; carrying in his heart the dark memory of Virginia's death. He could see her as she lay on the straw bed in the little cottage at Fordham. It had been January and very cold. He had wrapped her in his overcoat and laid upon her bosom the big tortoise-shell cat. Virginia was cold and dying, with only the overcoat and cat to warm her. He and Mrs. Clemm held her hands and feet, that the warmth from their own bodies might pass into hers. And thus Virginia—Virginia who was always a child—had died.

After that Poe had been desperately ill. With his recovery he began slowly to write again and to lecture. In a strange, distracted way he became involved with one woman and another. In Richmond he again met Elmira, now a widow; they had discovered that, in the long ago, Elmira's father had intercepted their letters; the inexplicable silence was at last explained. So finally they came once more together; Elmira, the rich widow, and Poe, broken by sorrow and drink and drugs; a threadbare Raven now, in his rusty black, but still a Raven of "stately mien"; with the distinguished manner of the Virginian of his day.

From Richmond, Poe wrote Mrs. Clemm about Elmira:

"My dear, dear Muddy: Elmira has just got home from the country. I spent last evening with her. I think she loves me more devotedly than any one I ever knew and I cannot help loving her in return. . . . On Tuesday I start for Philadelphia. . . . If possible I will get married before I start. . . ."

There was a postscript to say that the Richmond papers were praising him to death—that he was received everywhere with enthusiasm.

Poe's plan was to bring Mrs. Clemm to Richmond, which he would make his future home. But on his journey north he got no farther than Baltimore. After four days of delirium—of "constant talking—and vacant converse with spectral and imaginary objects on the wall . . . he became quiet and seemed to rest for a short time"; then once more he spoke: "Lord help my poor soul," he said, and with that he died.

He had been among those travelers whose feet were set upon the way that was to lead to Appomattox. Now he had fallen out of the procession.

And you wonder whether, in the mysterious depths of his poet's soul, unknown even to himself, the "impending doom" which so tortured him was perhaps not solely personal, but prophetic of that tragedy whose climax was to be Appomattox.

When Matthew Maury was a child a fall from a tree had altered the current of his life. Now, after a visit to his parents in Tennessee, traveling to New York to join his ship, the stagecoach upset. Maury fractured a knee joint and a thigh bone. He was far from home and it was three months before he could travel.

Lying helpless, his mind went back to the day when, riding over the mountains into Virginia, he had resolved to make everything bend to his profession.

But suppose he should be lamed for life and unfit for active service, how was he to carry out that resolution? Well, if he couldn't follow his profession actively, then he must follow it in his mind. He would "cultivate," he said, "a few little patches of knowledge." Such a wilderness of subjects needed to be studied; should he choose ship building or ship sailing, winds or tides, storms or currents? Perhaps the destiny which had upset the coach would answer the question for him. After all, he insisted, "it is the talent of industry that makes a man. I don't think so much depends upon intellect as is generally supposed; but industry and steadiness of purpose, they are the things."

He wrote a series of articles on the reorganization of the navy; writing under the name of "Harry Bluff." One by one he discussed in detail the deficiencies of the service, and suggested remedies; documenting every point with facts and figures. The articles were published in the *Messenger*. Harry Bluff became a sensation. Naval officers had the articles reprinted, and widely circulated, at their own personal expense. And out of the words of the crippled Maury there eventually came into being a new navy.

The Harry Bluff articles brought him an assignment to the Department of Charts and Instruments at Washington. In the beginning it was a small routine position, but it decided what was to be the great work of Maury's life.

As master of the *Falmouth,* making accurate notes on his experiences around the Horn, he had dreamed of a science of navigation that would map the seas:

Suppose captains were provided with abstract logs on which to enter every day "the temperature of air and water, the direction and set of the currents, and the height of the barometer . . ." And suppose these captains "cast overboard at stated periods bottles tightly corked, containing on a slip of paper the latitude and longitude, and the day and month of the year." Suppose also that the bottles thus set afloat were picked up, "the latitude and longitude of the place where they were found noted in the captains' logs, with the day of month and year. Then—the logs returned to Washington, and a careful study made of their records—might it not be possible to map winds and currents along the ocean routes and to furnish navigators with reliable sailing directions?

It was a great dream—the dream of a new science of navigation.

Maury, now established in the Department of Charts and Instruments, began to study old logbooks found stored in Washington; at the same time he distributed to sea captains the abstract log which he had himself prepared. Very soon he had more than a thousand captains recording their voyages. And from study of their logs he compiled Wind and Current Charts and Sailing Directions.

Mariners who used the Maury charts found that the dangers of the sea were lessened, and that they were able to reduce voyages by many days. Clipper ships cut the journey from New York around the Horn to California by as much as fifty days. A new route was plotted for the voyage between England and Australia, cutting nearly fifty days off the round trip.

The seaman's path, Maury said, "has been literally blazed through the winds—mile-posts have been set up on the waves, finger-boards planted, and time-tables furnished for the trackless waste."

All over the world mariners were now using the Maury charts, and from every part of the globe captains were constantly adding to the information upon which Maury based these charts. At the end of eight years he had collected records covering twenty-five million sailing days. The result was a lessening not only in time and in peril, but a saving of millions of dollars a year to all nations which used the Maury sailing directions.

Meanwhile visions were crowding his mind; he saw not only the charting of the ocean, but the establishment of a Navy Academy, the digging of a canal across the Isthmus of Panama, and the formation of a Weather Bureau which would aid farmers, as the mapping of winds and currents was guiding the navigators of the sea.

But Maury . . . dreaming his great dreams . . . could not know that soon he was to see that terror which, like a "fire-bell in the night," had come to the heart of Thomas Jefferson.

The Falls of the James at Richmond

CHAPTER EIGHTEEN

Miss LaSalle Corbell and Young Mrs. Pryor

WHEN LaSalle Corbell was a little girl, perhaps
four or five years old, she went on a visit near Old Point
Comfort, at the mouth of James River. She had been sent
from home in the hope of escaping whooping cough. Sallie
was having a beautiful time on this visit. She was a gay little
thing; she could dance and sing, and found herself very
popular. Then she came down with whooping cough. Now
mothers cried out when they saw her: "Run away, little girl.
My children can't play with you."

One day walking forlornly on the beach she saw a young
man sitting on the sand under an umbrella. She had observed
this young man before; he was often on the beach; reading,
or watching the waves roll in and break. Like herself, he
was alone, and suddenly, an idea occurred to her.

She crept under his umbrella, giving him quite a start,

for he 'had not seen her coming. "Have you got whooping cough?" she inquired earnestly.

Whooping cough? . . . Why in the world should she think he had whooping cough? The young man was amused. Sallie explained. She had seen him alone, not dancing with the others; and so she thought he must have whooping cough. She herself had whooping cough; that was why she was so lonely.

But no, it was not whooping cough that he had; he was troubled in his heart, he told her, because someone he loved very much had died; and that, he explained, was worse than whooping cough. Sallie was sympathetic. She would comfort him and when she grew up to be a lady she would marry him.

Years later, she herself told the story of this meeting, in a book which she called *What Happened to Me*.

The young man under the umbrella was George E. Pickett, of the United States Army. He was born in Richmond in that year when Edgar Poe was falling in love with Elmira Royster and Robert E. Lee had just entered West Point as a cadet. Later Pickett, too, had gone to West Point. And, like Lee, he also had been in the Mexican War. As a young lieutenant he had scaled the parapet of the famous castle of Chapultepec, and under enemy fire had planted there the flag of his country.

Pickett was diverted by the child who had established herself under his umbrella, calmly adopted him and arranging for him his future.

To Sallie whooping cough no longer mattered, for she had her soldier to play with. They were every day together. Sometimes Pickett brought his guitar to the beach and sang to her. At other times he amused her by making little boats of bark and sailing them on pools left by the tide. He showed her how to dam up the water in larger pools, and how to build forts and garrisons in the sand.

Three years later Sallie and her soldier met again. Now he was Captain Pickett, and had come to Fortress Monroe to take passage on the United States transport *St. Louis;* his destination, Puget Sound on the Pacific coast. Sallie watched the ship sail out of the mouth of James River, and grief filled her child-heart.

When it was decided that she was old enough to go away to boarding school, her father took her to the seminary at Lynchburg, and they traveled by train. At Richmond a tall handsome man in the uniform of a colonel came on board. Even had Sallie's heart not been susceptible to all uniforms, because of her absent soldier, she would have noted this man; for none who ever saw him could forget the noble beauty of his presence.

She remembered so well that in her memoirs she recalled the man, and what he said that autumn day on the train. For he was Colonel Robert E. Lee, a man never to be forgotten.

Lee stopped to greet her father, who then turned over a seat, making room for the colonel to sit down. He was a gallant gentleman, making himself charming to Sallie, teasing for one of her curls; those brown curls. But playful as he was with Sallie, Lee was serious enough in his talk with her father. He was home on furlough from Texas, he said, and had been summoned from Arlington in an emergency; ordered to Harpers Ferry, in command of troops to quell John Brown's raid on the arsenal and on the town. But all was now quiet, the colonel said: the hostages had been rescued and the insurgents turned over to the civil authorities, but before this was accomplished, several citizens had been killed by the raiders; one of them a free Negro, who had no part in the uprising. The colonel thought the whole thing but the scheme of a madman; it was not John Brown's first exhibition of violence.

"I am glad we did not have to kill him," the colonel said, "for I believe he is an honest old man . . . a madman, but honest and conscientious."

And Sallie's father said that he had asked his Negro foreman whether he thought John Brown ought to be hanged if the authorities convicted him. The foreman, shaking his head, had replied very slowly: "I know dat po' Marse John

done brok' de law killin' all dem mens; but den . . . even
ef he did . . . don't you think, suh, dat hangin' him would
be a lil' *abrupt?*"

Today, so many years after Robert E. Lee talked to
LaSalle Corbell's father on the train to Lynchburg, "Truth
crown'd with freedom" is at last "from danger free," and
the writer who brings facts out of hiding surely no longer
needs to fear being censured or misunderstood. Gerald Johnson, writing with the modern freedom from danger, and
always with illuminating freedom from inherited prejudice,
has described John Brown as "plainly crazy . . . a homicidal
maniac," who "should have been locked up in an asylum.
. . . His mother had died insane. So had his maternal grandmother. So had one of his aunts. So had five of his cousins.
So did two of his sons." It was fantastic to idealize him;
tragic to have executed a man so obviously mad.

At Lynchburg, where Sallie was left to be educated,
James River, the familiar river of her life, flows past the
town on its way to Richmond, and to Old Point Comfort
where she had first met her own soldier. And in Lynchburg
she was no more than twenty miles from Appomattox Court
House; a placid little place where nothing epochal had ever
occurred.

Meanwhile, a certain young Mrs. Pryor was writing to
her friend, Mrs. Cochran:

"Dear Mrs. Cochran: May I have your receipt for
brandy peaches? You know Roger is speaking all over the
country, trying to win votes for a seat in Congress. I'm not
sure he will be elected, but I *am* sure he will like some brandy
peaches! If he is successful they will enhance the glory of
victory—if he is defeated, they will help to console him."

Into the Washington life that followed his victory, Mrs.
Pryor threw herself completely, her heart full of patriotic
pride in the capital of her country. She even enjoyed listen-

ing to wearying speeches in the House and the Senate. "None of it was very clear," she admitted, "but surely everything was coming out right; everybody was working for the good of his country; we belonged to it and were part of it; this thought glorified all around us."

The Thirty-sixth Congress was long in session; the country still seething over the trial and execution of John Brown; and the men who, Mrs. Pryor so confidently believed, were to "make all come right"—those men were denouncing and insulting each other on the floor of the House and the Senate. And the fateful words "irrepressible conflict" were beginning to be heard.

Then upon a certain December day official Washington presented itself at a fashionable wedding. There, in an armchair at one end of the room, was President Buchanan. He looked aged, Mrs. Pryor thought, as he turned to speak to her: "Do you suppose the house is on fire?" he asked. "I hear an unusual commotion in the hall."

"I will inquire the cause, Mr. President," she said.

When she came back, she stooped over his chair to say gently: "It appears, Mr. President, that South Carolina has seceded from the Union."

Appomattox - the old Jail and site of the Court House

CHAPTER NINETEEN

The Road to Appomattox

"IT APPEARS, Mr. President, that South Carolina has seceded from the Union."

And the president had whispered, like a man stunned: "Madam, might I beg you to have my carriage called."

It was December, and by the first of February, Mississippi, Florida, Alabama, Georgia, Louisiana, and Texas had one by one followed South Carolina out of the Union.

What would Virginia's decision be?

A strong Union had been the dearest wish of George Washington. And now, at the request of Virginia, a "Peace Convention" met in Washington early in February; it was attended by twenty-one states. Its purpose was if possible to save the Union by some compromise on which all could agree. But the convention failed.

In Boston, Edward Everett exclaimed: "The idea of a Civil War, accompanied as it would be, by a servile insurrection, is too monstrous to be entertained for a moment. If our sister states must leave us, in the name of Heaven, let them go in peace."

But that was not to be. Lincoln, the new president, sent out a call for troops to subjugate the seceded states. And now Virginia felt that the great principle of consent of the governed was violated. In accepting the Constitution she had reserved the right to secede, if that should ever seem necessary. In bitter sorrow she now left the Union.

Colonel Robert E. Lee, on active duty in Texas, had been summoned to Washington, to report to General Scott, commander in chief of the United States Army. Lee had been all his life an army man. General Scott was aging. Lee, it was taken for granted, would succeed him. The highest honor for which a soldier might hope would then have been his. But Lee could not accept command of the army that was now to be brought into the field.

"Though I was opposed to secession," he said, "I could take no part in an invasion of the Southern States. . . . If I owned the four million slaves in the South, I would sacrifice them all to the Union," but how could "I draw my sword upon Virginia, my native State?" He felt that he had no choice: he must resign his commission in the United States Army; resign from that service to which, as he put it, he had devoted the best years of his life and all the ability he possessed.

On the same day that Lee sent from Arlington his resignation from the United States Army, Matthew Maury in Washington resigned his commission in the navy. All that he as an individual could do to prevent the war, he had done. He had written personal appeals to the governors of Pennsylvania, New Jersey, Maryland, and Delaware, begging them to throw their influence against the "fratricidal strife"; urging for the South equal rights in the Union, for he, like all

Southerners, had long felt a discrimination against the South in the matter of tariff and in the spending of public funds. But when Virginia seceded, Maury resigned from that position which gave him opportunity to carry on the geographic work that was the passion of his life; he resigned and went to Richmond to offer his services to his state. Like Robert E. Lee, Maury renounced personal prosperity and ambition.

At Lexington, in the Valley of the James a deeply religious, heavy-bearded man with fearless grey-blue eyes was professor of mathematics at the Military Institute. He was a West Point man, and in the Mexican War had been an officer in Magruder's battery. But he had retired from the army, and settled down in the serenity of little Lexington among the lovely hills of the Blue Ridge. Of Scotch-Irish ancestry, he was a devout Presbyterian, to be found every Sunday in his pew. But when Virginia seceded, he resigned his professorship and entered the Confederate Army, where he came to be known as "Stonewall" Jackson.

So, the sons of Virginia laid their all at her feet, to fight —not for slavery, for it is said that scarcely one in thirty of the soldiers of Virginia had ever owned a slave, or ever expected to—but to fight, as they believed, for the principle of government by the consent of the governed. And the men who made this vain sacrifice could not know that their heroic courage and the magnitude of the disaster that came to them would place them among the immortals in the hearts even of those who utterly disagreed with their decision; for they have become a shining company riding in the sky of history; led by a sublime figure mounted on an immortal horse whose name is "Traveller."

Thus the war had come; the tragic war which Thomas Jefferson had so feared that the prospect of it had filled him with terror. Later, General Sherman, of the Union Army, was to say: "The Press made the war."

The Press made the war, and now it was to be fought under leaders who would have saved the nation from it if they could.

Young Mrs. Pryor watched the first troops march out of Petersburg; flags waving and bands playing:

> From Dixieland we'll rout the band,
> That comes to conquer Dixie,
> To arms! To arms! and rout the foe from Dixie,
> Away, away, away down South in Dixie.

The available military strength of the North outnumbered that of the South three to one; in wealth it was nearly doubled; in the North were most of the railroads, most of the factories and the shipyards; the North had a navy with power to keep her harbors open and to close all southern ports. But men marching to the stirring tune of "Dixie" did not count the odds. They did not know that they marched along a road that was to lead to Appomattox.

It is not known why LaSalle Corbell was not at school in Lynchburg on the eighth day of March in the year 1862. Perhaps it was the spring vacation. But whatever the reason, the young lady, on that balmy Saturday, was sitting upon her horse on the riverbank opposite Newport News.

Hundreds of people crowded the bank, and the eyes of all were fixed upon the new ironclad ship, the *Virginia*. The *Virginia* was the old *Merrimac*, a 3,500-ton frigate, burned and sunk when the United States Navy had abandoned the yard at Norfolk.

While Matthew Maury had been mining James River, and experimenting with torpedoes, the *Merrimac* had been raised, rebuilt as an ironclad, and named the *Virginia*. It was because such a ship was something new in the world that people had gathered in great numbers to see her make her trial run. The waiting crowds did not know that this was to be anything more than a tryout; for the *Virginia's* engines had scarcely been tested since their long submersion; not one of her guns had been fired; her crew was as yet untried. In fact, workmen had been busy aboard her up to the moment when she left her dock. It was a strange craft which the crowd saw steaming slowly down Elizabeth River and out into Hampton Roads; an iron ram was bolted to her prow, and her gun deck was covered with a sloping wooden casement to which were attached plates of iron.

Would her armor really safeguard her against gunfire? Or was she just a huge metal coffin in which all aboard would be buried? Of course, she was not designed to fight in heavy seas; her purpose was to protect the harbor of Norfolk. And few had faith that she could do even that. As for use in the river, drawing twenty-two feet of water, she could not be of service much above its mouth. The most that you could say was that she was a hope. . . .

Sallie Corbell, sitting lightly on her horse, her field glasses focused upon the *Virginia,* heard people about her thus questioning.

Yet because the *Virginia* was a hope, however uncertain, the crowd cheered as she slowly steamed out of Elizabeth River, and into Hampton Roads. Breathless they watched her round Craney Island. Straight ahead, about four miles distant slightly to the right, the Federal fleet was anchored off Fortress Monroe; and to the left, at about the same dis-ance, lying in the mouth of James River, were two United States men-of-war—the *Congress* and the *Cumberland.* To-ward these ships the *Virginia* headed.

It was washday on the *Congress* and the *Cumberland,* for you could see clothing hung to dry in the rigging. Daz-zling sunlight glinted on the unruffled water of the flood tide. The air was soft, and warm, as though it were May instead of early March. The boats of the two men-of-war were attached to their swinging booms; and in the boats men lay idly, unsuspicious of trouble; while slowly the *Vir-ginia* approached across the smooth shining water. As she drew nearer, the men in the boats sat up, and at the port-holes faces appeared, staring at the apparition that was the *Virginia.*

Then Sallie, seated on her horse, saw suddenly a "flash of fire, pale against the white day, a puff of smoke drifting, wreathing . . . floating off into space."

So she described it later, and with that apparently innocent puff of smoke there came to her a deep roar, as of a dreadful thunder. Guns from the *Congress* and from the *Cumberland* hurled broadsides against the *Virginia;* and the *Virginia* answered in kind.

The crowds sent up shouts of triumph; seeing the *Virginia* proceed steadily ahead, unharmed; forging ahead toward the *Cumberland,* firing as she went; plowing ahead —straight into the wooden side of the Cumberland.

Then, reversing her engines, the *Virginia* slowly backed away; the batteries from Newport News and the guns of the *Congress* and the *Cumberland* simultaneously pouring fire upon her. Yet all that they could do availed them nothing; every volley glanced off from her sloping metal sides.

But the *Cumberland*—Sallie saw that the *Cumberland* reeled; and then with a great terrible shudder, began to sink; sinking with her guns roaring; going down with all aboard her . . . sinking . . . until at last there was nothing visible above the yellow waters but the Union flag fluttering for a final moment before it also vanished.

"For days we had seen her," Sallie afterward said, "threatening us . . . but it was pitiful to watch her go down."

The *Cumberland* was gone, and laboriously the *Virginia* was manipulating her rusty engines to turn back and attack the *Congress* which, in trying to escape, had run aground.

Three Federal frigates appeared, coming from Old Point Comfort—the *Minnesota,* the *St. Lawrence,* and the *Roanoke* —hurrying to the rescue of the *Congress* which was now in flames; the flames "like banners flapping in the rigging." Her defense was gallant but at last she hoisted the white flag of surrender.

The *Virginia* then sent out a launch to take off men from the burning ship; and two Confederate gunboats also went to her aid, under heavy fire from the frigates and the shore batteries.

At midnight the magazine aboard the *Congress* exploded; and briefly, before her end, the *Congress* stood forth, a ship of fire in the darkness.

Sallie Corbell was up early on the following morning. Her uncle was just putting off in his boat, and she ran to ask if she might not go with him. Of course, she might *not* go.

Her uncle stepped aboard, and Sallie stepped after him. The boat was off before he turned and saw her.

"You little daredevil, you! I've a good mind to drown you." But a laugh went with those ferocious words.

And so it came about that Sallie saw the first battle between two ironclad ships ever to be fought in the world. For a second armored craft had arrived during the night. It was Ericsson's invention, the *Monitor,* come down from New York.

There had been rumor of the strangeness of the *Monitor,* but no one had expected it to be half so queer at it actually was. "It's just a tin can on a shingle," somebody said; for its circular revolving turret rose from a flat, water-level deck; that was all there was except a low square pilothouse. The whole thing was not a quarter the size of the *Virginia*; but more easily handled, and with the advantage of drawing only twelve feet.

In the battle of the previous day the *Virginia's* smokestack had been perforated, and her prow had been broken off in ramming the *Cumberland;* so that it was like a dilapidated fighting cock that she returned to the fray. Now for four hours on that Sunday morning in Hampton Roads, the pygmy *Monitor* and the *Virginia* bombarded each other. Once, when the *Virginia* ran aground, the *Monitor* circled round and round her, seeking in vain some vulnerable point.

Finally the *Monitor* turned in the direction of Fortress Monroe to replenish her ammunition, and the *Virginia,* unable to pursue her into low water, steamed back to her base while the tide was yet high enough to let her pass. The two ships never again met in battle; but the contest which Sallie Corbell that day watched from her uncle's boat changed forever the naval warfare of the world.

The London *Times* exclaimed that on the day before the *Monitor* met the *Virginia* England had possessed one hundred and forty-nine first-class warships, but of that number on the day after the battle in Hampton Roads one hundred and forty-seven were no longer of the first class; since only two of the fleet could do battle against ironclads.

Young Mrs. Pryor and Sallie Corbell were living in Richmond at the time of the battle of Seven Pines. Sallie's soldier, returned from Seattle, to fight for the Confederacy, and Mrs. Pryor's husband, both now generals, had fought at Williamsburg, and side by side they headed their brigades in this battle of Seven Pines, which, in the irony of war, took its name from a clump of pines standing green and fragrant in a serene landscape converted by war into a scene of horror.

Throughout the days of fighting the thunder of guns shook the heart of Richmond, while on the field marked by seven pines McClellan's army of a hundred thousand met the Confederate force of sixty-three thousand.

Then the wounded and the dead poured into Richmond. Hospitals overflowed into private homes, and black streamed from doors where the dead lay.

Sallie thought she had never seen roses so lovely as in that June when the battle of Seven Pines was fought; that June when ambulances left a trail of blood in the streets through which they passed; when in the dead-wagons stiffened bodies were heaped one upon another; when those of the wounded who were able to walk marched weary and sick into the city. But the roses seemed never to have bloomed so bright in the gardens, while from the open windows there came often a scream of mortal agony.

Anesthetics—morphine and chloroform, opium—were

contraband of war. The South had only such merciful relief
as could now and then be smuggled through Federal lines.

Could it be that Richmond had ever been gay, that once
from its open windows there had floated light laughter and
song? Only the mockingbirds singing in the gardens and on
the chimneytops seemed to remember song:

> Listen to the mockingbird,
> Listen to the mockingbird.
> The mockingbird is singing all the day.

The *Virginia* and the *Monitor*, the sinking *Cumberland*,
and the burning *Congress* had been great spectacles of warfare; their death and agony had not been present to the
eyes of those who looked on. But the battle of Seven Pines
flooded Richmond with all the hideous anguish that is war.

Mrs. Pryor, like other women of Richmond, became,
overnight, a nurse. And through the crowded hospitals there
often passed the powerful black figure of the slave Jasper.
Soldiers who were sufficiently well to listen loved to hear
his picturesque version of the Bible stories; his deep tender
voice lifted in song took them back to the plantation homes
so dear to them, and his reverent faith brought them peace.

At Gaines's Mill—the name is placidly suggestive of
fruition, of sowing and harvesting, of farmers bringing their
grain to be converted into flour and meal—on a level field
of oats at the foot of a wooded cliff, the Confederates attacked McClellan's army which defended the cliff with tiers
of artillery and infantry. And charging at the head of his
brigade, Pickett was shot from his horse and a ball penetrated
his shoulder. But he led on, cheering though his arm hung
helpless, while his horse followed as if its master still guided
the reins. When the doctor came up he ordered Pickett from
the field; insisting that the ball should be immediately
extracted.

"No, doctor, take the bullet out here; quick! I must go
back. See, my men need me."

The doctor obeyed, and Pickett went back into the

battle until, weakened from loss of blood, he had to be sent home to Richmond; leaving his brigade to continue with Lee's army in pursuit of McClellan's retreating forces.

It was September before Pickett was able to return to the army; the September of Lincoln's warning of Emancipation.

In that month, too, Sallie went back to school; but in a year she was to be graduated, and then—so they planned in Pickett's weeks of illness—then they were to be married.

But before that marriage took place there were to be yet other battles. . . .

In early May of the following year, at the battle of Chancellorsville, Lee with sixty-five thousand men defeated the Union forces, under Hooker with a hundred and thirty-two thousand men. But Stonewall Jackson was mortally wounded. It was night, and Jackson with several of his staff had ridden out to reconnoiter, and on returning he was struck down by mistaken fire from the watchful sentries of one of his own regiments, and severely wounded. It was necessary to amputate one arm, and after a week of great suffering he died. The devotion of his men was such that he had absolute control over them. He required of them nothing that he did not exact of himself: all that they endured he endured. He was famous for what has been called "the portentous rapidity of his marches," delivering battles, people said, "as a thunder-cloud discharges bolts." His every decision was decided by prayer, and his faith in Lee was second only to his faith in God. "I would follow Lee anywhere, blindfold," he had once said. His loss to Lee was beyond words.

It had been Stonewall's wish to be buried at Lexington. They carried his body to mourning Richmond, where it lay in state before being taken by train to Lynchburg, and there transferred to the packet boat *Marshall*—the "queen" of the James and Kanawha Canal boats. The *Marshall* proceeded then by canal up James River; and someone has said that the tramping feet of the horses on the towpath took the place of muffled drums in a funeral march; the journey made in such

silent solemnity that even the wind in the trees and the gentle
lapping of the river against the sides of the boat were recorded and remembered.

At the terminus of navigation on North River, the
Marshall was met by a corps of cadets from the Military Institute, who bore the coffin to Jackson's old lecture room, and
placed it before the chair from which he used to deliver the
lectures to his classes.

On the following day Stonewall Jackson was buried in
the little cemetery at Lexington. And two months later Lee
was defeated at Gettysburg.

In that same summer, Sallie Corbell was assembling a
Confederate bride's trousseau. She had dresses of home-woven
fabrics dyed with homemade dyes. Buttons were carved from
peach stones. Trimmings were made from various sorts of
seeds, and laces were hand-knit of thread spun from flax.
She had a poke-shaped hat of grey straw, braided by the
family servants. Another hat was fashioned from the lace-
like tissue lining of gourds. Milkweed balls supplied its deco-
ration, and picked cotton shaped into balls and tinted any
color you liked furnished bunches of grapes or pink roses
which were very becoming. Her party dresses were made from
the court robes of her great-grandmother, and friends presented a wedding gown of white satin, which became, in a
manner, a community wedding gown, used by succeeding
brides.

So at last LaSalle Corbell was married to Major General
George E. Pickett; the tall soldier with, now, the memory of
Gettysburg in his eyes.

And in their honor guns were fired, bugles blew, and
bells chimed; while for a moment war paused, for these two
who had loved so long, so deeply, and so romantically.

"I have a queer feeling in my stomach, mamma . . .
No, it doesn't ache . . . but it feels like a nutmeg grater."

It was one of Mrs. Pryor's little brood, her son Theodorick Bland, who was speaking. "A queer feeling . . . like
a nutmeg grater."

His mother well understood what was the trouble; for
famine had come to Petersburg. Once there had been flocks
of pigeons, but they were gone now. Constant cannonading
had driven the fish from the river. The very rats and mice
had disappeared. Venturing one day under shellfire to the
market, Mrs. Pryor found on sale only some jugs and cakes
of sorghum molasses, and a single frozen cabbage.

The long siege of Petersburg had begun.

General Grant's army had come down into Tidewater
Virginia. In trying to hold him back from Richmond, General Lee had fought his last great successful battle—the battle
of Cold Harbor.

But the Cold Harbor victory had delayed only briefly
the inevitable siege which had now begun; it had but put
off for a little the doom of Richmond and of Petersburg. For
within a fortnight Grant had transported his great army
across the James, uniting with the forces under General
Butler. And at Petersburg the combined armies confronted
what remained of Lee's Army of Northern Virginia.

The siege was on and the famine began.

Soldiers were hungry, so weak that the slightest wound
was almost certain to mean death. Horses were dying of
starvation. And Mrs. Pryor's little son was saying that his
stomach felt like a nutmeg grater.

Federal guns swept the city, their shells screaming,
ricocheting, bursting. People made dugouts where they might
take refuge in times of the heaviest bombardment.

"Grant knows all about *me*," General Lee said one day
to General Pryor. Actually he had sent a message to say that
he knew what General Lee had for breakfast every morning.
And Lee's reply had been that surely that could not be pos-

sible; for if he did know, he would certainly send him something better. "Yes, Grant knows all about me," Lee said. "And I know too little about Grant. Now, General Pryor, you were a schoolboy here, and have hunted in all the by-paths around Petersburg. Knowing the country better than any of us, you are the best man for this important duty."

The idea was that General Pryor should head a small squad of men and scout the country, to learn of Grant's operations. It was dangerous business. And at the end of November, General Wilcox came to tell Mrs. Pryor that her husband had been taken.

"You have to know it," he said, and she saw that his face quivered. "You have to know it. The general won't return. The Yankees caught him this morning."

And through the window she saw her husband's horse, standing riderless.

General Wilcox tried to console her with hope that he might soon be exchanged. But when he had gone she could feel no hope; she huddled over the fire, sick with fear.

Then—as she often told the story—the click of an officer's spurs aroused her. An officer came to say that General Lee sent her his "affectionate sympathy."

Outside in the yard she saw a grey figure mounted upon a grey horse—General Lee on his horse Traveller; waiting until his message had been delivered, when, not intruding upon her grief, he rode slowly back toward the lines.

And only the enemy could tell Mrs. Pryor her husband's fate. She could only hope, and somehow provide food for her children.

The first information was printed in the New York *Herald,* which stated that a rebel officer, waving a paper for exchange, had appeared in front of the Union lines. He had been taken, and proved to be the "famous Roger A. Pryor." Later, a "personal" inserted in a northern paper told Mrs. Pryor that her husband was imprisoned in Fort Lafayette. After some weeks elapsed she began to get letters sent to her through the lines.

In the long months of the siege of Petersburg, General Lee often passed Mrs. Pryor's door, and she thought how he had aged under the agony of the hopeless, desperate responsibility he carried. Jeb Stuart, who, Lee said, had never brought him a false piece of news—Jeb Stuart was dead. Stonewall Jackson, whom Lee called his "right arm," was dead. They and many others on whom he had relied were gone. She knew that he took upon himself a responsibility almost beyond endurance. She knew that when there had been defeat, he had assumed the blame. After Gettysburg he had said: "All this has been my fault. It is I that have lost and you must help me out of it the best way you can."

As he rode past her door, she knew that he was breaking his heart. He had but forty-five thousand men; men crazed with hunger. Grant had a hundred and sixty thousand, well-fed and fit.

Day after day Mrs. Pryor watched Lee riding by mounted on Traveller, the horse that was dear to all the South because of faithful service to his master.

Then, on a morning in March, Traveller stopped before her door and General Lee came into the room where she sat sewing. He stopped and took her little girl up in his arms. Mrs. Pryor, raising her hazel eyes, saw that he had news which he would break to her; yet because of the light in his face she was not alarmed.

He spoke of her husband. "You let the Yankees catch him," he said. "Now he is coming back to be with you again, on parole until he is exchanged. You must take better care of him in the future."

After a few minutes' talk Lee walked to her window, and stood there looking out.

"Is it worth my while, general," Mrs. Pryor asked, "to put the plowshare into those fields?"

"Plant your seeds, madam," he said. And then he added: "The doing it will be some reward."

She thought then that he must have hope . . . a little hope, perhaps.

But in just twenty days the long road was to arrive at Appomattox.

In Washington, General Pryor received his parole from President Lincoln, who remembered that at Manassas, when Pryor had captured a camp of Federal wounded, he had at once paroled them and their surgeons and ambulances.

Lincoln, lonely in the isolation of his crushing responsibilities, talked freely to this paroled Confederate: of his grief at the failure of the Hampton Roads conference, where, on board a ship lying in the harbor, he had met representatives from the president of the Confederacy, in a vain attempt to negotiate a peace. It was obvious that Lincoln hoped the Southern people might reopen negotiations. But Destiny was not to be turned aside from the road to Appomattox. There had followed the final battle at Petersburg. And General Lee was leading the Army of Northern Virginia in retreat.

Jefferson Davis had fled, and Richmond was burning.

George Pickett's young wife watched the wind carry the flames from building to building. She saw the fire devour warehouses and shops, public buildings, and mansions which had known Washington and Jefferson, Patrick Henry, John Marshall, Poe, and the notorious Aaron Burr. Above the great roar of the flames, and the crash of falling buildings, there were cries of terror and of agony. Drunken, looting mobs added horror.

On the following day, Federal troops took possession of the city, raising once more the Stars and Stripes above the Capitol.

And Lincoln was unexpectedly again in Virginia, coming by river steamer to City Point; for the purpose of an interview with Grant. Federal victory was near, and Lincoln's mind full of the future. "Let them down easy," he said. He would not hear of persecution when the war was over. He would have no part in vindictiveness or hate. He believed that slavery was the sin not of the South alone, but of the nation. He had wanted to bring the war to an end by offering four hundred million dollars to the South in payment for their slaves; provided they accepted the Union and abolition. When his Cabinet refused, he had said sorrowfully: "You are all opposed to me."

On the eve of victory he was insisting that there should be no hatred, no persecution.

Lee

CHAPTER TWENTY

He Smote His Hands Together

O<small>N</small> the morning of Sunday, the ninth of April, General Lee dressed himself in his best. In the field he ordinarily wore a plain grey uniform, high cavalry boots, and a wide-brimmed grey hat, low on the forehead; only the stars on his collar marked his rank. But on the morning of April ninth he put on dress uniform, a red silk sash, gold spurs, and a sword in a handsomely decorated scabbard.

He did not trouble about breakfast.

There was a little corn meal; and a small tin can in which each man in the order of military precedence boiled his share of the meal; eating this gruel as soon as it was cool enough, and then passing the can to the next in line. But no one remembered seeing General Lee eat anything. While others were cooking their gruel over a small fire of twigs, the general was dressing himself in his best.

It had been long since the army had seen him in anything but his simple field kit. And now on this desperate morning he amazed them by the elegant dress which so became his distinguished person.

"I have probably to be General Grant's prisoner and thought I must make my best appearance," he explained quietly.

When you see him standing there it seems incredible that such as he should speak of being any man's prisoner.

Two years before, Viscount Wolseley had visited Lee in camp at the front; and was so deeply impressed that he said afterward: "I have met many of the great men of my time, but Lee alone impressed me with the feeling that I was in the presence of a man who was cast in a grander mould, and made of different and finer metal than all other men. He is stamped upon my memory as a being apart and superior to all others . . . I have met but two men who realize my ideas of what a true hero should be: my friend, Charles Gordon was one, General Lee was the other."

Gordon of Khartoum and Lee of Virginia were thus linked in Wolseley's mind.

Sitting in a tent at the Confederate front, Wolseley had had a long talk with Robert E. Lee.

Lee had explained that he hated slavery, but that he thought it wicked to give freedom suddenly to some millions of people, incapable yet of using it with profit to themselves or to the country. But it was not, he said, for this that he fought; he fought, he believed, for those same rights which had led George Washington into revolution.

Now, on that Sunday morning in April, in the green gay spring, with peach and cherry and apple trees in bloom, dogwood white in the woods and everywhere frogs piping, Robert E. Lee stood among his officers, saying that probably, before the day was done, he would be General Grant's prisoner.

In his conduct of the war Lee had never been free to act entirely as he thought best. For the past year he had wished to lead his army to the base of the Blue Ridge, where he might have found food for the men and for their horses; at the same time drawing General Grant into the interior, away from James River, by which food and recruits were continually supplied to the great Union army.

But Petersburg was the key to the defenses of Richmond, and Richmond was the capital of the Confederacy. It was decided that the capital must not fall.

So Lee had remained entrenched about Petersburg, his men on less than half rations, then on less than one-third rations; a little meal each day, and every few days a small portion of bacon. They were ragged—these hungry men—and thousands of them were barefoot; their horses were starving; and for all this Lee's heart was breaking, though no disaster had yet daunted his spirit.

In February President Lincoln had come down to Hampton Roads to confer with the Confederacy, but nothing had come of their discussions.

And in March it was conceded that the one hope was to withdraw Lee's army and unite it with Johnston's forces which were to come up from North Carolina. But if this were to be done, it must be done quickly, for already Sheridan was marching through Virginia, and might at any moment cut off communications to the south. The sole hope lay in speed.

The Confederates must strike Sheridan before Grant could join him.

Speed . . . only speed could save them. And already the heavy spring rains were making of every road a slough of despond.

It was just a few days after Lee had stood at Mrs. Pryor's window, looking out over the fields, saying, "Plant your seed . . . The doing it will be some reward," that he had ordered Pickett to march at once to Five Forks, some twelve miles away, to prevent capture of the Southside Railroad.

At the same time the army must be immediately withdrawn. But before that was accomplished Grant had made another assault. Lee held his position throughout the day; and then, in the protecting blackness of night, with no beat of drum, or bugle call, Lee began the retreat, his heart heavy with the news just come, that at Five Forks Pickett's forces had been crushed. And General Hill had been killed.

So, in rain and darkness, what was left of the Army of Northern Virginia moved out of the lines about Richmond and Petersburg, with orders to destroy all bridges after passing over them.

The plan to join Johnston was desperate; but not altogether without hope.

The retreating forces—from Richmond and Petersburg, and what remained of Pickett's division—were to proceed to Amelia Court House, some days' march inland. Lee had commanded that rations and ammunition should meet them there. From Amelia—with all possible haste—they were to hurry south to Danville, to unite with Johnston.

This was the plan with which Lee began the retreat.

And on that retreat a young Englishman marched with Lee's army. When it was all over, he told what he saw. He saw mules and horses give up the struggle. He saw their abandoned wagons burned that they might not be taken by the pursuing Federals. He saw famished soldiers drop from exhaustion; their rifles falling from hands too weak to carry them longer. Men, mules, and horses were laid down side by side to die. Their dead bodies cluttered the roads, and from the blazing wagons ammunition, set off by the flames, burst with deafening, terrifying roar, and great pillars of smoke rose through the grey rain. And behind was the oncoming Union Army, well-fed and fit.

But at Amelia Court House there would be rations. Thirty thousand Confederates, faint with hunger, marched, thinking of the food that would be waiting at Amelia.

All this was written upon General Lee's mind to be forever remembered.

The army reached Amelia in the early morning. But in Amelia it was found that no rations had arrived. Supplies of ammunition were waiting, but there was no food.

Lee sent out wagons to scour the countryside, begging meat, meal, corn. Time—precious time—must be lost while he awaited their return; and from all directions the Federals were advancing upon them.

Yet there remained spirit in Lee's weary, hungering, disappointed army, spirit to cheer their commander; spirit even for the banter and laughter so dear to the gallant Army of Northern Virginia.

They waited for the wagons another day; again it was raining. In Richmond, Union forces had taken possession of the city which was in flames. The wagons which had gone out with Lee's appeal for food were coming back, most of them empty; for the farms, too, were destitute. And, below Amelia, Federal troops blocked the way south. There now remained but one direction in which he might move; he might advance along the road which, passing through Appomattox, led to Lynchburg. He would telegraph to Lynchburg to have rations sent to meet them; and he would march the army; he would march it throughout the night; for messengers had brought news that on his very heels were the Federal armies of the James and the Potomac. Without respite, his own weary men must march, march, march, through the deep mud of the rain-soaked roads. March— they stumbled now, rather than marched.

Yet, on the next day, as so often on that long retreat, they rallied against Federals blocking the way. So the Army of Northern Virginia fought as it retreated.

And to the end, on the very eve of Appomattox, the Confederate soldiers sang:

> The race is not to them, that's got
> The longest legs to run,
> Nor the battle to the people
> That shoots the biggest gun.

It was after dark on the fifth day of the retreat that a courier came with a letter from General Grant to General Lee.

General Grant expressed himself as sure that the results of the past week must convince General Lee of the hopelessness of further resistance. "I feel that it is so," Grant wrote, "and regard it as my duty to shift from myself the responsibility of further effusion of blood, by asking of you the surrender of that portion of the C.S. Army, known as the Army of Northern Virginia."

Lee replied at once that, while he could not agree on the hopelessness of resistance, he shared Grant's desire to avoid bloodshed, and he therefore asked the terms of surrender which Grant would offer.

And in the morning Lee moved his army forward, toward Appomattox where he hoped to find that rations had arrived from Lynchburg. If he could get food, he might even yet march his men by another route south to join General Johnston.

It was Saturday, a bright sunlit day; so quiet a day that almost it seemed as though they had outstripped the Federals in that race for Appomattox.

At dusk there came to Lee, on the march, a letter from General Grant, giving the terms of surrender; they were simple, requiring merely that the "officers and men who were surrendered should be disqualified to bear arms until properly exchanged."

Lee made immediate reply; he did not think that the emergency demanded surrender, but he would be pleased to meet General Grant for discussion on the following morning at ten o'clock "on the old stage road to Richmond, between the picket lines of the two armies."

That night Lee's army camped in the woods about two miles from Appomattox and twelve miles south of James River. With the fall of night they saw themselves surrounded by a ring of glittering campfires. The Federal forces lay now across their line of advance. If they were cavalry it might be possible to cut a passage for the army. But if they were infantry, then Lee feared he must surrender.

With this knowledge he rose early and dressed himself carefully in his best.

Yet he still hoped it might be cavalry that blocked the way. Fog lay upon the scene, veiling the truth.

A general sent out to investigate was attacked by cavalry and a strong force of infantry. "I have fought my corps to a frazzle," he reported, "I can do nothing more unless I am supported."

"Then," said General Lee, knowing support impossible, "then there is nothing for me to do but to go and see General Grant, and I would rather die a thousand deaths."

"Oh, general," an officer exclaimed, "what will history say of the surrender of the army in the field?"

"They will say hard things of us. They will not understand how we were overwhelmed by numbers. But that is not the question, colonel: the question is, is it right to surrender this army. If it is right, then I will take all the responsibility."

He might have sent officers to discuss the business of surrender. Grant, in order that Lee might be spared the humiliation, had suggested it. But Lee did not shirk.

And out of the far past, like an echo in the halls of memory, there come to you the words of Light-Horse Harry: "Robert was always good."

Thus Lee, taking an escort of two members of his staff and their orderlies, rode to meet General Grant.

In the parlor of the house chosen for the conference he waited.

And in half an hour General Grant arrived. There came with him some dozen Federal officials. The expectant hush of the moment was broken by their arrival, by their jangling spurs and clanking swords. Removing a pair of yellow gloves, Grant came directly forward and shook hands with Lee, who was standing at the end of the room opposite the door.

They had not met since the Mexican War, and the

conversation began with some talk of that campaign. It was Lee who first spoke of the momentous matter which had now brought them together.

Grant again stated the terms as Lee had understood them; and at Lee's suggestion they were put into writing. Grant lit a pipe, and while he wrote, puffs of smoke drifted upward in the room.

When the document was put into Lee's hands, he took out his spectacles and wiped them carefully with his handkerchief; and then slowly read Grant's conditions of surrender: ". . . officers to give their individual parole not to take up arms against the Government of the United States . . . arms, artillery and public property to be stacked and turned over to the officer appointed. This will not embrace the side-arms of the officers; nor their private horses or baggage. This done . . . officers are then to be allowed to return to their homes not to be disturbed by the United States authority so long as they observe their paroles."

"That will have a very happy effect," Lee said.

Grant asked for suggestions. Had Lee any suggestions?

Yes, there was just one. In the Confederate Army, he said, the cavalrymen provided their own horses. They would want them to plow ground for planting corn.

General Grant agreed; he would give orders that those who owned horses or mules might take them home.

Marshall was then directed to write out Lee's acceptance of the terms.

And Lee spoke of the Federal prisoners he was holding— a thousand or more such prisoners whom he was unable to feed properly, and he explained that he was expecting several trainloads of rations from Lynchburg; he would like to have them for his men when they arrived. He did not know then that his trains had been captured by Sheridan.

As to the prisoners, Grant said he would, of course, be glad to receive them in the Federal lines; and he would send over to Lee twenty-five thousand rations.

"That will be a great relief."

Then Lee signed the acceptance which Marshall had written out.

So ended the long road to Appomattox.

And Marshall, grandson of the great chief justice and aide-de-camp to General Lee, in describing the scene of surrender, would have you know that he "cannot give any idea of the kindness and the generosity and magnanimity of Grant and the officers with him."

Among the Federal officers who waited outside the house there was General George A. Forsyth. He saw Lee as he came from the interview. He watched him cross the porch to the head of the steps. He saw him pause there, and the look in Lee's eyes impressed General Forsyth. "His eyes," he says, were "fixed in the direction of the little valley . . . in which his army lay."

Standing at the head of the steps, Lee "slowly drew on his gauntlets, smiting his gloved hands into each other several times . . . evidently utterly oblivious of his surroundings. Then, apparently recalling his thoughts, he glanced deliberately right and left, and not seeing his horse, he called in a hoarse, half-choked voice: 'Orderly! Orderly!' "

And Forsyth describes how, when the soldier brought the horse, Lee went down the steps and stood at Traveller's head while he was being bridled. "He reached up," Forsyth says, "and drew the horse's forelock out from under the brow-band, parted and smoothed it, and then gently patted the grey charger's forehead in an absent-minded way, as one who loves horses, but whose thoughts are far away."

Then, still like a man in a dream, he mounted, and as he settled into the saddle, Forsyth heard break from him "unguardedly . . . a long, low, deep sigh, almost like a groan in its intensity."

And at once, through a countryside fair with blossoming fruit trees, Lee rode away . . . back to his army.

When they saw him coming, they began to cheer; then seeing the look on his face, they cried out to know if they were surrendered.

Lee halted. "We have fought the war together," he said, "and I have done the best I could for you. You will be paroled and go to your homes until exchanged."

Tears filled his eyes.

"General, we'll fight 'em yet!"

"General, say the word, and we'll go in and fight 'em yet."

And they stretched out their hands to him, hoping to touch him, or failing that, to touch Traveller; to pat the horse which was inseparable in their minds from his master.

Then Lee turned aside from the road into an apple orchard; there walking back and forth in the warm bright sunshine, he fought the despair that welled up within him.

It was sunset before he rode on toward his headquarters, under the great white oak.

And one who saw him has described how General Lee rode between "two solid walls of men . . . formed along the whole distance . . . awaiting his coming. . . . As soon as he entered the avenue of these old soldiers . . . who had stood at their duty . . . in so many battles, wild heartfelt cheers arose which so touched General Lee that tears filled his eyes and trickled down his cheeks."

When the men saw his tears, their "cheers changed to choking sobs . . . each group began in the same way with cheers, and ended in the same way with sobs, all along the route to his headquarters."

And they were thus moved, not by the surrender of their lost hopes, but by love for the general who broke his heart for them.

News of Lee's surrender reached Abraham Lincoln in Washington, on his return from City Point. He had thought that he could never again be glad. Now the load was lifted, and he was happy. It might be given to him to prevent hatred and persecution. The very city bloomed as if to celebrate his joy, the gardens fragrant with lilac blossoms.

Then General Grant arrived in Washington and was invited to be present at the Cabinet meeting which met on the morning of April fourteenth; there he heard Lincoln urge liberal terms of peace, declaring that he would have no part in revenge.

And in the evening Lincoln went to the theater, his face serenely joyful that there was to be peace.

Three days later news came to James River that Abraham Lincoln had been shot at the theater, and that he was dead.

"My God!" George Pickett cried. "My God! The South has lost her best friend and protection in this her direst hour of need!"

It was just seven days before his death that Lincoln had left City Point. The Confederate prisoners there had cheered him on his return from visiting Richmond. The last journey of his life had been that trip to James River; and he had come with "malice toward none," with "charity toward all." He had walked in the streets of stricken Richmond, and had visited Petersburg during the siege. On his way back to Washington his eyes had rested upon the tender green and the magic whiteness of dogwood along the riverbanks.

"I want you to meet Mr. Lincoln," Grant had said to Lee on the day after the surrender at Appomattox. "Whatever you and he agree upon will be satisfactory to the reasonable people of North and South."

The bullet fired in Washington had made that impossible.

Old Ferry on the James at Indian Rock.

CHAPTER TWENTY-ONE

Out of Defeat

THE VIRGINIA through which the soldiers traveled to their homes, after stacking their arms at Appomattox, was a land stripped bare, a battleground where railroads and bridges had been destroyed, homes and barns burned, farmyards raided; a land whose money was now so much worthless paper.

Virginia was prostrate.

After the surrender, Mrs. Pryor returned to the home outside Petersburg from which she had fled on the morning of Grant's final assault. In the last years of her life she often described to me the devastation she found: "Grass and flowers were gone, the carcasses of six dead cows lay in the yard. . . . The evening air was heavy with the odor of decaying flesh. As the front door opened millions of flies swarmed forth. . . . Within, pieces of fat pork lay on the floors, molasses trickled from the library shelves . . . nothing was left in the house except one chair out of which the bottom had been cut, and one bed-stead fastened together with bayonets. Picture frames were piled against the wall. Every one was empty. One family portrait of an old lady was hanging on the wall, with a sabre-cut across her face."

Mrs. Pryor's old servant, Aunt Jinny, appeared and helped put the children to bed, on quilts laid down upon the floor. She described how, in the absence of the family, the house had been sacked, and the cellar been dug up, seeking treasure; the outhouses, she said, were full of strange Negroes, come from nobody knew where.

Then, while her children slept, Mrs. Pryor watched beside her window, afraid to lie down to sleep. Heavy rain fell, and then the moon slowly straggled out. Its light revealed the uncovered arm of a dead soldier buried just outside the window where Mrs. Pryor watched.

In the weeks following the surrender Lee's soldiers turned to him asking what they should do.

"Go home," he said, "all you boys who fought with me. Go home and help to build up the shattered fortunes of our State . . . make her great again . . . all must get to work, and if they cannot do what they prefer, they must do what they can."

For himself, he would set Southerners an example of loyalty to the Union. He refused the invitation of an English nobleman who offered him for life a "mansion and an estate commensurate with his individual merits and the greatness of an historic family."

He was deeply appreciative. But he refused: "I cannot desert my native State in the hour of her adversity. I must abide her fortunes and share her fate."

Many offers came to him, but he declined them all. "I am looking," he said, "for some little quiet home in the woods, where I can procure shelter and my daily bread. . . ."

It was at the end of the summer following the surrender that an offer was made to Lee which he did accept. He was elected president of Washington College at Lexington. In the final year of the war, Hunter's soldiers had sacked Lexington; the college library had been broken up, and the buildings so wrecked that they were almost uninhabitable. Only four professors remained, and about forty students.

Still Lee accepted the position. He said that he had led the young men of the South in battle; he had seen many of them die; now he was comforted that his remaining years might be given to training other young men "to do their duty in life." He was fitted for the task by his experience as superintendent of West Point.

But the vengeful minority grudged him even so poor a position as president of a college in ruins.

"Satan," they said, "wouldn't have him to open the door for fresh arrivals." They thought the president of the United States should forbid his holding such an office.

But this time the agitators failed, and Lee, mounting Traveller, rode to Lexington.

The town of Lexington, on the western side of the Blue Ridge, stands on the bank of North River, and North River flows southward into the James; with all about a lovely world of mountains. And Cornelia MacDonald of Lexington was at her window on the day when General Lee rode into the town, come to take over the presidency of Washington College. "I saw him," she says, "riding on his old war horse, Traveller . . . erect and straight, looking like the great old soldier that he was . . . his bright dark eyes and kind smile lighting up a face that was noble as well as handsome. . . .

"Slowly he passed, raising his brown slouch hat to those on the pavements who recognized him, and not appearing conscious that he more than anybody else was the object of attention. He wore his military coat divested of all marks of rank; even the military buttons had been removed. He doubtless would have laid it aside altogether, but it was the only one he had, and he was too poor to buy another."

So opened the final chapter of General Lee's life, and at the same time began the terrible period of reconstruction in the South: the era of the carpetbaggers, like a horde of vermin infesting the conquered states; betraying the last wishes of Abraham Lincoln; the carpetbaggers, symbols of "forty years of economic bondage" for the South.

The South, Lee prophetically feared, "has yet to suffer many evils and it will require time, patience and fortitude to heal her affliction." Silence and patience, he thought her only course. But he believed that one day reason and charity would prevail.

His own consolation he found in his work for the now wrecked little college which bore the name of the man whom he had worshiped all his life—Washington.

At Washington's death it was found that he had willed to this college—then known as Liberty Hall Academy—the shares which he held in the James River Company; the will explaining: ". . . as it has always been a source of serious regret with me to see the youth of the United States sent to foreign countries for the purpose of education, often before their minds were formed, or they had imbibed any adequate ideas of the happiness of their own; contracting too frequently not only habits of dissipation and extravagance, but principles unfriendly to republican government, and to the true and genuine liberties of mankind . . . for these reasons it has been my ardent wish to see a plan devised on a liberal scale . . . to do away with local attachments and State prejudices, as far as the nature of things would, or indeed ought to admit, from our national councils."

Washington, at Lexington, and later Jefferson, at Charlottesville, both expressed their belief in the supreme importance of education in the functioning of our form of government.

And now, Robert E. Lee set to work to repair the buildings of Washington College, to plant the grounds in trees and shrubs and roses. The number of students was increased, new professors were added and new courses of study. And always, everywhere, Lee urged: "Make your children Americans."

He would not consciously dwell on the past, nor fear the future; he believed that human virtue should equal human calamity; he spoke little of the war, and always reluctantly; his genius for delight in simple things, his gentle humor shone upon the daily life of the college, and of his home, as light plays upon the surface of a river; while, beneath, the deep water flows unseen.

You feel that only with Traveller did he permit himself really to remember. He and Traveller had been through it together; together they had known the brilliant victories, together they had known defeat. Now, still together, they went out into the lovely hills about Lexington. "Traveller and I," he said, "whenever practicable wander into the mountains, and enjoy sweet confidence."

An artist once wrote him, asking for a description of Traveller. His reply was that if he were an artist he would picture him as of fine proportions, a muscular figure with a broad forehead, delicate ears, and a quick eye. And if he were a poet, Lee said, he would sing of Traveller's endurance of toil, of hunger, thirst, heat and cold, and of the dangers and sufferings through which he had passed.

But, being neither artist nor poet, Lee adds that he can only say that Traveller is a Confederate grey, and that he carried him through the Seven Days' Battles around Richmond, the Second Manassas, Sharpsburg, Fredericksburg; through to the end at Appomattox, and that in all that time the saddle was scarcely off his back.

And you must know, Lee concludes, "the comfort he is to me in my present retirement."

Once, when absent from home, Lee wrote: "How is Traveller? Tell him I miss him dreadfully, and have repented of our separation but once—and that is the whole time since we parted."

One day, riding through the mountain forest, he met a solitary old Confederate soldier, also riding through the forest. When the man recognized Lee he stopped:

"General Lee, I am powerful glad to see you, and I feel like cheering you."

Then the old soldier waved his hat high: "Hurrah for General Lee!" he shouted. And when the general had said good-bye and ridden away, the cheers followed him until he was out of hearing. "Hurrah for General Lee! . . . Hurrah! . . ."

Lee himself described the incident to his family, and his son, Robert, relates it in the *Recollections and Letters* of his father.

When his son, Fitzhugh, was married, Lee was persuaded to go to Petersburg to the wedding. He went reluctantly, for he had melancholy recollections of the place, but his presence at the marriage was so much desired that he could not refuse. And all along the way people crowded to see him, and in Petersburg the streets were thronged.

After he went home to Lexington, he wrote Fitzhugh how happy the experience had been. "When our armies were in front of Petersburg," he explained, "I suffered so much in body and mind on account of the good townspeople, especially on that gloomy night when I was forced to abandon them, that I have always reverted to them in sadness and sorrow. My old feelings returned to me as I passed well-remembered spots and recalled the ravages of the hostile shells. But when I saw the cheerfulness with which the people were working to restore their condition and witnessed the comforts with which they were surrounded, a load of sorrow which had been pressing upon me for years was lifted from my heart."

Reading this, you understand something of his thoughts on those solitary rides with Traveller; something of what flowed beneath the playful gallant serenity with which he met each day of life.

When he returned from a journey he would say, yes, he had had a pleasant time, but "they make too much fuss over the old Rebel." And everywhere he urged: "Work for Virginia . . . build her up . . . make her great again. . . . And make your children Americans."

He was ever thinking what he himself might do to build up Virginia. In childhood he had learned to assume responsibility. His whole life had tended to develop in him resourcefulness. In the army he had belonged to the Engineer Corps: that training had made him practical and exact. As construction engineer he had shown a great gift for handling laborers. War had later proved him one of the world's greatest generals. And whatever life had taught him he longed to contribute to the service of defeated Virginia.

Now, as head of the college at Lexington, all that he had learned he would make of practical value to youth.

But he would do more. In the Valley of Virginia there was rich farm land, mineral springs, iron, and natural wonders to attract the traveler. The Valley needed a railroad. To reach Lexington at that time you had to journey by canal, or by stage over a rough mountain road. There must be a railroad through the Valley, linking the southwest with the northeast. It would certainly bring prosperity.

Lee went to Baltimore to help raise money to build it. And in the following year he was made president of this road which was one day to be; though he himself was not even to see its first rail laid.

Matthew Maury was on his way home from England, and in the dazzling harbor of St. Thomas, where the sun shines bright upon houses yellow and blue, red and white, among foliage brightly green, all rising from an azure bay, he heard of the collapse of the Confederacy, and the death of Abraham Lincoln.

Maury had now to decide what he must do. In England he had represented the Confederate Navy. It had been necessary to leave his family in Richmond, taking with him only his youngest son. The separation had been long and anxious, and he was eager to be at home; but realizing the danger of arrest, that might not yet be; he knew that he must live for a time in exile.

He wrote, surrendering his sword; making it clear that he considered himself bound by whatever terms had been granted to General Lee and other Confederate officers.

By degrees a grandiose scheme shaped itself in his mind. Maximilian was Napoleon the Third's puppet emperor of Mexico. Maury went to Mexico and was at once appointed director of the Imperial Observatory; he then submitted to the emperor his scheme for a Virginia colony in Mexico. Maximilian was enthusiastic, and Maury wrote eagerly to General Lee, recalling the Huguenots—his own ancestors— fleeing from persecution, and establishing themselves upon James River.

But Lee did not approve the great scheme. "I have a great admiration for Mexico," he explained, "but I shall be very sorry if your presence is lost to Virginia . . . the thought of abandoning the country and all that is left in it is abhorrent to my feelings, and I prefer to struggle for its restoration, and share its fate, rather than to give up all as lost."

Early in the New Year, Matthew Maury left Mexico to meet his family in England. He knew the Mexico plan was opposed by most of his Virginia friends, but he did not realize that the United States government was insisting on the withdrawal of French troops from Mexico. Within a month after Maury's departure, Maximilian wrote that he could no longer back the new colony. In fact, Maximilian himself was now powerless, and abandoned to his fast-approaching doom. Maury could not therefore go on with the colonization, nor was it yet safe to return to Virginia. He must wait. Meanwhile, in London, he opened a school of instruction in the science of electric torpedoes.

Then at last a general pardon was proclaimed in the United States and Matthew Maury came home. He spent the first winter in Richmond, writing a survey of the material resources of Virginia, and in the spring he went to Lexington as professor of physics at the Virginia Military Institute. Only a fence, in which there was a gate, separated Maury from the grounds of Washington College, now the home of his old friend, Robert E. Lee.

Long ago, a penniless boy riding over the mountains from Tennessee into Virginia, Maury had vowed to make everything bend to his profession. But he had sacrificed his profession to his state; now he came home to make his profession serve Virginia in that struggle which Lee called "making her great again." Like Jefferson, Washington, and Lee, Maury also had become deeply concerned in the education of the youth of the United States of America.

But in what time might be spared from his work as professor of physics, Maury traveled up and down the country, making speeches on agriculture, urging a system of forecasting weather, which would do for the farmer what his wind and current charts were doing for the navigator. At intervals, as new editions were called for, he revised his physical geography of the sea; and he wrote a general geography for use in schools.

So the years passed, and Lee wrote to his son, Fitzhugh that Traveller's trot was harder to him than it used to be. And finally so great a weariness came upon him that he was no longer able to ride.

In March of the year following Maury's coming to Lexington, the doctors sent Lee south for his health. Everywhere an ovation greeted him. Had you not known the facts you would have thought him a conquering hero, and not a general who had surrendered his army. On the way home he made his last journey to James River, visiting once more the old home at Shirley. In September, 1870, he was in Lexington for the opening of the college, and early in October—exactly five years and six months after Appomattox—he was gone; sinking without complaint or repining, gently, serenely into death.

At the end it was clear that his mind had wandered back to those days of which he had been so reluctant to

speak; for he was heard distinctly to command: "Tell Hill
he must come up" . . . Hill, who was killed during the week
that preceded Appomattox.

Then after a pause came the last words: "Strike the
tent."

After his death there were found in Lee's old army
satchel various papers which had remained undisturbed since
his return from Appomattox. Among them was the parole
which he received from General Grant at the surrender. And
there were other papers on which Lee had written, evidently
for his own comfort and strength, those thoughts which he
would keep near him.

Upon one of the papers he had put these words: "There
is a true glory and a true honor: the glory of duty done—
the honor of integrity of principle."

Two years later Matthew Maury, returning from a lecture trip, said to his wife, "My dear, I am come home to die."
But he lingered yet four months, well enough, now and then,
to dictate the final revision of his famous *Geography*.

When he was gone he left the world richer in knowledge
than he had found it. He was a man of dreams, and he seldom failed to dream true. The first transatlantic cable was
laid upon a course charted by him. The Naval Academy of
which he had dreamed came into being, as did the railroad
across the continent, and the canal spanning the Isthmus
of Panama, all of which he had foretold; the Weather Bureau
which he worked to establish is a reality; and he himself saw
the charting of the seas which his studies had made possible.

Of all the honors which came to him, that which would
perhaps touch him most deeply, could he know it, is that
every chart sent out by the Hydrographic Office in Washington is headed by the words: "Founded upon the researches
made in the early part of the nineteenth century by Matthew
Fontaine Maury, while serving as a lieutenant in the United
States Navy."

That, you feel, would mean more than all else; just as
General Lee would find profound and humble gratification

in the fact that after his death Washington College was called "Washington and Lee"; uniting his name with that of the man he most revered.

As soon as treason charges against the leaders of the Confederacy had been dropped, General Pickett returned to James River, where he built a cottage to take the place of his home, burned during the war by order of General Butler. And two years after Matthew Maury's death, George Pickett, lying mortally ill, called his Sallie to his arms. And so he died. His descendants have fought in the United States Army, in the Spanish-American War, in World War I, and now in World War II—the Global War.

After Lee's surrender at Appomattox, Roger Pryor, late of the Confederate Army, with hope of somehow earning a livelihood for his wife and their seven young children, settled in New York City.

I have heard Mrs. Pryor (who was my grandmother) describe their life in a city where they were considered "Rebels."

"You know," one of her little sons confided to her soon after they had finally moved to the North, "you know, mamma, I'm going to change Rebel's name. I'm going to call him Prince."

Rebel was the child's dog; so named not with any political significance, but by reason of the dog's temperament.

"I'll call him Rebel at home, but Prince in the street, because when I call him Rebel in the street the boys stone him."

That was a way out for the dog, but for the family there could not be one name for the public and another for the home. Yet, since they had come in that spirit of reconciliation which General Lee preached, that spirit which Abraham Lincoln had urged, they made friends, and much kindness brightened the bitter struggle against poverty, of the years before the success which was later theirs.

General Grant came often to the modest hospitality which Confederate General Pryor was able to offer. And Mrs. Pryor one day showed the met-bullets which had been picked up outside her door in Petersburg.

"Those are Minie-balls," Grant commented. "They were shot from rifles of equal calibre, and met precisely equidistant to a hair . . . I have seen one other. It came from Vicksburg. Where was this found? At Peterburg, possibly?"

"Yes," she said, "but not when you were shelling the city. It was picked up after the last fight."

"Now, Mrs. Pryor," Grant smiled, "don't you go about telling people that I shelled Petersburg."

In writing the James River story, I have purposely omitted all details of the shameful era of the carpetbaggers, and of the cruel folly of setting an alien race, just emerging from savagery, above brother Americans in whose veins flowed the blood of the Founding Fathers.

I have preferred to pass over whatever was as a turn of the screw in the agony of defeat.

As General Lee, visiting Petersburg two years after the surrender, had said that a load of sorrow was lifted from his heart when he saw the cheerfulness with which the people were working to restore their condition, so I would have this story of the James dwell upon the gallantry of their acceptance of defeat.

Many years later Mrs. Pryor told of meeting a friend in the streets of Petersburg soon after the long siege had been lifted and the port opened again to trade. The friend explained that, with the last five dollars she possessed, she was going to buy citron and raisins and currants, sugar, butter and eggs, brandy and spice.

"Mercy!" Mrs. Pryor exclaimed. "Are you planning to open a grocery store?"

"A grocery? No, I'm going to make a fruit cake!"

Never to lose heart, to rise gamely, often gaily, from

the ashes of ruin, to go back loyally into the Union, demonstrates a resilience, a spirit of good sportsmanship, which is a heritage of which any nation should be deeply proud.

The war was an appalling and needless tragedy, but there is a glory in what has come out of the defeat.

I like to think that the little colored girl, Maggie Walker, was a Richmond child; educated at the Lancaster School, whose teachers were Southern white women, with great interest in the colored children under their charge. After school hours Maggie helped her mother, who took in washing for a livelihood. And when she had graduated from high school, Maggie went back as teacher to the old Lancaster School. In Baltimore an ex-slave-woman had founded a society whose object was to provide for Negroes in sickness and death. Branches of this organization were formed in the James River towns, and early in the century Maggie Walker became a member. Out of this grew her idea to found a penny bank. She called it the St. Luke Penny Savings Bank. Its aim was to encourage thrift; even children, who sold papers and ran errands, must be taught to save. Maggie Walker's bank also made loans for home building. With the bank's help, many Richmond Negroes built and owned their own homes. Maggie Walker was the first woman in the United States to become the founder and president of a bank. Eventually the institution became the Consolidated Banking and Trust Company, with a hundred thousand dollar building of its own. And one of Virginia's governors said that, if all the money spent by the state on Negro education in fifty years had done no more than educate Maggie Walker, the state would have been fully repaid.

And in the years since Appomattox writers have made the James great in Letters. Mary Johnston, born at Buchanan in the Valley of the James, was the author of historical novels which brought to life earlier days in Virginia. Douglas Southall Freeman's biographies of Robert E. Lee and of Lee's lieutenants are magnificent achievements. James Branch Cabell created the land of Poictesme as the setting for his unique art. Ellen Glasgow, the first novelist to write realistically of the South, heads the list of America's writers of fiction. Emily Clark, in her *Innocence Abroad*, quotes Miss Glasgow as saying: "Because I am a Virginian in every drop of my blood and pulse of my heart I may speak the truth as I understand it . . . at least the faults of Virginia are my own faults, just as I hope the peculiar virtues of Virginia are my own also."

And Senator Carter Glass from Lynchburg on the James, in insisting upon "personal honesty and national honesty" as "things more precious than gold," carries forward a creed by which man must live, or in the end perish.

It was in a slowly disintegrating Williamsburg that Dr. W. A. R. Goodwin dreamed of the restoration of colonial Williamsburg, and because he believed with profound intensity, made his dream come true; declaring the "hope and purpose" of the restoration to be that "the future may learn from the past."

Then, in the momentous year 1944, I came upon an editorial in the New York *Herald Tribune*, which seems to belong at the conclusion of this study of James River; for in speaking of the instant reaction of the South to World War II, the editorial says: "Resistance to tyrants came naturally to men of Southern upbringing, and willingness to fight for liberty and against aggression has been part of their history since the landing in Jamestown. . . ." Their "far-sighted view of affairs across the oceans . . . is the more remarkable when it is remembered what might have been the South's natural preoccupation with its growing interest in foreign markets, and particularly in export of cotton and tobacco. It is reassuring to find that older parts of the United States, undisturbed by economic changes and the terrific ordeal of civil war, maintain their patriotism and that it responds instantly to challenge."

I say that I place this editorial at the conclusion of the story, and yet the story of a river can really have no conclusion; the life of a river being endless, its history, like itself, continuous, flowing out of the past, through the present, and into the future . . . that future for which the present is solemnly responsible.

A certain African explorer once had this significant experience: Traveling, as they say, on safari, across the black continent, he came upon his Negro porters seated quietly on the jungle trail, his boxes of provisions and equipment beside them. The porters had marched energetically for ten days, and the explorer was puzzled to find them sitting thus idle beside the trail.

Asking an explanation, he received this reply: "We have come so far, and so fast, that we have left our souls behind. We wait now for our souls to catch up with us."

Similarly, in the material world, the world of science, man has come so fast, and so astoundingly far, that it is vitally necessary for him to pause so that his soul may catch up with him; and while pausing, to attempt an understanding, not only of the road he has traveled, but of himself as man.

The writing, and the reading, of the story of a river is such a pause; such a waiting for our souls to join us; seeking, while we wait, that deeper understanding of ourselves which will again set a new bright light in the lighthouse.

The Oaks

Personal History

THE JAMES RIVER story is a plantation epic; from its beginning more than three centuries ago, with the Venturers who sailed from England in those little ships—the *Sarah Constant*, the *Goodspeed*, and the *Discovery*. In that far-off time Virginia was as often called a plantation as a colony. It was natural that men who had left their homes to sail a wide fearful sea, and to conquer a savage wilderness, should each have come to look upon his own individual plantation as though it were the world. Virginia has now, of course, many villages and towns and cities, but because my childhood home happens to have been a river-plantation, the story is to me an epic of plantation and of river.

My father's plantation as I first knew it, was thirteen miles from a railroad station, over a road always bad, sometimes impossible, and so lonely that you might drive the whole way without meeting another human creature; so remote that a child could scarcely believe in the existence of anything beyond its horizon.

The house stood half a mile from the big road. And from the big road a wide driveway, cut through the forest, led to a grove of enormous oaks and hickories. The drive ended in the flourish of a circle, around a plot as grassy as the great trees growing in it permitted. And the drive was of sand, white like the green-shuttered house. A large square porch opened into a hall where a graceful horseshoe staircase mounted to the second floor. At the end of the hall was a library with rectangles of colored glass in the upper sash of its windows, and doors to the right and left of the hall led into parlor and dining room—vast, square, high-ceilinged rooms, with fireplaces. The upper story had bedrooms of the same great size, and since every plantation house sooner or later developed wings, there was at the south a wing with more halls and bedrooms and porches, and at the north a chapel with stained-glass windows. An archway separated the south wing from a long one-story extension so thickly covered with English ivy that its windows seemed to have been cut into a wall of vines. Beside this wall was a walk passing between flowering shrubs and ending at the garden gate.

The extension contained kitchen, storerooms, and a harness room. Its doors, facing the rear of the establishment, opened upon an arcade where on rainy days bedraggled chickens sought protection. At the rear also was a high-roofed smokehouse, and an icehouse sunk into the earth, with its squat roof practically on the ground. A row of white cabins marked the limit of the back yard, and a little distance away were the carriage house and the orchard.

Beyond the garden stretched the fecund low-grounds to the river, whose presence was marked by willows growing along its banks. On the west, pastures rolled to the horizon and black-and-white cattle grazed in the pastures. To the east were cultivated fields, with here and there a tobacco barn or a stable, a clump of trees about a spring, or a little cluster of two or three cabins. To the north were the woods.

And the plantation, with its fields, its river, its gardens, its barns, the little whitewashed dwellings of tenants and hired laborers—this was then the world, and I saw it with the exploring eyes of one to whom it was birthplace.

As a plantation child, my education began with the dark people. The influence of parents came later; the earliest impressions were from the more primitive race which thought in terms of proverbs and drama, and which, like the child itself, lived close to nature.

"After you, is manners" was my introduction to courtesy.

"When the peacock looks at his feet, his tail drops" proved to me the importance of holding your head high.

"Dogs see spirits" convinced me of a world beyond the material and the visible.

"When chickens drink they lift up their bills to thank God" waked in me a sense of worship, never achieved by the pompous, catechism demanding:

"Q.: What is man's chief end?

"Ans.: Man's chief end is to glorify God and to enjoy him forever."

And something is born in the heart of any child who has tended a newly hatched chick, or coaxed a wobbly orphan calf to take milk from a nursing bottle.

My first feminine playmate was a small colored girl named Milly. As very little children we would lie for hours at a time beside an anthill, calling softly over and over:

"Doodle-bug, Doodle-bug, yo' house is on fire!"

And we were fond of snuggling under a snowball bush, and singing:

> Ole Molly har, what you doin' dar?
> Settin' in de cornder smokin' a cigyar?

Far off we would hear an older voice singing:

> I looked over Jordan, an' what did I see?
> Comin' fo' to carry me home,
> A band of angels comin' after me,
> Comin' fo' to carry me home.

> Oh, swing low, sweet chariot
> Comin' fo' to carry me home.

But the little friends under the snowball bush preferred songs of the animal world:

> De coon's got a long-ringed bushy tail,
> De 'possum tail is bare,
> De rabbit's got no tail a 'tall
> But a little bush o' hair.

> Oh, de 'possum is a cunnin' thing
> Smilin' in de dark.
> Nothin' 'tall disturb his mind
> But to hear my bulldog bark.

Then sliding into another tune we would sing:

> As I was gwine 'long de road,
> 'Pon a stump dar sot a toad.
> De toad he winked at de tadpole's daughter
> An' kicked de big frog in de water.

Later, after Milly and I had learned to read, we read *Little Women* together, and used to act out the story. Milly always wanted to take the part of the blond Amy of the tale. She would dress for the rôle by pinning to her own black frizzy hair the fragrant yellow pine shavings that fell from the carpenter's bench.

Although the War between the States was ever so long past, yet among my dark friends there were a few old enough to have known slavery. When the emancipation came, one of these, whom everyone called "Aunt Lethe," had remained with my grandmother, and later nursed the grandchildren as they came along. She lived to help her aged mistress in the passage from life to death.

The scene impressed itself unforgettably upon my memory.

My majestic old grandmother was dying. A light burned

low in the room. Aunt Lethe lay upon a pallet beside the deathbed, her dark face obliterated by the shadows. And in hushed awe I sat beside her.

Aunt Lethe could remember . . . oh, how much she could remember! The war, and how there was so little and you must do the best you could with what you had. The men of the house were gone to fight. Sometimes when you put your ear to the ground you could hear the guns—almost like thunder when a storm is coming up. She remembered that, as the war went on, so many were killed that at last even the boys went off to join the Confederate Army. And when boys like that went into battle, Jefferson Davis had said that now Virginia was using up her "seed corn." Then finally there had come what Aunt Lethe called "Lee-Surrender." After that you didn't hear the guns any more, but a terrible sickness went over the country.

Outside in the hot August night a whippoorwill was calling. Aunt Lethe broke into her whispered memories to exclaim:

"Listen to dat whippo'will. . . . Listen! De night my ole mammy die a whippo'will call jus' like dat. It call an' it call . . . an' . . . an' I look out an' see it settin' on de chimney . . . callin'.

"When de bref left my mammy . . . den de bird stop callin'. . . .

"An' in de mornin', when I walk out in de yard, dar was dat whippo'will, dead too."

My righteous austere old grandmother who died on that August night lives on in my memory. Every day she had commanded me to sit on a hassock beside her chair, hemming napkins and handkerchiefs. Every day my brothers and I must learn a verse from the Bible. On Sundays there were the ponderous questions and answers in the *Shorter Catechism*. On weekdays we were paid a cent an hour for weeding flower beds or garden walks. There was an obstinate little plant known as the "bluebottle," which seemed to have been created especially that we might understand that in return for money you must work. A tenth of the pennies thus earned were always deducted for the missionaries; the rest might be spent on sticks of lemon or peppermint candy kept for the purpose in a glass jar locked in a black-walnut wardrobe.

Then . . . this wise, strict, loving dictator of our early years had died, while out in the summer night the whippoor-will called.

Spring came early to the plantation garden. On the day when I found the first white hyacinth blooming under the shelter of the thick glossy foliage of a tree-box, I knew that it was spring. The flower was so small, so frail; daring to bloom while patches of snow still lingered in shady spots. I would go many times a day to raise up the low branches of the box and look again, to convince myself that the flower was truly there, as lovely and fragrant as I remembered it.

And then almost overnight the garden was a huge bouquet of daffodils, violets, and hyacinths. Every day birds were arriving from the south. It was time to plant and sow, and my brothers and I were permitted a part in it all. We cut potatoes into the proper segments: each must contain two "eyes," and the eyes must be so placed in the earth that they faced up and not down. Then when the leaves of the dogwood were as large as a squirrel's ear it was time to plant the corn, four grains to the hill:

> One for the blackbird, one for the crow,
> One for the cutworm, and one for to grow.

It was a season of excitement. Suddenly all the trees were in leaf. Birds were hanging nests from their branches, or tucking them away in the shrubbery. And mockingbirds sang all day.

Summer came. Now you must wear your sunbonnet. Cherries were ripening on the garden trees. Sometimes you found pale-blue or speckled eggs in a cleverly hidden nest,

and on the ground under one of the tree-boxwoods that
bordered the flower square a quail once laid a nestful of oval
white eggs.

Every day was busy, from the early breakfast to twi-
light, when it is too dark to tell a hawk from a buzzard.
Raspberries, strawberries, and cherries must be canned and
jellied for the winter. So much was going on in so many
places at once that I fluttered from one event to another;
from the garden to the kitchen, from the kitchen to the
dairy. And as my mother went about the duty of supervision,
often a pet squirrel sat in the black leather key basket on
her arm; and an obese white gander waddled after her
everywhere, even climbing the porch steps into the house.

Summer quickly became midsummer—the hot summer-
time. Nests squirmed with chirping young birds. All the
roses were in bloom; white and yellow jasmine gave the garden a tropic fragrance, and the crape myrtles—pink and
white and purple—blossomed above the heads even of grown
people.

And while still a child I felt the stately repose of the
flower square with its geometric beds edged by hedges of
dwarf box, separated by narrow gravel walks; the whole
design surrounded by a wider walk shut in by tall tree-box
trimmed in conical shape.

To those newly arrived in the world, life everywhere
must have a quality of magic, but I am persuaded that on
such a plantation the sense of magic is magnified; enhanced
by isolation from the rest of the world, by the mystery of
loneliness, and by the closeness of human life to nature, the
intimate personal relationship to every living growing thing.

In the dark of the moon the plantation was a world
blackly mysterious. It shimmered when the moon was full.
The trees cast shadows of unbelievable loveliness. A tiny
screech owl spoke. Magic was a reality, and the glow of a
will-o'-the-wisp traveling low over the ground was an unearthly thing. Sometimes majestic awful storms thundered
and crackled, profoundly stirring a child to strange ecstacy.

Skies cleared, and among flowers brilliant in a sedate garden, mockingbirds sang, and in the late afternoon wood thrushes called and were answered. Tobacco marched in long green rows through the fields. The river flowed like hammered copper in the sun. And far off a voice was singing: "I looked over Jordan, an' what did I see?"

The enchantment of summer would pass, and autumn would come, to write upon our child minds its own unforgettable details.

Tobacco was cut and hung to be cured in the tall tobacco barns. Wine must be made from the ripe grapes; peaches and figs preserved, pickled, and brandied, or dried on long tables in the sun, and when a cloud appeared on the fringe of the sky you must hurry to take in the drying fruit before the rain. Everywhere young birds were practicing for the long migration south. All day geese in V-shaped formation flew honking high overhead; soon such of the garden birds as planned to winter farther south had departed, and all but the evergreens and holly trees now lifted bare branches to the sky. Frost fell. Trees turned red and yellow. Persimmons ripened. The cider press was busy. Hickory nuts and walnuts were gathered. Apples were stored in barrels, potatoes filled the bins, and beets were put into kilns. The squirrels scampered about the grove, hiding away nuts for the winter.

Autumn was the season when my father got down his gun, and taking the dogs, went to hunt quail. We loved to follow, tramping all through golden afternoons in fields of yellow broomstraw as high as a child's head. When the sun dropped behind the pastures we came home to lamp-lit suppers of broiled quail and hot beaten biscuit. And fires crackled on the hearths, while outside in the early night the quail were calling forlornly to each other as the scattered coveys reassembled.

The great festival of the winter—for all but the hogs—was hog-killing time. It began in the cold of dawn before I was out of bed, and I would pull the covers over my head, and put my fingers in my ears, for I dreaded to hear the far-off squeals of the doomed pigs. But when the slaughter was over, I, like the others, would heartlessly scurry excited to the scene.

A great fire blazed outdoors, as well as in the kitchen fireplace. And every child—black or white—roasted pigs' tails over the flames. Lard was tried out in enormous caldrons suspended above the fires. The sausage grinder was turning all day. Fragrance of thyme and sage filled the kitchen, and laughter took material form in the condensation of breath in the chill air.

The revelry of hog-killing time lasted for days. And then there was Christmas! If you heard a rooster crowing in the night you knew he was "crowin' fo' Christmas." At other seasons he would be merely "crowin' fo' day," but in the weeks before Christmas it was for Christmas that he crowed.

On the great day at the crack of dawn, Negroes waited at the door crying "Christmas gif'! Christmas gif'!" Then there were firecrackers and Roman candles. After Christmas the cold weather set in. The house was heated only by its open fires. Long sandbags were laid on the doorsills to keep out drafts. The opening of a door automatically produced the caution: "Put the sandbag back." But of course it must be cold, or there would be no ice for the hot summer that was coming.

Thus the cycle of the year revolved until again the pale frail white hyacinth bloomed under the tree-box.

The big road passed in front of the colored church. The road was of brilliant red Virginia clay and the church was a small rectangular wooden building showing white against the pine forest which on three sides stood close about it. And a narrow sandy road through the trees connected the plantation and the church.

It was along this road that my brothers and I once walked in a funeral procession.

Matilda had died. She had been a servant in the house before her marriage to one of the tenants on the place, and her dying request had been that her white folks should go to her funeral. In after years my mother told me that Matilda had died in an unearthly ecstasy, but that, naturally, a child could not appreciate.

I was impressed only by the details of death, the sound of old Uncle Thomas, the plantation carpenter, sawing the planks for the coffin, and then a visit to Matilda's cabin where she lay dressed for the grave, appallingly motionless upon the best bedquilt. And there was a saucer of salt on her chest.

Those things which are odd to an adult are seldom the things which appear strange to a child. I did not wonder about the presence of the salt in the stranger presence of death, and I cannot now explain it, except as one of those dark superstitions imported in slave ships from Africa. With many such superstitions plantation childhood had made me familiar. I knew that the evil forces of the invisible world haunted crossroads, but that by whistling or singing as you passed you might protect yourself from them. I knew that you need not fear witches if before you went to bed you laid a broom across the doorsill, for the witch must count every straw before she could enter the room. By that time it would be morning, and with the coming of day witches lost their power. And of course I knew of the good magic of a rabbit's foot and of the evil that might come through conjuring. But I never understood the placing of a saucer of salt on the body of the dead. I had never seen it before and I never saw it again.

When Matilda's coffin was ready, they put her in it, and an oxcart bore it through the forest to the church, where under the trees the empty grave waited; the cart wheels creaking as the oxen moved with slow solemnity along that narrow road between walls of trees.

With the exception of my mother, my brothers, and

myself, those who followed were black. And from time to time they broke into song:

> Asleep in Jesus, blessed sleep
> From which none ever wake to weep.

Quiet words ... yet as they were sung on that slow procession through the forest they might have been the wild wailing of a savage world. It was strange to me, as a child, that among the singers were my familiar friends who laughed with such abandon about the kitchen fire.

At the grave those who came to mourn Matilda stood like a black tapestry hung close about the coffin. The coffin, decorated with a wreath of garden flowers made by my mother, was ready to be lowered. And Uncle Abel, the colored parson, stood at the coffin's head, lining out the hymn:

> How blest the righteous
> when he dies!

Suddenly he stopped and handed the hymnbook to my mother. "You all know," he said, "I ain't got but one eye, an' de sweat is runnin' down in de yuther, so I can't see. I gwine ax Mis' Gordon to line out de hymn."

There was a moment's silence, with no sound but the soft mourning of the wind in the pines.

My mother stood straight and slender, her face strangely white against that human curtain of black; black unbroken even by the whites of eyeballs, since the gaze of all was lowered to rest upon the coffin.

After an instant of shy hesitation, my mother's voice clear as the sweet notes of a flute lined out the words:

> How blest the righteous
> when he dies. . . .

And the swelling roll of many voices sang:

> How blest the righteous
> when he dies. . . .

At long-spaced intervals, usually in the late summer and early autumn, when the harvest was over and before the roads became impassable, the plantations exchanged visits, often all-day affairs with imposing midday dinners.

In the kitchen it would be said, "Today we gwine put de big pot in de little one," which meant that the feast was to be as grand as it was possible to make it. The children must have been exasperatingly underfoot on those occasions, for we were in and out of the kitchen and dining room, or under the trees helping to turn the crank of the ice-cream freezer, our mouths open like those of a nestful of young birds, eager for a taste of everything.

Then, by the time the company had driven down the long approach to the house, and around the circle to the door, we had been freshly washed and combed, feeling elegant because our feet, accustomed in summer to running bare all over the grove and garden, were now so wretched in the confinement of patent-leather pumps. We were shy, wild creatures, congealed into solemn silence by the presence of the guests, by the company magnificence of the table, and by the fact that two little colored children, instead of the everyday one, were waving beautiful peacock feather brooms above the table to shoo flies away from the feast.

When the guests said good-bye and drove away, leaving the prints of their horses' hoofs in the driveway, the plantation returned to its accustomed busy tranquillity; the drive so undisturbed by carriage wheels or horses' hoofs that the "frogs' houses" which we were fond of making in the sand, patting each into shape over a bare foot, and then carefully removing the foot, remained intact until there came a rain to wash them away. Or until we, in turn, drove off to repay visits; calling upon the descendants of Patrick Henry at Red Hill, ten miles away, upon Edmunds and Carringtons on adjacent plantations, being poled across the river to visit Clarks and more Carringtons, or driving up the long steep gravel roadway leading to beautiful Staunton Hill where the Charlotte County Bruces lived.

But all these were occasions in plantation life: it was the plantation itself that was our world.

I often wonder now how one woman accomplished all that my mother did; and yet without any sense of haste. On the plantation there seemed always to be time for everything; people were no more hurried than nature; they lived in its rhythm.

But the traditional picture of an indolent South was not true of the plantation. Everyone worked, whatever the sex or color or age. Laziness was so unusual as to be a matter for comment. "Ez lazy ez a dawg dat leans against de house to bark" was the simile applied to a loafer. Perhaps it is the gift of tranquillity in toil that has established the myth of an idle South. Because you never see the hurrying pace that kills, the conclusion is—a lazy people.

Though much was done on the plantation, it was done without drive and bluster. The work of that world proceeded as bees make honey, or spiders spin glistening webs on the tree-box, or ants construct tunnels, or birds build nests, feed young, and twice a year perform great journeys of migration. Like the industry of nature, the plantation was never at high pressure; song and laughter, relaxation and worship, were as essential and as much a part of living as work.

In the faded ink of an old recipe book you may find proof of the manifold activities of a plantation mistress of the time of my grandmother's marriage. The recipes include directions for compounding remedies for sick headache, for toothache and sore throat, remedies for scalds and burns, for felons and warts and corns, for distemper in cattle, for wounds in cattle, directions for fattening fowls, for making blacking, for a cement which resists fire and water, and an "everlasting fence post, so that there is not a man who will live long enough to see it rotten"; instructions for mulching the melon patch, for stopping leaks, for cleaning wallpaper,

marble and matting, for making various wood stains—black
walnut and mahogany—and many recipes for dyes.

There are recipes, too, for preserving beef in brine, for
curing bacon and hams, for making cooling summer drinks,
for wines and cordials, for making vinegar and yeast and
soap, preserving fruits and vegetables in bottles, for making
"ising-glass jelly," and every sort of hot breads and desserts.

When my brothers and I arrived at an age to require
lessons, our instruction was added to my mother's many
duties. Also, she had formed a class of the sons of white
"sharecroppers" which met at the plantation house several
nights during the week. The young men had worked all day
in the fields. At night they washed off part of the odor of
toil and of earth; they plastered their hair close to their heads,
and walked, often several miles, to be taught by my mother.
On Sundays she held a Sunday-school class. Through correspondence with Northern friends she collected used clothing,
to distribute to the poor, both black and white. In the same
way she sent to schools and colleges many Negroes and "poor
whites." She built churches in different parts of the country.
And at Christmas we provided for each a great glittering
tree. I say "we", because, as children, my brothers and I had
some small part in these many activities to which my mother
devoted her leisure; as well as having our childish share in
the busy plantation life.

It was not until I came to the North that I heard of
the indolence of the South. I never saw it anywhere. To me
it is no more true than that all Southern girls are beautiful
and bewitching, and stand everlastingly in the shade of mag-
nolia trees.

All my childhood, and the long vacations of youth, I
spent on that plantation. I have since gone back again and
again; and in preparation for writing *The James*, I have
traveled the length of the river; from its beginning in the

union of the Jackson and Cowpasture rivers below Iron Gate, through the Valley, the Piedmont and Tidewater sections, to the sea. I have wandered up and down the Valley, and re-visited other parts of the watershed, already long familiar. I have studied the social background from which came the English, the Ulster-Scots, and the Huguenots, who settled Virginia. I have studied Africa in the days of the slave trade. I have pored over records and reports, over letters, diaries, reminiscences, and old newspapers, over the accounts of early voyages, and the impressions of visitors to Virginia through the centuries.

And I inherit my interest in Virginia history. Early in the seventeenth century my forebears settled on Tidewater James River. One of these long-ago ancestors, Richard Bland, the "Virginia Antiquary," was for more than thirty years a member of the House of Burgesses; and ten years before the American Revolution he wrote a treatise which he called *An Inquiry into the Rights of the British Colonies*. He saw the colonies as "distinct states, independent as to their internal government of the original Kingdom, but united with her as to their external policy, in the closest and most intimate league and amity, under the same allegiance."

Writing in 1931 of Richard Bland's treatise of 1766, James E. Pate (professor of Political Science at the College of William and Mary) says: "This American scholar had worked out in 1766 the principle on which the British Com-monwealth of Nations is based to-day."

When Richard Bland was later named as delegate to the First Continental Congress, Roger Atkinson (also an ances-tor) described him as "staunch and tough as whiteleather, with something of the look of musty old Parchments which he handleth and studieth much."

Fifteen years after the publication of Richard Bland's treatise on the Rights of the British Colonies, another ances-tor, David Rice (born in the northern watershed of the James, and a pioneer preacher and founder of schools and colleges) wrote what is said to be the first antislavery pamph-let published in America. In this pamphlet he exclaims:

"Slavery of the Negroes began in iniquity, a curse has attended it, a curse will follow it. . . . Has the King of Heaven given this extraordinary right to white men over black men? Where is the charter? In whose hands is it lodged? . . . "

And in our own century, my grandmother has written books on the *Founding of Jamestown* and *The Mother of Washington and Her Times*.

I come to the writing of *The James* with this inherited interest in Virginia, as well as with personal feeling for what was my earliest home. To this is added a perspective of some little knowledge of the rivers of the world; the Thames, the Ganges, the Irrawaddy, the Yangtze, the rivers of Borneo, of the Malay Peninsula and of South America—the delta of the Orinoco, the Essequibo, the Mazaruni, the Surinam, the Maroni, the Urubamba, and the Magdalena.

Rivers have flowed through much of my life, so that while I naturally see the James with eyes of affection, I hope that the eyes are not provincial.

And I would like to repeat here (for those who do not read prefaces) that in telling the story it has been my desire to convey the liberty-loving, resilient spirit of James River, which has been alien always to the era of cynicism now surely destined to perish in the light of that vision of freedom and of faith which has come to men in foxholes, to men fighting on perilous seas, and in the air.

Acknowledgments

FOR the opportunity to fly over Tidewater Virginia I am indebted to Captain E. V. Rickenbacker of the Eastern Air Lines; to Beverly Griffith for planning the route of the flight; and to the pilot, Captain Richard Earle Fell.

For his kindness in putting at my disposal all the resources of the Williamsburg Restoration, I am most grateful to B. W. Norton; to Helen Bullock, formerly of the Restoration Department of Research; and to a Thomas C. Miller of the National Park Service.

For valuable suggestions regarding source material I am indebted to the late Reverend W. A. R. Goodwin, of Bruton Parish Church; C. L. Lewis, Professor at the United States Naval Academy; J. D. Eggleston, President of Hampden-Sydney College; Dr. E. G. Swem, Librarian of William and Mary College; Dr. W. H. T. Squires; Benjamin Morton; my cousin, Lucy Atkinson McIlwaine; my mother's old friend, Miss Emma C. Venable.

For courteous response to my various inquiries I wish to thank Mrs. Littleton Fitzgerald, granddaughter of Matthew Fontaine Maury; Mrs. Wilfred Epes; R. F. Nelson, of the Virginia State Chamber of Commerce; Captain L. R. Leahy, of the Hydrographic Office in Washington; Joseph W. Krutch; Rebecca Johnston, the late Robert A. Lancaster, Jr.; Clayton Torrence, Corresponding Secretary of the Virginia Historical Society; Dr. J. D. Eggleston, President Emeritus of Hampden-Sydney College; Matthew Page Andrews; John Corbin, and Mrs. Archibald Montgomery McCrae.

I am most appreciative of the kindness of Mr. S. Bywater and Mr. Boughey Bywater, through whom I have obtained a letter from the head of the College of Arms in London; in which he states that the grant of arms to John Smith is there "recorded in full and there is nothing to suggest that the original was not a genuine document."

I am grateful also for the courtesy of the Library of Washington and Lee University, of the Virginia Military Institute, and of the Public Library of Lynchburg, Virginia. As always I wish to express special appreciation to Miss Florence S. Garing and her staff at the New York Mercantile Library, and to Miss Dorothy P. Miller, Mr. Sylvester L. Vigilante, and Mr. F. Ivor D. Avellino of the American History Department of the New York Public Library, for their co-operation throughout my many months of research.

I have been fortunate in having had the use of Mr. George Arents's unique collection of books relating to tobacco.

And, as always, on the completion of a book I am deeply grateful for the encouragement of my brother, Henry I. B. Rice, and of my husband, Robert Niles.

Selected Sources

ADAMS, JAMES TRUSLOW, *The Living Jefferson.* New York and London, 1936.

ADAMS, NEHEMIAH, *A South-side View of Slavery.* Boston, 1854.

ADDEY, MARKINFIELD, *The Life and Military Career of Thomas Jonathan Jackson.* New York, 1863.

ALLEN, HERVEY, *Israfel, The Life and Times of Edgar Allan Poe.* New York, 1926.

ANBURY, THOMAS, *Travels Through the Interior Parts of America.* London, 1789.

ANDREWS, CHARLES M., *The Colonial Period of American History.* New Haven, Conn., 1934.

ANDREWS, MATTHEW PAGE, *Virginia, The Old Dominion.* New York, 1937.

ASHTON, JOHN, *Social Life in the Reign of Queen Anne* (2 vols.). London, 1882.

ATKINSON, ROGER, Letters of, 1769-1776, *Virginia Magazine of History and Biography,* Vol. XV, April, 1908.

BACON, NATHANIEL, "Letters, Reports, Proclamations," *Virginia Magazine of History and Biography,* Vols. I, IV, V, IX.

———— *Winder Papers (Virginia State Library),* "A True Narrative of the Rise, Progresse, and Cessation of the Late Rebellion in Virginia. Most Humbly and Impartially Reported by His Majesty's Commissioners appointed to enquire Into the affaires of the Said Colony," *Virginia Magazine of History and Biography,* Vol. IV.

BAGBY, GEORGE W., *The Old Virginia Gentleman and Other Sketches.* New York, 1910.

BALLAGH, JAMES CURTIS, *A History of Slavery in Virginia.* Baltimore: Johns Hopkins Press (Extra Series), 1902.

———— *White Servitude in the Colony of Virginia,* Johns Hopkins University Studies, Series XIII, VI-VII. Baltimore, 1895.

BELLET, L. P. DU, *Some Prominent Virginia Families*, Vol. II. Lynchburg, Va., 1907.

BEVERLY, ROBERT, *The History of Virginia, in Four Parts by a Native and Inhabitant*. London, 1722.

BIRKBECK, MORRIS, *Notes on a Journey in America*. London, 1818.

BLAND, RICHARD, *An Inquiry into the Rights of the British Colonies*. Williamsburg, Va., 1766.

BOTSFORD, JAY BARRETT, *English Society in the Eighteenth Century*. New York, 1924.

BOWERS, CLAUDE G., *Jefferson in Power*. Boston, 1936.

BOYD, THOMAS, *Light-Horse Harry Lee*. New York and London, 1931.

BRADFORD, GAMALIEL, *Lee the American*. Boston, 1912.

BROOKE, FRANCIS T., "A Narrative of my Life for my Family," Chapter XI in *Some Prominent Virginia Families*. (See L. P. du Bellet.)

BROOKS, W. E., *Lee of Virginia*. Indianapolis, Ind., 1932.

BROWN, ALEXANDER, *Genesis of the United States of America*. Boston, 1890.

——— *The First Republic in America. An Account of the Origin of this Nation. Written From the Records Then (1624) Concealed by the Council, Rather than From the Histories then Licensed By the Crown*. Boston and New York, 1898.

BRUCE, PHILIP ALEXANDER, *Economic History of Virginia in the 17th. Century*. New York and London, 1896.

——— *Social Life of Virginia in the 17th. Century*. Lynchburg, Va., 1927.

——— *The Virginia Plutarch*, Chapel Hill, University of North Carolina Press, 1921.

BUCKINGHAM, J. S., *The Slave States of America*. London, 1842.

BULLOCK, WILLIAM, *Virginia Impartially Examined*. London, 1649.

BURK, JOHN DALY, *The History of Virginia* (2 vols.). Petersburg, Va., 1804.

BURKE, EDMUND, *European Settlements in America* (2 vols.). London, 1785.

BURKE, WILLIAM, *The Mineral Springs of Virginia with Remarks on Their Use*. Richmond, Va., 1851.

BYRD, WILLIAM, "Personal Letters," *Virginia Magazine of History and Biography*, Vol. 32, 1924.

——— *The Secret Diary of William Byrd of Westover, 1709–1712*. Edited by Louis B. Wright and Marion Tinling. Richmond, Va., 1941.

BYRD, WILLIAM, *Another Secret Diary, With Letters and Literary Exercises, 1697–1726*, Edited by Maude H. Woofin, and collated by Marion Tinling, Richmond, Va., 1942.

———*Writings of Colonel William Byrd of Westover, Virginia*, Edited by J. S. Bassett. New York, 1901.

CALDWELL, T., *A Tour Through Part of Virginia in the Summer of 1808*. New York, 1809.

CAMPBELL, CHARLES, *History of the Colony and Ancient Dominion of Virginia*. Philadelphia, 1860.

CAREY, H. C., *The Slave Trade Domestic and Foreign: Why it Exists, And How it May Be Extinguished*. Philadelphia, 1853.

CARROLL, JOSEPH CEPHAS, *Slave Insurrections in The United States, 1800–1865*. Boston, 1938.

CASKIE, J. A., *Life and Letters of Matthew Fontaine Maury*. Richmond, Va., 1928.

CHASTELLUX, MARQUIS DE, *Travels in North America, 1780–1782*. New York, 1827.

CHILDS, BENJAMIN GUY, *The Negroes of Lynchburg, Virginia*. Charlottesville, Va., 1923.

CHINARD, GILBERT, *A Huguenot Exile In Virginia*. New York, 1934. (For edition in the original French, see Durand.).

CHRISTIAN, W. ASBURY, *Lynchburg and Its People*. Lynchburg, Va., 1900.

COOK, JOHN ESTEN, *Virginia, A History of the People*. Boston, 1896.

CORBIN, DIANA FONTAINE MAURY, *A Life of Matthew Fontaine Maury*, Compiled by his daughter. London, 1888.

CORBIN, JOHN, *The Unknown Washington*, New York, 1930.

COTTON, MRS. AN, *An Account of Our Late Troubles in Virginia*, written in 1676. Published from the original manuscript in the *Richmond* (Va.) *Enquirer*, September, 1804. Reprinted in Vol. I of Peter Force's *Tracts Relating to the Colonies in North America*. Washington, 1835.

COUPER, COLONEL WILLIAM, *One Hundred Years of V. M. I.* (4 vols.). Richmond, Va., 1939.

DANDRIDGE, NATHANIEL PENDLETON, *The Discovery of the Valley of Virginia by Governor Spotswood*. Cincinnati, Ohio, 1903.

DANIELS, SADIE IOLA, *Women Builders*. Washington, 1931.

DAVIS, JOHN, *Travels of Four Years and a Half in the United States, 1789, 1799, 1800, 1801*. London, 1803.

DODDRIDGE, REV. JAMES (See Kercheval, Samuel, *History of the Valley of Virginia,* for chapters by Doddridge.)

DODSON, LEONIDAS, *Alexander Spotswood.* Philadelphia, 1932.

DUNAWAY, W. F., *History of the James River and Kanawha Co.* New York, 1922.

DUNBAR, S., *History of Travel in America.* Indianapolis, Ind., 1915.

DURAND, DE DAUPHINÉ, *Un Français en Virginie. Voyages D'un Français Exilé pour la Religion. D'après l'édition originale de 1687.* Avec une Introduction et Des notes par Gilbert Chinard. Baltimore, 1932.

ECHOLS, CAPTAIN EDWARD, Account of Frank Padget in the Lexington *Gazette,* January and February, 1854.

EGGLESTON, EDWARD, "Nathaniel Bacon, the Patriot of 1676," *Century Magazine,* July, 1890.

EGGLESTON, GEORGE CARY, *A Rebel's Recollections.* New York, 1875.

———— *The History of the Confederate War* (2 vols.). New York, 1910.

ELLIOT, JONATHAN, *Debates on the Federal Constitution,* Washington 1827–1830.

FITHIAN, PHILIP VICKERS, *Journal and Letters:* 1773–1774, Tudor at Nomini Hall in Virginia. 1775–1776; on the Virginia-Pennsylvania frontier. 1775–1776. Edited by John Roger Williams. Princeton, N. J., 1934.

FITZPATRICK, JOHN CLEMENT, *George Washington: Colonial Traveler, 1732–1775.* Indianapolis, Ind., 1927.

———— *George Washington Himself; a common-sense biography written from his manuscripts.* Indianapolis, Ind., 1933.

———— *The Spirit of the Revolution. New Light From Some of the Original Sources of American history.* Boston, 1924.

FONTAINE, JOHN, *Journal* (1710–1716), printed in *Memoirs of a Huguenot Family,* translated and compiled by Ann Maury. New York, 1853.

FORCE, PETER, *Tracts and other Papers relating to the origin, settlements and progress of the colonies in North America, from discovery of the country to the year 1776* (4 vols.). Washington, 1836–1846.

FORD, H. J., *The Scotch-Irish in America.* Princeton, N. J., 1915.

FORSYTH, GENERAL GEORGE A., "The Closing Scene at Appomattox," *Harper's Magazine,* April, 1898.

FREEMAN, DOUGLAS SOUTHALL, *R. E. Lee, A Biography* (4 vols.). New York and London, 1934.

"French Traveler in the Colonies, 1765, A," *American Historical Review,* Vols. XVI and XVII.

GEISER, K. F., "Redemptioners and Indentured Servants in Pennsylvania," *Yale Review,* New Haven, 1901.

GLASGOW, ELLEN, *A Certain Measure.* New York, 1943.

GOODWIN, R., *Williamsburg in Virginia.* Williamsburg, 1936.

GREEN, RALEIGH T., *Notes on Culpeper County, Embracing a Revised and Enlarged Edition of Dr. Philip Slaughter's History of St. Mark's Parish,* Culpeper, Va., 1900.

GRIGSBY, HUGH BLAIR, *A History of the Federal Convention of 1788.* Richmond, Va., 1890–1891.

HAKLUYT, RICHARD, *Divers Voyages touching the discovery of America and the islands adjacent.* Collected and published by Richard Hakluyt. London, 1850.

HALE, JOHN PETER, *Trans-Allegheny Pioneers.* Cincinnati, Ohio, 1886.

HAMILTON, S. M., *Letters to Washington* (as assembled by) 5 vols. Boston, 1898–1902.

HAMOR, RALPH, *True Discourse of the Present State of Virginia.* London, 1615.

HARLOW, A. F., *Old Towpaths.* New York and London, 1926.

HARROWER, JOHN, "Diary, 1773–1776" (printed from the document in the Library of the Virginia Historical Society), *American Historical Review,* Vol. VI.

HART, FREEMAN H., *The Valley of Virginia in the American Revolution.* Chapel Hill, N. C., 1942.

HENING, WILLIAM WALLER, *The Statutes at Large, Being a Collection of All the Laws of Virginia From the First Session of the Legislature in the Year 1619.* (First 4 vols.) Vols, 1, 2, and 3, New York, 1823; Vol. 4, Richmond, Va., 1820.

HERRICK, C. A., *White Servitude in Pennsylvania.* Philadelphia, 1926.

HODGSON, ADAM, *Remarks During a Journey in America.* New York, 1823.

HULBERT, ARCHER BUTLER, *Historic Highways of America* (Vol. 2). Cleveland, Ohio, 1902.

"Indians' and Civil Wars in Virginia in the Years 1675 and 1676" (published from the original manuscript, found among the papers of the late Capt. Nathaniel Burwell of King William County), *Collections of the Massachusetts Historical Society,* Vol. 1. Boston, 1814.

JEFFERSON, THOMAS, *Autobiography of, 1743–1790, Together with a Summary of the Chief Events in Jefferson's Life.* Introduction and Notes by Paul Leicester Ford and a Foreword by George Haven Putnam. New York and London, 1914.
——— *Notes on Virginia.* (See *Writings of Thomas Jefferson*). Washington, 1905.
——— *Writings.* Collected and edited by Paul Leicester Ford. New York, 1904.
JERNEGAN, M. W., *Laboring and Dependent Classes in Colonial America, 1607–1783.* Chicago, 1931.
Jesuit Relations and Allied Documents. Travels and Explorations of the Jesuit Missionaries in New France, 1610–1791. Cleveland, Ohio, 1896–1901.
JOHNSON, GERALD W., *American Heroes and Hero-Worship.* New York, 1943.
——— *The Secession of the Southern States.* New York, 1933.
JONES, REV. HUGH, *The Present State of Virginia.* London, 1724.
JONES, J. WILLIAM, *Life and Letters of Robert Edward Lee.* New York and Washington, 1906.
——— *Personal Reminiscences, Anecdotes and Letters of General Robert E. Lee.* New York, 1876.

KEGLEY, F. B., *Virginia Frontier, 1740–1783.* With Introduction by Samuel M. Wilson. Southwest Historical Society, Roanoke, Va., 1938.
KEMPER, CHARLES E., "Some Valley Notes," *Virginia Magazine of History and Biography,* 1921.
——— "The Early Westward Movement of Virginia, 1722–1734," *Virginia Magazine of History and Biography,* Vols. 12 and 13, 1905–1906.
KERCHEVAL, SAMUEL, *History of the Valley of Virginia, Woodstock, Virginia* (1st ed.), 1833.
KINGSBURY, DR. SUSAN M. (Compiler), *Records of the Virginia Company in London.* Washington, 1905.

KOONTZ, LOUIS K., *The Virginia Frontier, 1754–1763*, Johns Hopkins University Studies in Historical and Political Science. Series XLIII No. 2. Baltimore, 1925.

LANCASTER, R. A. JR., *Historic Virginia Homes and Churches*. Philadelphia, 1915.

LEDERER, JOHN, *The Discoveries of John Lederer in the Several Marches from Virginia to the West of Carolina and Other Parts of the Continent, in the Years 1669 and 1670*. Collected and translated out of the Latin by Sir William Talbot. London, 1672.

LEE, ROBERT E., *Recollections and Letters* (by his son, Robert E. Lee), New York, 1904.

LELAND, JOHN, *The Virginia Chronicles, With Juditious and Critical Remarks*. London, 1790.

Lexington *Gazette*, January and February, 1894.

Lynchburg, Virginia, The Saga of a City. Compiled by the Lynchburg Sesqui-Centennial Association, Inc., Lynchburg, Va. 1936.

McCLUNG, JAMES W., *Historical Significance of Rockbridge County. Virginia*. Staunton, Va., 1939.

MARSHALL, CHARLES, *An Aide-de-Camp of Lee*. Edited by General Sir Frederick Maurice. Boston, 1927.

——— *Papers of*. Edited by Major General Frederick Maurice. Boston, 1927.

MARTINEAU, HARRIET, *Retrospect of Western Travel*. London, 1838.

——— *Society in America*. London, 1837.

MASON, EMILY V., *Popular Life of General Robert E. Lee*. Baltimore, 1874.

MASSE, DR. PHILIP, "Memoirs of the Life and Voyages of," *William and Mary College Quarterly*, Series 2, Vol. I.

MATHEW, THOMAS, *The Beginning, Progress, And Conclusion of Bacon's Rebellion in Virginia, In the Years 1675 and 1676*. Reprinted in Vol. I of Peter Force's *Tracts Relating to the Colonies in North America*. Washington, 1835.

MAVERICK, MAURY, *A Maverick American*. New York, 1937.

MAYO, BERNARD, *Jefferson Himself*. Boston, 1942.

MEADE, BISHOP WILLIAM, *Old Churches, Ministers and Families of Virginia*. Philadelphia, 1857.

MELISH, JOHN, *Travels in the United States of America, in the Years, 1806, 1807, 1809, 1810 and 1811*. Philadelphia, 1812.

MILLER, WILLIAM, *The Effects of the American Revolution On Indentured Service*. Philadelphia, 1840.

MORDECAI, S., *Richmond in Bygone Days*. Richmond, Va., 1860.

MORTON, OREN F., *Annals of Bath County, Virginia*. Staunton, Va., 1917.

———— *Centennial History of Alleghany County, Virginia*. Dayton, Va., 1923.

———— *History of Rockbridge County*. Staunton, Va., 1920.

MUNFORD, BEVERLEY, *Virginia's Attitude Toward Secession*. New York, 1909.

NEILL, EDWARD D., *Virginia Carolorum*. Albany, N. Y., 1886.

———— *Virginia Company of London*. Washington, 1868.

———— *Virginia Vetusta*. Albany, N. Y., 1885.

NORTON, JOHN & SONS, *Merchants of London and Virginia: Being the Papers of Their Counting House for the Years 1750 to 1765*. Edited by Frances Norton Mason. Richmond, Va., 1937.

OLMSTED, FREDERICK LAW, *A Journey in the Seaboard Slave States*. New York, 1859.

———— *The Cotton Kingdom*, New York, 1861.

ORR, MRS. LUCINDA (LEE), *Journal of a Young Lady of Virginia*, Edited by Emily Mason. Baltimore, 1871.

OSBORNE, J. A., *Williamsburg in Colonial Times*. With an Introduction by the Rev. W. A. R. Goodwin. Richmond, Va. 1935.

PAGE, THOMAS NELSON, *Robert E. Lee, Man and Soldier*. New York, 1911.

PATE, JAMES E., "Richard Bland's Inquiry into the Rights of The British Colonies," *William and Mary College Quarterly*, (2) Vol. XI.

PEYTON, J. LEWIS, *History of Augusta County*. Staunton, Va. 1883.

PICKETT, LaSALLE CORBELL, *The Heart of a Soldier*. New York, 1913.

———— *What Happened to Me*. New York, 1917.

POE, EDGAR ALLAN, *Works*, Edited by John H. Ingram (4 vols.). With a *Memoir* of his Life. Edinburgh, 1881.

POLLARD, E. A., *The Lost Cause*. New York, 1867.

PORTER, GENERAL HORACE, *Campaigning With Grant*. New York, 1897.

PRYOR, MRS. ROGER A., *Reminiscences of Peace and War*. New York, 1905.

PURCHASE, SAMUEL, *Pyrchas, his Pilgrimage*. London, 1614.

RANDALL, HENRY S., *Life of Thomas Jefferson*. New York, 1858.

RICE, REV. DAVID, *Slavery Inconsistent With Justice and Good Policy*. Philadelphia, 1792.

ROBIN, ABBÉ (CLAUDE C.), *New Travels Through North America; in a series of letters, exhibiting the history of the victorious campaign of the allied armies . . . in the year 1781*. Translated from the original of Abbé Robin; one of the chaplains of the French Army in America. Philadelphia, 1783.

Rockbridge Historical Society, *Proceedings*, Lexington, Va., 1941.

ROSCOE, E. S., *The English Scene in the Eighteenth Century*. New York, 1912.

ROYALL, ANN, *Sketches of History, Life and Manners in the United States*. New Haven, Conn. 1826.

——— *Southern Tour, or Second Series of The Black Book*. Washington, 1830.

RUSSELL, JOHN H., *The Free Negro in Virginia*. Johns Hopkins University, Studies in Historical and Political Science, Series XXXI, No. 3. Baltimore, 1913.

SAMPSON, ANNIE ELIZA (WOOD), *Kith and Kin*. Richmond, Va., 1922.

SCHAFF, MORRIS, *The Sunset of the Confederacy*. Boston, 1912.

SCHOEPF, J. D., *Travels in the Confederation, 1783–1784*. Translated from the German and edited by Alfred J. Morrison. Philadelphia, 1911.

SCOTT, W. W., *A History of Orange County, Virginia*. From its formation in 1734 (O.S.) to the end of the Reconstruction in 1870. Compiled mostly from original records. Richmond, Va., 1907.

SCRUGGS, PHILIP LIGHTFOOT, *First Adventure*. Lynchburg, Va. 1935.

SEMPLE, ELLEN C., *American History and Its Geographic Conditions*. Boston, 1903.

SEWARD, WILLIAM HENRY, *Autobiography from 1801–1834. With a Memoir of his life and selections from his letters*. Compiled by Frederick W. Seward (3 vols.). New York, 1877–1891.

SLAUGHTER, DR. PHILIP, *History of St. Mark's Parish*. (See Raleigh Travers Green's *Notes on Culpeper County, Virginia*). Culpeper, Va., 1900.

SMITH, CAPTAIN JOHN, *Works, 1608–1631*. Collected and edited by Edward Arber. Birmingham, England, 1884.

SMITH, RIXEY AND BEASLEY, NORMAN, *Carter Glass. A Biography.* With an Introduction by Senator Harry Flood Byrd, and a Preface by Douglas Southall Freeman. New York and Toronto, 1939.

SMYTH, J. F. D., *A Tour in the United States of America* (2 vols.). London, 1784.

SPEED, THOMAS, *The Wilderness Road.* Louisville, Ky., 1886.

STANDARD, MARY MANN PAGE (NEWTON), *Colonial Virginia, its peoples and customs.* Philadelphia, 1917.

———— *Virginia's First Century.* Philadelphia, 1928.

Statutes at Large, Being A Collection of all the Laws of Virginia, From the First Session of the Legislature in the Year 1619. Philadelphia, 1823.

STILES, ROBERT, *Four Years Under Marse Robert.* New York, 1903.

STROUDE, G. M., *A Sketch of the Laws Relative to Slavery in the Several States of the Union.* Philadelphia, 1827.

SUMMERS, LEWIS PRESTON, *Annals of Southwest Virginia, 1769–1800.* Abingdon, Va., 1929.

SWEM, EARL GREGG, *Virginia historical Index.* Roanoke, Va., 1934–1936.

TAYLOR, FRANK H., *To the Shenandoah and Beyond.* New York, 1885.

THACKERAY, WILLIAM MAKEPEACE (For Letters from Richmond, Va., in 1853, see Ritchie, Hester Thackeray, *Thackeray and his Daughter* New York, 1924.

THWAITES, REUBEN GOLD, AND KELLOGG, LOUISE PHELPS, *Dunmore's War.* Compiled and edited from the *Draper Manuscripts.* Madison, Wisc., 1905.

TOMPKINS, E. P., AND DAVIS, J. LEE, *The Natural Bridge and Its Historical Surroundings.* Natural Bridge, Va., 1939.

TYLER, LYON GARDINER, *Narratives of Early Virginia, 1606–1625,* Edited by Lyon Gardiner Tyler. New York, 1930.

TYLER, MOSES COIT, *Patrick Henry.* Boston and New York, 1898.

Virginia Gazette, Old Files of,

Virginia Magazine of History and Biography. 1894-1942, Richmond, Va.

WADDELL, JOSEPH ADDISON, *Annals of Augusta County, Virginia, From 1726–1871* (2nd ed., revised and enlarged). Staunton, Va., 1902.

WALKER, DR. THOMAS, *Journal of An Exploration in the Spring of the Year 1750*. Boston, 1888.

WASHINGTON, GEORGE, *Diaries*. Edited by John Clement Fitzpatrick. Boston, 1925.

—— *Writings* (from the original sources, 1745–1799). Edited by John Clement Fitzpatrick. Washington, 1931.

—— *Writings*. Edited by Jared Sparks. New York, 1847.

—— *Writings*. Collected and edited by Worthington Chauncey Ford. New York, 1889–1893.

WEDDELL, ALEXANDER WILBOURNE, *A Memorial Volume of Virginia Historical Portraiture*. With an Introduction by Ellen Glasgow. Richmond, Va., 1930.

—— *Virginia in Old Prints*. Richmond, Va., 1932.

WELD, ISAAC, JR., *Travels Through the States of North America and the Provinces of Upper and Lower Canada During the Years 1795, 1796, and 1797*. London, 1807.

WERTENBAKER, T. J., *Planters of Colonial Virginia*. Princeton, N. J.: Princeton University Press, 1922.

—— *The First Americans*. New York, 1927.

William and Mary Quarterly, 1892–1943. Williamsburg, Va.

WILLIAMS, EDWARD, *Virginia Truly Valued*. London, 1650.

WILLIAMS, GEORGE W., *History of The Negro Race in America*. New York, 1883.

WIRT, WILLIAM, *Sketches of the life and Character of Patrick Henry*. Philadelphia, 1840.

WITHERS, ALEXANDER SCOTT, *Chronicles of Border Warfare*. Edited and annotated by Reuben Gold Thwaites. Cincinnati, Ohio, 1895.

WOLSEY, GARRET JOSEPH WOLSELEY, 1ST VISCOUNT, *General Lee*. Rochester, N. Y., 1906.

WRIGHT, LOUIS B., *The First Gentleman of Virginia. Intellectual Qualities of the Early Colonial Ruling Class*. The Huntington Library, San Marino, Cal., 1940.

YANCEY, ROSA FAULKNER, *Lynchburg And Its Neighbors*. Richmond, Va., 1935.

Index

A

Adams, John, 163, 164, 165, 178, 227, 228
Adams, Reverend Nehemiah, 198, 199, 201
Africa, 66-70, 75, 192, 202-205, 292, 302
Alleghenies, 3, 88, 123, 139, 148, 151, 208
Allegheny County, 5
Alexandria, 222, 225
Aliquipa, 139
Allan, Frances, 223-226, 228-230, 240
Allan, John, 223, 224, 228-231, 240
Amelia Court House, 270-271
Anne, Queen, 50, 54, 128
Appomattox, 7, 220, 232, 243, 249, 254, 265, 271-278, 282, 286-288
Appomattox River, 113
Argall, Captain Samuel, 36, 43-44, 47
Arlington, 232, 234, 248
Armada, Spanish, 76
Atkinson, Roger, 161, 165, 180, 307

B

Bacon, Nathaniel, 8, 84-99, 101-102, 111
  Declaration of the People, 94, 98
  epitaph, 98, 99
Bacon, Nathaniel, Senior, 87, 89, 91
Bacon, Mrs. Nathaniel, 84, 87, 89-90
Bacon's Assembly, 92
Bacon's laws, 92, 98
Bagby, George W., 207-208, 210-211, 220
Balcony Falls, 6, 211, 218
Baltimore, 222, 230, 243, 284, 290
Bartram, John, 110
Bateaux, 206-208, 215-217, 220
Berkeley, Sir William, 85-99, 101-102, 112, 126
Bermuda Hundred, 8
Beverly, Robert, 103, 121-122
Beverley's Manor, 146
Bible, King James version, 76
Bill of Rights, 162, 163, 188, 201

Dennis, Josiah, 147, 151, 153
Dessalines, 233
Dickinson, Colonel, 176, 178
Dinwiddie, Governor Robert, 135-136, 138-139, 149, 208
Discovery, 293
Dissenters, 77, 128
"Dixie," 254
Doddridge, Reverend Joseph, 131-132
Drummond, William, 88, 96, 97
Duke, Sir Edward, 84, 87
Duke, Elizabeth (*see* Bacon, Mrs. Nathaniel)
Duke of Gloucester Street, 134-145, 155, 158-159
Dunmore, Governor, 160, 182
Dutch, slave trade, 58, 69, 75

E

Echols, Captain Edward, 218, 219
Elizabeth, Queen, 128
Elizabeth River, 255
England, 63-64, 66, 70, 72, 75, 82, 102-103, 128, 136, 156, 181-185, 195, 222, 258, 284-285
  settlers, 7, 9, 10, 15-55, 307
  slaves freed by, 233
  social contrasts, 104-110
Ericsson, John, 257
Everett, Edward, 252

F

Fairfax, George, 137
Fairfax, Sally Cary, 138, 142

Fauquier, Governor, 157
Ferryboats, 6
Fithian, Philip, 170-178
Five Forks, 269, 270
Fontaine, John, 121-123, 238
Fontaine, Reverend Peter, 238
Forrest, Thomas, 26
Forsyth, General George A., 275
Fortress, Monroe, 230, 232, 233, 247, 255
Forts, 142, 149-150
  Duquesne, 139, 144, 145, 150
  Lafayette, 263
  Necessity, 140
  Vause, 148, 150
  Young, 153
France, 69, 130
  aid in Revolution, 179-184
  (*See also* Huguenots)
Freeman, Douglas Southall, 290
French and Indian War, 138-144, 147-154, 159, 176-177
Frethorne, Richard, 64-65

G

Gaines's Mill, 259
Gambia River, 67-68
Gates, Sir Thomas, 36, 37
George III, 159, 160, 162, 163, 193
George, Mount, 122, 127
Germans, Palatine, 130
Gettysburg, 261, 264
Gilbert, Sir Humphrey, 23-24
Glasgow, Ellen, 291
Glass, Carter, 291

Gooch, Governor, 134
Goodspeed, 293
Goodwin, Dr. W. A. R., 12, 291
Goody Bull and her Daughter,
182, 184
Goosley, Mrs. Martha, 118
Gordon of Khartoum, 268
Grant, Ulysses S., 262-265, 268-
270, 272-277, 287, 289
Grasse, Comte de, 180, 183
Grigsby, Hugh, 190

H

Haiti, 233
Hamilton, Alexander, 184
Hamor, Ralph, 44, 55
Hampton Roads, 11, 255, 257,
258
conference, 265, 269
Hansford, Colonel, 97
Harpers Ferry, 248
Harrison, Benjamin, 161, 189
Henry, Patrick, 12, 116, 120,
156-162, 182, 186-187
opposes Constitution, 188-191
protest against Stamp Act,
159-160
speech at Richmond Conven-
tion, 161-162
Henry, Patrick, Negro, 193-195,
205
Henry, Cape, 18
Herndon, Ann, 238, 240
Hessians, 180
Hill, General, 270, 287
Hooker, General Joseph, 260
Horsemanden, Warham, 101,
102

Houston, Sam, 236
Huguenots, 74, 77-78, 121, 128,
238, 285, 307
Humboldt, 237
Hunt, Robert, 18, 23

I

Indenture papers, 59-60
Indentured servants, 57-60, 64-
66, 70-74, 104, 132, 168-
169
Negro, 66-67, 74
protection to, 72-74
voluntary, 58-59, 65-66
Indian Trading Path, 100-102,
113
Indians, 3-5, 14, 16-55, 114,
122, 169
"Great Path," 5, 89, 129-131,
133, 147
massacre of settlers, 61-64,
177
trade with, 20, 24-25, 29, 101
villages, 38-39, 41, 49
warfare against, 4-5, 8, 19,
43-90, 101-103
(*See also* French and Indian
War)
Ireland, colonists from, 127-129,
199
Iron Gate, 3, 307
Iroquis tribe, 5
Isham, Henry and Katherine, 8
Isham, Mary, 8

J

Jackson, "Stonewall," 253, 260-
261, 264